Religious Education

FAITHformation2020

"This is an extremely important book. Without presuming to prescribe a formula for faith formation and the future, John Roberto offers a wealth of wisdom that is grounded in excellent research, concrete suggestions, and accessible resources. Templates are strategically presented throughout the book with practical use for congregations to evaluate their current ministry in ways which will encourage visioning for the future. *Faith Formation 2020* is a book of hope."

Susan H. Hay, Director, Effective Practices in Young People's Ministry
GBOD, The United Methodist Church, Nashville

"Thank God John Roberto wrote this book now. It assists the church in the vital task of addressing the diversity of today's spiritual landscape in the United States. Through the innovative and helpful tool of "scenario thinking," four distinct narratives are explored as a way for the church to face the need for life-long faith formation by the year 2020. Roberto's approach to Christian ministry takes the long view (as opposed to simply addressing the pressing issues of today), looks at ministry from the outside-in (instead of shaping ministry from the perspective of the internal concerns of one's own faith community), and considers multiple possibilities for the future as a way to widen the church's perspective.

Fundamentally, Roberto is interested in leadership competencies that anticipate, plan for, and act on behalf of the church in contemporary society. His work presents strategic, research-based, and field-tested ideas that encourage the church to be proactive instead of reactive. The book identifies critical factors in promoting and nurturing the Christian faith, including digital media, web technologies and the role of the family. The scenarios and strategies recognize the life of the home as that center of religious socialization that has been in the past and continues to be in the present a critical—yet often overlooked—inspiration for faith formation. *Faith Formation 2020* creates a sense of urgency and energy for outreach and Christian discipleship. I highly recommend this book to all who have the passion for leadership in the church that seeks to advance Christian faith formation."

David W. Anderson, Author of From the Great Omission to Vibrant Faith
Vibrant Faith Ministries, Minneapolis

"Read *Faith Formation 2020* and you will have a blueprint for the future! John Roberto provides a wealth of essential information along with practical strategies for forming Christians in all their diversity. Comprehensive and thought-provoking, this book faces reality with joy and hope."

Pam Coster, Executive Director
Charis Ministries, Chicago

"For those congregations who are serious about lifelong Christian formation, John Roberto has laid out a strategy for planning and implementing a full-court press for the future. Tapping into recent research done by the Pew Research Center, Christian Smith and cohorts, the "Faith Communities Today" study at Hartford Seminary, and many others, Roberto has synthesized and applied their statistics into possible scenarios and responses churches can address. Proposing that every congregation develop a Lifelong Faith Formation Network, questions and processes are offered to help leaders address challenges, opportunities, and implications for their future. The goal of lifting up lifelong Christian formation in the Church is not a new one, but this guidebook offers strategies, steps, and concrete tasks similar to how the Lifelong Faith Journal has given countless Christian educators tools for developing strong programs for supporting and strengthening the faith of their members. This is not a book for the faint hearted; it is for those who desire to step up to the plate and get serious about how collaborative leadership and long-range planning can make a difference in the life of the Church."

Sharon Ely Pearson, Christian Formation Specialist
Church Publishing Inc., New York City

"Roberto draws his readers into the twenty-first-century reality by casting light on the significant driving forces that are impacting how churches are to engage in faith formation. The current era demands that a radical new perspective for defining the parameters of where, when, and how faith formation is presented if faith formation is to have impact in the lives of those who are searching for a deeper relationship with God. The scenario planning process is the ground for Roberto's approach. It involves the comprehensive in-depth engagement of the entire faith community to bring about change. This rich treasury of resources and best practices is a supportive guide for navigating church leaders toward an effective pastoral plan for faith formation."

Angela Ann Zukowski MHSH is the Director of the Institute for Pastoral Initiatives
and Professor in the Department of Religious Studies of the University of Dayton

"John Roberto has brought vision and innovation into productive conversation in *Faith Formation 2020: Designing the Future of Faith Formation.* John has utilized the evidence of trends already prevalent in our society and in the field of faith formation to design forward-looking models that are both responsive to the current context as well as to the likely milieu of faith formation ministry in 2020—and in the rising decade along the way! Rather than reacting to what will be operative in 2020, John's work guides the reflective practitioner through thinking and designing responses to the needs and desires of the spectrum of faith-seeking individuals now, in the future, and along the way. This is a must read for those who do not want to wake up unprepared in a ministry context in the next decade."

Brian A. Lemoi, Director, Office of Evangelization and Lifelong Faith Formation
Diocese of St. Petersburg, St. Petersburg

"In a thoughtful and evidence-based way, John Roberto has done the hard work of thinking through the alternative futures for faith formation that dioceses and parishes often struggle to consider due to the lack of time and resources. While some approaches to faith formation appear either too short sighted or piecemeal, John Roberto has thoughtfully assessed the current and potential future realities that successful faith formation will need to consider over the next ten years in order to be effective. With a solid grasp of Christian teachings, a holistic pedagogy, and a natural spirit of innovation, John Roberto has once again broken the mold of thinking about catechesis, helping us to consider the various possibilities for faith formation that will be necessary in order to reach current and future generations."

Peter Denio, Standards for Excellence Project Manager
National Leadership Roundtable on Church Leadership

FAITHformation2020

Designing the Future of Faith Formation

JOHN ROBERTO

LifelongFaith Associates

VIBRANT FAITH PUBLISHING

FAITH FORMATION 2020
Designing the Future of Faith Formation

Cover images: Divorced © iStockphoto.com / Franz Pfluegl; Family Safe © Amy Walters / fotolia.com; Figurine Crowd © iStockphoto.com / AdShooter; Little Men © iStockphoto.com / Lara Seregni; Miniature Home and Family © Amy Walters / fotolia.com; People in Motion © iStockphoto.com / Andrew Johnson; Spend Money © Farang / Dreamstime.com

Cover and book design: Hillspring Books, Inc.
Faith Formation 2020 logo design: Brian Parda, Alias Creative, LLC
Publishing consultant: Huff Publishing Associates, LLC

Library of Congress Cataloging-in-Publication Data is available

ISBN 978-0-9823031-3-9

LifelongFaith Associates
40 Brighton Road
Naugatuck, CT 06770
www.LifelongFaith.com

The paper used in this publication meets the minimum requirements of American National Standard for Information Sciences—Permanence of Paper for Printed Library Materials, ANSI Z329.48-1984.

Manufactured in the U.S.A.

14   13   12   11   10   1   2   3   4   5   6   7   8   9   10

CONTENTS

CHAPTER FOUR
Bringing the Faith Formation 2020 Scenarios to Life

119

INTRODUCTION

Hope for the Decade

Hope is a state of mind, not of the world. Either we have hope or we don't; it is a dimension of the soul, and it's not essentially dependent on some particular observation of the world or estimate of the situation. Hope is not prognostication. It is an orientation of the spirit, an orientation of the heart; it transcends the world that is immediately experienced, and is anchored somewhere beyond its horizons. . . . Hope, in this deep and powerful sense, is not the same as joy that things are going well, or willingness to invest in enterprises that are obviously heading for success, but rather an ability to work for something because it is good, not just because it stands a chance to succeed. The more propitious the situation in which we demonstrate hope, the deeper the hope is. Hope is definitely not the same thing as optimism. It is not the conviction that something will turn out well, but the certainty that something makes sense, regardless of how it turns out.

—Vaclav Havel, *Disturbing the Peace*, 1986

▶ This is a book about hope. Hope in the future of faith formation. Hope in the next generation. Hope in churches that are resilient and adaptive in the face of great challenges and opportunities. Hope and trust in God who will do marvelous and wondrous things in our churches and world through us, even if we do not know how it happens. "The kingdom of God is as if someone would scatter seed on the ground, and would sleep and rise night and day, and the seed would sprout and grow, he does not know how. The earth produces of itself, first the stalk, then the head, then the full grain in the head. But when the grain is ripe, at once he goes in with his sickle, because the harvest has come" (Mark 4:26–29).

The Faith Formation 2020 Initiative was created to guide churches to envision and design dynamic, engaging, and inspiring faith formation in the second decade of the twenty-first century—to imagine the possibilities for faith formation in 2020. The last two decades have seen dramatic political, economic, social, and cultural changes affecting virtually every dimension of American Christianity. Churches across the United States are facing significant challenges in their efforts to provide vibrant faith formation for all ages and generations in the faith community. The new environment in which Christian faith formation will operate in the decade from 2010-2020 will demand new thinking and new models, practices, resources, and technologies to address the spiritual needs of all generations.

The Faith Formation 2020 Initiative is focused on three overarching questions: What could faith formation in Christian churches look like in 2020? How can Christian congregations provide vibrant faith formation to address the spiritual and religious needs of all ages and generations over the next ten years? How can churches envision the shape of faith formation in the year 2020 and design initiatives to respond proactively to the challenges and opportunities in the second decade of the twenty-first century?

The goal of the Faith Formation 2020 Initiative is to inspire creative action in the present through anticipation of possible futures. The four scenarios developed through the initiative are stories that address significant forces affecting faith formation and stimulate new ways of thinking about the present and the future. No one knows what lies just beyond the horizon but these four scenarios of the future can inform church leaders of potential challenges and opportunities they may want to prepare for now rather than react to later. The four scenarios are not predictions, projections, or prophecies but rather an attempt to provoke a realization that the future need not simply be more of the same.

The book is organized into four chapters. Chapter 1 describes eight significant driving forces that are influencing faith formation in churches today and into the future. This chapter presents four scenarios to guide churches in envisioning the possibilities for the future by addressing the spiritual and religious needs of: (1) people of vibrant faith and active engagement in the parish community, (2) people who participate occasionally in parish life but are not actively engaged or spiritually committed, (3) people who are spiritual but not religious, and not participating in parish life, and (4) people who are uninterested in the spiritual life and unaffiliated with religion.

Chapter 2 develops the principles and practices for developing a Lifelong Faith Formation Network that addresses the diverse spiritual and religious needs of people in all four scenarios. Chapter 2 presents a step-by-step process and application tools for moving from needs to action by designing innovative programs, activities, strategies, and resources to shape the future of faith formation in a church.

Chapter 3 presents six of the most important leadership competencies necessary for leading faith formation today and into the future: adaptive leadership, innovative leadership, "Blue Ocean" thinking, change facilitation, and culturally intelligent leadership. The sixth leadership competency, curating content, reflects the importance today of identifying, selecting, and providing high quality faith formation resources from a variety of sources: print, audio, video, and online. Chapter 3 includes a variety of application tools.

Chapter 4 presents sixteen core strategies with practical ideas and resources for addressing the challenges and opportunities in each scenario. The sixteen strategies are not just "good ideas." Each one is grounded in practices that are already being implemented in one form or another in congregations and religious organizations today. The good news is that there are proven strategies, ideas, and resources that can bring the four scenarios to life in a congregation. The sixteen strategies are offered as a starting point for designing the future of faith formation in each scenario. They are not intended as a definitive list, but as a helpful guide. Many of the strategies can be customized for use in multiple scenarios. Every church can learn from the experience of these strategies and innovations, and adapt them to the size, geography, people, and cultures of a particular church.

To launch the Faith Formation 2020 Initiative, I invited a group of faith formation leaders from a diversity of Christian traditions to explore, discuss, and create the outline of the scenarios. They were instrumental in launching the project. I want to thank each of them for their contribution: David Anderson, Tonya Y. Burton, Pam Coster, Peter Denio, Fred Edie, Susan Hay, Mary Hess, Michael Horan, Lisa Kimball, Dion Kitching, Brian Lemoi, John McGinty, Patricia Nederveld, Sharon Ely Pearson, Janet Schaeffler, Susanna Singer, Rudy Vargas, Karen-Marie Yust, and Angela Ann Zukowski.

So Let Us Plant Dates

The next ten years can be a decade of hope for churches and faith formation, despite evidence to the contrary. Developing the Faith Formation 2020 Initiative and writing this book have reinforced my hope for the future because of the exciting and transformative approaches and practices that so many churches around the country are developing, and because of the innovative spirit that is infectious and holds so much promise. Even if we never see the fruits of our labors, the spirit of hope and innovation can permeate everything we do. In the end it is all about our children and grandchildren and the quality of church life and faith formation that they will come to experience. I hope this book inspires you to action and provides you with hope for the decade.

I am closing this introduction with an inspiring poem from the Brazilian author Rubem Alves. It captures the spirit of hope and courage and perseverance. As you read his words, remember that it make take up to ten years for a date tree to produce its first fruit.

What Is Hope?

It is a presentiment that imagination is more real
and reality less real than it looks.
It is a hunch
that the overwhelming brutality of facts
that oppress and repress is not the last word.
It is a suspicion
that reality is more complex
than realism wants us to believe
and that the frontiers of the possible
are not determined by the limits of the actual
and that in a miraculous and unexpected way
life is preparing the creative events
which will open the way to freedom and resurrection....
The two, suffering and hope, live from each other.
Suffering without hope
produces resentment and despair,
hope without suffering
creates illusions, naivete, and drunkenness....
Let us plant dates
even though those who plant them will never eat them.
We must live by the love of what we will never see.
This is the secret discipline.
It is a refusal to let the creative act
be dissolved in immediate sense experience
and a stubborn commitment to the future of our grandchildren.
Such disciplined love
is what has given prophets, revolutionaries and saints
the courage to die for the future they envisaged.
They make their own bodies
the seed of their highest hope.

—Rubem A. Alves, *Tomorrow's Child*, 1972

ONE

Envisioning the Future of Faith Formation 2020

Imagine faith formation today in a church community. A variety of high-quality faith formation programs for grade-school children, youth, and adults are offered throughout the year. The children's program consists of weekly classes and occasional special activities and events. The youth program is a mix of confirmation classes, youth meetings, service projects, and special events and trips. Adult programs include courses on a variety of topics, seasonal presentations like a Lenten series, and small group Bible study. Family programs are offered several times a year to connect families with the celebration of the church year seasons. In the summer, children and their parents participate in a Vacation Bible School program, while young people are engaged in service projects and mission trips locally and across the country. Milestones and sacraments provide opportunities for faith formation at baptism, first communion, receiving the first Bible, and confirmation. For people interested in becoming Christian, there is a yearlong process of faith formation to prepare them for baptism and joining the church.

It is a huge undertaking for the church and their faith formation leaders to provide this level of faith formation programming. But is it enough? Even though the community is very positive and supportive of faith formation and the great work that is being done, there is a feeling among the leaders that something is missing. They wonder why teens leave the church after confirmation. Why are parents bringing their children to classes but not to worship on Sunday? Why do some families get involved only when they are celebrating a milestone or sacrament? Why don't more adults participate in the adult faith formation programs? Where are all the people in their twenties and thirties? Why do parents have their child baptized and then never return to church again? How can we reach the new ethnic groups that are moving into our community? How can we reach those who have left the church?

The pastor, staff, and faith formation leaders see the changes occurring in their church, in their community, and in the world, and wonder what the future holds for them. If present trends continue what impact will they have on the future of the church? What will happen if the church doesn't respond to the challenges, if faith formation is not aligned well with the life situations and the spiritual needs of people today and in the future? The pastor, staff, and faith formation leaders feel that the pressing demands of the present preclude the possibility of imagining the future of faith formation in their church. Yet they must envision the future and design new initiatives to provide vibrant faith formation for all ages and generations if they are to thrive as a church community.

The Faith Formation 2020 Initiative was created to guide churches to envision and design dynamic, engaging, and inspiring faith formation in the second decade of the twenty-first century—to imagine the possibilities for faith formation in 2020. The last two decades have seen dramatic political, economic, social, and cultural changes affecting virtually every dimension of American Christianity. Churches across the United States are facing significant challenges in their efforts to provide vibrant faith formation for all ages and generations in the faith community. The new environment in which Christian faith formation will operate in the decade from 2010–2020 will demand new thinking and new models, practices, resources, and technologies to address the spiritual needs of all generations.

- *What could faith formation in Christian churches look like in 2020?*
- *Specifically, how can Christian congregations provide vibrant faith formation to address the spiritual and religious needs of all ages and generations over the next ten years?*
- *How can churches envision the shape of faith formation in the year 2020 and design initiatives to respond proactively to the challenges and opportunities in the second decade of the twenty-first century?*

The goal of the Faith Formation 2020 Initiative is to inspire creative action in the present through anticipation of possible futures. The four scenarios developed through the initiative are stories that address significant forces affecting faith forma-tion and stimulate new ways of thinking about the present and the future. No one knows what lies just beyond the horizon but these four scenarios of the future can inform church leaders of potential challenges and opportunities they may want to prepare for now rather than react to later. The four scenarios are not predictions, projections, or prophecies but rather an attempt to provoke a realization that the future need not simply be more of the same.

Scenario Thinking and the Future

To help church leaders envision the future of faith formation the Faith Formation 2020 Initiative employs a process called *scenario thinking.* Jay Ogilvy and Peter Schwartz of Global Business Network describe scenarios as "narratives of alternative environments in which today's decisions may be played out. They are not predictions. Nor are they strategies. Instead they are more like hypotheses of different futures specifically designed to highlight the risks and opportunities involved in specific strategic issues." The point is not to gather evidence for some "most probable" future. The point is rather to entertain a number of different possibilities in order to make better choices about the future of faith formation in the face of inevitable uncertainties.

Scenarios are created and used in sets of multiple stories that capture a range of possibilities, good and bad, expected and surprising. They are designed to stretch our thinking about emerging changes and the opportunities and threats that the future might hold. They allow us to weigh our choices more carefully when making short-term and long term strategic decisions. At their most basic, scenarios help people and organizations order and frame their thinking about the long term while providing them with the tools and confidence to take action soon. At their most powerful, scenarios help people and organizations find strength of purpose and strategic direction in the face of daunting, chaotic, and even frightening circumstances.

Over the last forty years, in the face of increasing uncertainty and complexity, corporations and organizations have begun to apply scenario processes to their work. A famous example occurred in South Africa in 1991, when the creation of the Mont Fleur scenarios catalyzed a nationwide discussion about the possibilities for post-Apartheid South Africa. These scenarios were developed as the political negotiations between the ANC and the apartheid-era National Party were taking place. The scenarios were presented as alternative outcomes to difficult decisions that the key stakeholders in South Africa would have to make (for example, about reconciliation versus revenge, about the role of private property, and about minority rights for whites). The dialogue that stemmed from these scenarios enabled the stakeholders to think through the implications of their decisions and consequently adjust their strategies.

The Smithsonian Institution engaged in scenario thinking when it decided to generate a new vision for the Institution and create a strategic plan that would help to decide how and where to allot its billion dollar annual budget over the next decade (2010–2020). The focus question was: How might the Smithsonian best create and diffuse knowledge in the future? A core piece of the process was to understand what the future would require the Institution to become. During the scenario workshops in 2009, roughly one hundred participants worked together to explore the external forces—from economic and geopolitical influences to demographic and technological change—that might affect the Smithsonian in the near, mid, and long term. They then developed and refined four alternative scenarios for the future and considered what role the Smithsonian could best plan in each:

- **Citizen of the World**: a globalized future in which borders become more porous, the United States becomes more intertwined with other nations, and the global and transnational elements of the Smithsonian activities come to the fore
- **Global Prosperity**: a "bright future" scenario in which national economies recover and thrive, and the Smithsonian is free to develop new opportunities without major economic constraints
- **Global Challenges**: a world in which the Smithsonian plays a role in addressing big challenges facing the United States and the world, including climate change issues, the need to improve education, and threats to the planet's cultural and national heritage
- **Most Respected Nation**: a world in which the Smithsonian embodies and represents what is best about the United States and grows its reputation as an institution that values and embodies knowledge, learning, and progress

One interesting realization that came out of the workshop was just how interconnected the future of the Smithsonian—steward of the United States' material culture and history—is with the future of the United States itself. In each scenario, the Smithsonian becomes an expression of the changing American identity. Another key realization was the increased importance of digitizing the Institution's collections and incorporating new interactive technologies into the museum experience in order to reach and attract broader audiences.

In recent years, scenario thinking has become one of the most popular strategy and long-term thinking tools, used by many of the world's top companies, influential government agencies, and community organizations and foundations to make sense of and succeed in a turbulent, uncertain world.

Three principles underpin any successful scenario thinking approach. Applied to religious congregations, the three principles are:

1. **Take the Long View.** The day-to-day work of most churches is driven by near-term concerns and one- to three-year planning horizons. However, in reality, most strategic choices—from new projects to new leadership—are

choices that will play out a long way into the future. Taking the long view offers a more proactive and anticipatory approach to address the forces affecting church life; to see both challenges and opportunities more clearly; and to consider the long-term effects and potential unintended consequences of actions that a church might take.

2. **Think from the "Outside-in."** Like other organizations, most churches are surprised by discontinuous events because they spend their time thinking about what they are most familiar with: their own congregation. They think from the inside—the things they can control—out to the world in which they operate. Conversely, thinking from the outside-in begins with pondering external social, technological, environmental, economic, religious, and political shifts—changes that might, over time, profoundly affect the community and church, creating new risks and opportunities in the process.

3. **Embrace Multiple Perspectives**. The introduction of multiple perspectives helps one better understand and challenge assumptions while painting an expansive picture of an issue or idea. The result is the broadening of a church's peripheral vision; new threats and opportunities are seen that otherwise might have been missed.

Ultimately, the point of scenario thinking is to arrive at a deeper understanding of the world in which the church operates, and to continue to use that understanding to address the most critical challenges—from faith formation priorities, programming strategy, and innovation to visioning and leadership. In every context, scenario thinking improves upon the ability to make better decisions today and in the future.

Although scenario planning is a highly imaginative and interactive exercise, the process is systematic with five distinct phases. These phases are:

1. **Orient.** The goal of this phase is to clarify the issue at stake, and to use that issue as an orienting device throughout the remaining phases.

2. **Explore.** The second phase explores the many "driving forces" that could shape your focal question. Driving forces are the forces of change outside the organization or community that will shape future dynamics in predictable and unpredictable ways. They might include new technologies, political shifts, economic conditions, or social dynamics. Driving forces can be either "predetermined elements"—forces that are highly likely to develop in a direction that is known and unchangeable; or "uncertainties"—forces that are important, but unpredictable in terms of how they may play out.

3. **Synthesize.** The next phase involves combining the identified driving forces to create a scenario framework. Usually frameworks are constructed from two of the most important, or "critical" uncertainties. Once a framework is in place, the next step is to develop the scenarios into narratives—stories that begin in the present and end in the future.

4. **Act.** In this phase, scenarios are used to inform and inspire action. The test of a good set of scenarios is not whether in the end those scenarios portray the future accurately, but whether it enables an organization to learn, adapt, and take effective action. After creating the scenarios, the next step is to imagine deeply living and working in each one. Individuals and organizations should ask themselves: What if this scenario is the future? What actions would I take today to prepare? Are there actions I could take to catalyze a desirable future, or to mitigate a negative one? The answers to your questions are scenario implications. The patterns and insights that emerge from the implications—across all possible scenarios—can set the priorities that will help you make progress on your long-term goals.

5. **Monitor.** The last phase involves creating mechanisms that will help your organization track shifts in the environment and adjust strategy accordingly.

What are the benefits of scenario thinking and planning for envisioning the future?

- Using a methodological structure that focuses on what is not known, scenario planning achieves greater impact by anticipating alternate outcomes and managing resources accordingly.
- Scenario planning is a powerful tool precisely because the future is unpredictable and shaped by many interacting variables. Scenarios enable us to think creatively and rigorously about the different ways these forces may interact, while forcing us to challenge our own assumptions about what we believe or hope the future will be.
- Scenarios embrace and weave together multiple perspectives and provide us an ongoing framework for spotting and making sense of important changes as they emerge.
- Perhaps most importantly, scenarios give us a new, shared language that deepens our conversations about the future and how we can help to shape it.

Envisioning the Future of Faith Formation Using Scenario Thinking

No one can definitively map the future of Christian faith formation. However, developing alternate futures can contribute to good decision-making processes that will determine the direction of faith formation. The four faith formation scenarios presented in this book can help frame key issues and developments that will shape what the future may hold for a church and help a church's leadership prepare more effectively. The scenarios are intended to begin a stimulating discussion about the future of faith formation in your church—not to propose readymade answers or solutions.

The Focus of Faith Formation 2020 (Orient)

Every scenario project has a focal question—a broad yet strategic query that serves as an anchor for the scenarios. For the Faith Formation 2020 Initiative the focal question is: What could faith formation in Christian churches look like in 2020? Additionally, how can Christian congregations provide vibrant faith formation to address the spiritual and religious needs of all ages and generations over the next ten years? How can churches envision the shape of faith formation in the year 2020 and design initiatives to respond proactively to the challenges and opportunities in the second decade of the twenty-first century?

Eight Significant Driving Forces Influencing Faith Formation 2020 (Explore)

What are the driving forces that will most directly impact the future of faith formation in Christian churches by 2020, and more specifically, the ability of congregations to provide vibrant faith formation over the next ten years? We cannot know what the future will hold beforehand. But we can see trends in the present, which, continuing on their current course, will have an impact on developing faith formation for 2020.

We know that Christian churches are confronted by a number of significant social, cultural, technological, and generational forces that make faith formation for all ages and generations quite challenging. There are driving forces that we can be reasonably certain will shape the worlds we are describing. These "predetermined elements" include the growing influence of Hispanic/Latino religious faith upon American Christianity, the rise of emerging adulthood—emerging adulthood, increasing numbers of adults sixty-five and older in American society, and increasing social, religious, and ethnic/cultural diversity in the United States. For example, it is a demographic certainty that there will be more adults over sixty-five years old in the United States population, and in churches, in 2020 than there are now.

Predetermined elements are important to any scenario story, but they are not the foundation on which these stories are built. Rather, scenarios are formed around "critical uncertainties"—driving forces that are considered both highly important to our focusing issue, the future of faith formation in Christian churches, and highly uncertain in terms of their future resolution. Whereas predetermined elements are predictable driving forces, uncertainties are by their nature unpredictable: their outcome can be guessed at but not known. While any single uncertainty could challenge our thinking, the future will be shaped by multiple forces playing out over time. The scenario framework provides a structured way to consider how these critical uncertainties might unfold and evolve in combination.

By reviewing research studies, analyzing trends, and consulting with leaders, the Faith Formation 2020 Initiative selected eight significant forces—critical uncertainties whose future direction is not known, but that are already having significant impact on faith formation and will likely continue to do so over the next decade. (See Appendix 1 for research summaries of each driving force.) The eight significant forces include:

1. Declining Number of Christians and Growing Number of People with No Religious Affiliation. The population of the United States continues to show signs of becoming less religious: In 2008, 15–16% of Americans claimed no religious affiliation, nearly double the 1990 figure. Among Americans ages 18-29, one in four say they are not currently affiliated with any particular religion. The number of American adults identified as Christians dropped 10% from 86% in 1990 to 76% in 2008. Similar to the general American public, Latinos have become less identified with Christianity—down from 91% in 1990 to 82% in 2008. Latinos claiming no religious affiliation increased fourfold in number, from 900,000 or 6% of the population in 1990 to nearly four million or 12% in 2008. It appears that the challenge to Christianity in the United States does not come from other religions but rather from a rejection of all forms of organized religion. This growing non-religious minority reduces the traditional societal role of congregations in family celebrations of life-cycle events. Forestalling of religious rites of passage, such as marriage and baptism, and the lowering expectations on religious funeral services, could have long lasting consequences for religious institutions.

2. Increasing Number of People Becoming More "Spiritual" and Less "Religious." A small but growing minority of the United States population describe themselves as Spiritual but Not Religious (meaning not connected to organized religion): 9% of Americans were Spiritual but Not Religious in 1998, rising to 14% in 2008; and 18% of eighteen- to thirty-nine-year-olds say they are Spiritual but Not Religious, compared to only 11% a decade ago. If what people mean when they say they are Spiritual but Not Religious is that they are generally concerned with spiritual matters but are not interested in organized religion, then this trend indicates a growing minority of the population whose spiritual inclinations do not lead them to become involved in churches, synagogues, or mosques. In our increasingly pluralistic society, to be "spiritual" is more likely to represent an eclectic spirituality, drawing not only from the various streams of Christianity, but including elements of other religious traditions.

3. Declining Participation in Christian Churches. By measure of participation such as worship attendance, marriages and baptisms in the church, and child and youth participation in faith formation programming, the trend is toward declining participation in church life in mainline Protestant and Catholic churches. Among young Hispanics, immigrants attend church services more regularly than do the native born (second and third generation). Combined with the trend toward fewer Christians and the growing numbers of religiously unaffiliated, it appears that succeeding generations of Christians are less likely to be exposed to formation in the Christian faith because worship attendance is down, and therefore participation in church life, education, and activities is likewise down. This means less exposure to the Christian tradition and teachings, reduced opportunities to experience the Christian way of life, and far less reinforcement of the Christian faith in church settings. The effect of these trends can be found in research on emerging adults (twenty- to thirty-year-olds): only 15% embrace a strong religious faith and another 30% believe and perform certain aspects of their religious traditions; at least 40% have no connection to a religious tradition (see *Souls in Transition*).

4. Increasing Diversity and Pluralism in American Society. American society reflects a growing diversity of ethnic cultures and nationalities and their traditions, customs, foods, and languages, and also a growing diversity of religious traditions from the East and the West. Pluralism creates both richness and tensions. We live next door to other nations; we're engaged in conversation with people from all parts of the world, with customs and expectations vastly different from our own. We also live in a pluralistic society in which no single authority exercises supremacy and no single belief or ideology dominates. Christian culture is no longer at the center of American life; it has been replaced by a tapestry of religious and spiritual alternatives and choices. The range of religious practice and belief in American society today is enormous, and it is all around us. The increasing diversity and the pluralism of belief and practice undermines the plausibility and truth-claims of any single religious tradition. The diversity of religious choice and openness to everything religious results in people crisscrossing religious boundaries as they construct their own personal spiritualities. We have become a society of "spiritual tinkerers" (Robert Wuthnow), which makes developing and sustaining a Christian identity and religious commitments exceeding difficult.

5. Increasing Influence of Individualism on Christian Identity and Community Life. The influence of individualism means that religious identity is more autonomous and deliberate today and that religion is less anchored in a sense of belonging. There is a decline in connectedness; a weakening or severing of the *social* basis of religion in family, marriage, ethnicity, and community; a decline in the perceived necessity of communal or institutional structures as constituent of religious identity. Religious identity today is not only less bounded by doctrine or creed; it is also less nurtured and reinforced by community. Significant numbers of Americans see little necessary connection between being spiritual and being part of a historic tradition, or part of a disciplined community of faith. This is reinforced by the mass media's not so subtle message that you don't need a religious community to engage "God issues." Nominal membership increasingly replaces active involvement, a development paralleling national civic trends. Religion is perceived less as an inherited phenomenon, or as a binding community of discipleship and obligation. Religious leaders and institutions, which traditionally provided the framework within which religious meaning was constructed, have become increasingly peripheral to the spirituality and "lived religion" of private personal enterprise.

6. Changing Patterns of Marriage and Family Life. It appears that one of the reasons for the decline in church participation is that younger Americans are marrying later, having fewer children, and having them later—all of which means that far more younger Americans are single and childless than was true a generation ago and that the same younger Americans are not settling into religious congregations at the same rate as their parents did in the 1970s. Religious practice is especially influenced by marrying, settling down, and having children and raising them. Since individuals who marry are more likely to attend religious services than are those who delay marriage, the postponement of marriage and childbearing has contributed to the decline in church attendance. Also, there has been a dramatic increase in religiously mixed marriages and partnerships: more than one in four (27%) American adults who are married or living with a partner are in religiously mixed relationships. If people from different Protestant denominational families are included, for example a marriage between a Methodist and a Lutheran, nearly four in ten (37%) marriages are religiously mixed.

7. Declining Family Religious Socialization. Family religious socialization has always been the foundation for the development of faith and faith practices in children, and for participation in church life and worship. As Christian Smith observes, "teenagers with seriously religious parents are more likely than those without such parents to have been trained in their lives to think, feel, believe, and act as serious religious believers, and that training "sticks" with them even when the leave home and enter emerging adulthood. Emerging adults who grew up with seriously religious parents are through socialization more likely (1) to have internalized their parents' religious worldview, (2) to possess the practical religious know-how needed to live more highly religious lives, and (3) to embody the identity orientations and behavioral tendencies toward continuing to practice what they have been taught religiously" (Smith, 232). Significant indicators, such as religious identification as a Christian, worship attendance, marriages and baptisms in the church, and changing generational patterns, point to a decline in family religious socialization across all denominations, but especially among Catholic and Mainline traditions. Religious practice among the next generation of parents (young adults in their twenties and thirties) is especially influenced by marrying, settling down, having children and raising them. Since individuals who marry are more likely to attend religious services than are those who delay marriage, the postponement of marriage and childbearing has contributed to the decline in church attendance. Complicating this picture, is the fact that an ever growing percentage of Christians (at least 30%) are not getting married in a religious ceremony. The less contact that young adults have with the Christian tradition through participation in a local church, the less family religious socialization that is likely to take place when they marry and have children.

8. Increasing Impact of Digital Media and Web Technologies. Technology and digital media are transforming the ways we live. Globalization and pluralism are driven by this unprecedented technological change. People meet on Facebook and share their inspirations on YouTube all the while Tweeting to an assortment of friends. Groups of people at opposite ends of a continent or around the globe don't need to leave their own contexts in order to meet in real time and in video, on Skype or some webinar format. Social connectivity is being leveraged globally online. People's use of the internet's capabilities for communication—for creating, cultivating, and continuing social relationships—is undeniable. However, time spent online often takes time away from important face-to-face relationships. As of 2010, virtually all of those twenty-nine and younger in the United States today are online, as are 93% of teens (12–17) and young adults (18–29), 81% of adults thirty to forty-nine years old, 70% of adults fifty to sixty-four years old, and 38% of adults sixty-five and over. Increasingly people are accessing the internet on smart phones like the iPhone to send or receive text messages, take a picture, play a game, check email, record video, instant message, play music, get maps or directions, or record and watch video. Media are among the most powerful forces in young people's lives today. Eight- to eighteen-year-olds spend more time with media than in any other activity besides (maybe) sleeping—an average of more than seven hours a day, seven days a week. The television shows they watch, video games they play, songs they listen to, books they read, and websites they visit are an enormous part of their lives, offering a constant stream of messages about families, peers, relationships, gender roles, sex, violence, food, values, clothes, and an abundance of other topics too long to list. How will these new digital technologies transform our lives and our religious identities? What will be the impact of this technological revolution on faith formation and Christian congregations?

Two Critical Uncertainties for Faith Formation 2020 (Synthesize)

After careful study of the significant driving forces, two uncertainties were selected from a longer list of potential uncertainties that might shape the broader context of church and faith formation over the next decade and longer. The framework for the final set of scenarios is a matrix with two axes that represent the two critical uncertainties in the external environment that will affect the future of faith formation from 2010–2020. The two chosen uncertainties, introduced below, together define a set of four scenarios for the future of faith formation in churches that are divergent, challenging, internally consistent, and plausible. Each of the two uncertainties is expressed as an axis that represents a continuum of possibilities ranging between two endpoints.

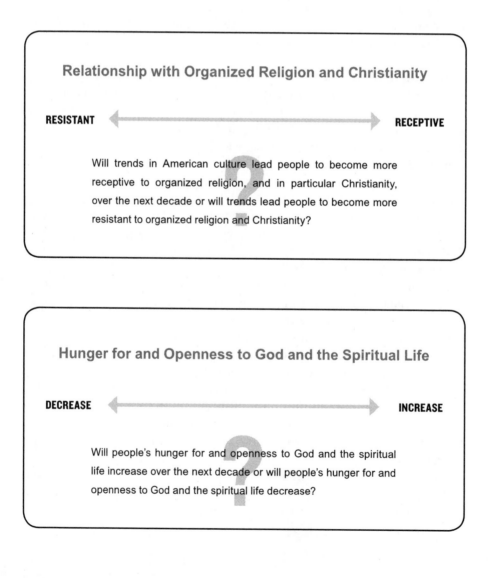

Relationship with Organized Religion and Christianity

RESISTANT ←————————————→ RECEPTIVE

Will trends in American culture lead people to become more receptive to organized religion, and in particular Christianity, over the next decade or will trends lead people to become more resistant to organized religion and Christianity?

Hunger for and Openness to God and the Spiritual Life

DECREASE ←————————————→ INCREASE

Will people's hunger for and openness to God and the spiritual life increase over the next decade or will people's hunger for and openness to God and the spiritual life decrease?

The "future of faith formation 2020 framework" was developed because the combination of *receptivity* to organized religion and Christianity, and *openness* or *hunger* for God and the spiritual life seemed to best express the American population's contemporary experience today and over the next decade.

Relationship with Organized Religion and Christianity

This uncertainty refers to the social and cultural trends regarding people's attitudes and responses to organized religion, and in particular Christianity, in the United States. Will people be more or less receptive to Christianity and involved in churches in the next decade? Several of the eight significant forces describe the current trajectory of this uncertainty: declining numbers of Christians; growing numbers of people with no religious affiliation; increasing numbers of people becoming more "spiritual" and less "religious;" declining participation in Christian churches; increasing influence of individualism on Christian identity and community life; changing patterns of marriage and family life, especially delaying marriage and having children later; and declining family religious socialization. Will these trends continue and, if they do, what will be the impact on Christian churches and faith formation? How will churches respond to this uncertainty over the next decade?

Hunger for and Openness to God and the Spiritual Life

This uncertainty refers to the importance of God and the spiritual life in the lives of people today. Will people's hunger and openness increase or decrease over the next decade? Several of the eight significant forces describe the current trajectory of this uncertainty: declining numbers of Christians; increasing number of people becoming more "spiritual" and less "religious;" declining participation in Christian churches; increasing diversity and pluralism in American society resulting in a tapestry of religious and spiritual alternatives and choices; increasing influence of individualism on Christian identity and community life resulting in "spiritual tinkering" and more individualized spirituality; declining family religious socialization; and utilizing the digital media and technological tools to access a diversity of spiritual traditions and resources, and to participate in online communities of support and spiritual growth. Will these trends continue and, if they do, what will be the impact on Christian churches and faith formation? How will churches respond to this uncertainty over the next decade?

Four Scenarios for Faith Formation 2020 (Synthesize)

When the two critical uncertainties are connected in a 2x2 matrix, a set of four stories—or scenarios—are created to describe how the future of faith formation in 2020 could evolve. This matrix represents a map of today and a projected future reality. That is, each of the four quadrants of this map represents a dynamic story that is based on a different future outcome of the two critical uncertainties.

Which of the scenarios will become dominant over the next decade? Where are people in our churches and culture moving? What will be the response of Christian churches to the four scenarios?

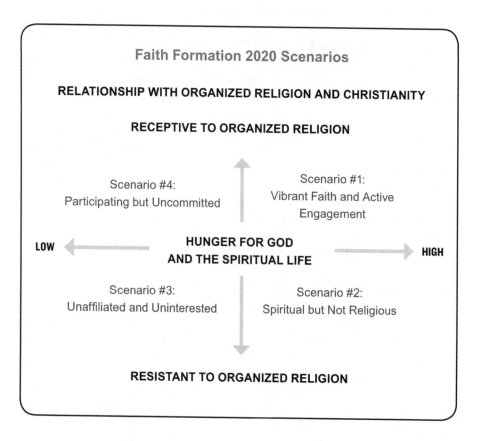

The scenarios express a range of possible futures facing congregational faith formation over the decade from 2010 to 2020. Each scenario story explains why the "main story" of faith formation in 2020 will be framed by the response of Christian churches to people's relationship—their attitudes and responses—to organized religion (receptive or resistant) and to people's hunger for and openness to God and the spiritual life (high or low).

The scenarios that follow are not meant to be exhaustive or prescriptive—rather they are designed to be both plausible and challenging, to engage your imagination while also raising new questions about what the future of faith formation might look and feel like. *Imagine what faith formation could look and feel like in your congregation if your church is responding to the challenges and opportunities in each scenario. Imagine the life of your congregation in 2020 if faith formation addresses the spiritual and religious needs of all ages and generations in each scenario over the next ten years.*

Scenario #1. Vibrant Faith and Active Engagement

The first scenario describes a world in which people of all ages and generations are actively engaged in a Christian church, are spiritually committed, and growing in their faith. People have found their spiritual home within an established Christian tradition and a local faith community that provides ways for all ages and generations to grow in faith, worship God, and live their faith in the world. Congregations are challenged to provide lifelong faith formation for all ages and generations, at home and at church, that develops vibrant faith, is continuous throughout life, and engages all people in the life and mission of the church community.

Scenario #2. Spiritual but Not Religious

The second scenario describes a world in which people are spiritually hungry and searching for God and the spiritual life, but most likely are not affiliated with organized religion and an established Christian tradition. Some may join a nondenominational Christian church focused on their spiritual needs, while others may find an outlet for their spiritual hunger in small communities of like-minded spiritual seekers, in local or global acts of service, or in online spiritual resources and communities. The Spiritual but Not Religious reflect a growing minority of the American population, especially among the eighteen- to thirty-nine-year-olds. Congregations are challenged to engage people where their live (physical and virtual communities), build relationships, engage in spiritual conversations, and offer programs and activities that nurture their spiritual growth.

Scenario #3. Unaffiliated and Uninterested

The third scenario describes a world in which people experience little need for God and the spiritual life and are not affiliated with organized religion and established Christian churches. The Unaffiliated and Uninterested reject all forms of organized religion and reflect a steadily increasing percentage of the American population, especially among the eighteen- to twenty-nine-year-olds. Congregations are challenged to find ways to "plant" themselves in the midst of the cultures and worlds of the Unaffiliated and Uninterested, build relationships, and be witnesses to the Christian faith in the world today.

Scenario #4. Participating but Uncommitted

The fourth scenario describes a world in which people attend church activities, but are not actively engaged in their church community or spiritually committed. They may participate in significant seasonal celebrations, such as Christmas and Easter, and celebrate sacraments and milestone events, such as marriage and baptism. Some may even attend worship regularly, and send their children to religious education classes. Their spiritual commitment is low and their connection to the church is more social and utilitarian than spiritual. Congregations are challenged to provide faith formation that recognizes that belonging (engagement) leads to believing (spiritual commitment) and a more vibrant faith, and develop approaches for increasing people's engagement with the church community and the Christian tradition.

Apply the Four Scenarios to Your Church

Use the following questions to explore how each scenario applies in your church community.

- Who are the people in your community in this scenario? How would you describe them?
- What are the religious and spiritual needs of people in this scenario? How would you describe one or two aspects of their religious and spiritual hopes or desires?
- How is your church addressing the spiritual and religious needs of people in this scenario through faith formation today?

The Impact of the Four Scenarios for Churches (Act)

Each scenario story explains why the "main story" of faith formation in 2020 will be framed by the response of churches to the challenges and opportunities in each scenario. While the questions that follow are only illustrative of the challenges and opportunities the scenarios present, they help to frame questions that churches need to ask about the impact of the four scenarios upon their congregation and its faith formation. Develop your own questions by studying the eight driving forces and how they apply to your church (see Appendix 1), and by exploring the implications of the four scenarios for your congregation. Use the following questions as a guide to begin your study of the impact—challenges and opportunities—of the four scenarios upon your church community.

Scenario #1. Vibrant Faith and Active Engagement

- Will churches develop continuous faith formation for all ages and generations, especially for adults (twenties-nineties), faith formation that engages people—mind, body, heart, and spirit—in a diversity of ways to grow in faith for a lifetime?
- Will churches strengthen family socialization by equipping parents and families to become centers of faith formation and practice?
- Will churches become "sticky"—keeping all ages involved in faith formation through a diversity of programs, activities, and resources at home and church that address their life situations and religious and spiritual needs?

- Will churches embrace the tremendous potential of digital media and web technologies to provide faith formation and engage people in lifelong faith growth 24/7/365?
- Will churches empower people of vibrant faith with the knowledge, faith sharing skills, and confidence to share their faith with those who are not involved in a church community or spiritually committed?

Scenario #2. Spiritual but Not Religious

- Will churches invest the time and resources to develop specialized faith formation around the life situations and spiritual needs of the Spiritual but Not Religious who are in their twenties and thirties?
- Will churches provide faith formation programming for spiritual seekers that is conducted in "Third Place" settings outside of the church facilities?
- Will churches see the potential in marriage and baptism for faith formation and the potential (re)engagement in church life for the "Spiritual but Not Religious?"
- Will churches provide a guided process and program for spiritually hungry people to investigate the Christian faith and join in small communities with other seekers for spiritual growth and support?

Scenario #3. Unaffiliated and Uninterested

- Will churches establish a "Third Place" gathering site as a platform for reaching the Unaffiliated and Uninterested through a variety of spiritual and/or life-centered programs, conversations, and activities?
- Will churches develop a "web-presence" that is inviting and attractive to the Unaffiliated and Uninterested so that they can investigate and experience the Christian faith online?
- Will churches sponsor programs, such as service projects and mission trips, that are designed so that people from the wider community can participate, interact with church members, and come into contact with the Christian faith in action?

Scenario #4. Participating but Uncommitted

- Will churches begin with the birth and baptism of children to strengthen family socialization by equipping parents and families to become centers of faith formation and practice?
- Will churches develop pathways for spiritual commitment and more active engagement by offering a formation process that helps people develop and deepen their relationship with Jesus Christ, explore the foundational teachings of the Christian faith, and live the fundamental Christian practices?
- Will churches utilize digital media and web technologies to extend faith formation—resources, social networking, faith practices—into the daily lives of people who only participate occasionally?

• Will churches use the occasions of participation, such as sacraments and milestones, to provide faith formation that involves the whole family and invites them into more active engagement in the church community?

Assess the Impact of the Four Scenarios on Your Church

Use the following questions to explore the impact of each scenario on your church community.

- What are the *challenges* that this scenario presents for the future of faith formation in your church community?
- What are the *opportunities* that this scenario presents for the future of faith formation in your church community?
- What are the *implications* of *not* addressing the future of faith formation in this scenario?
- What are the *implications* of addressing the future of faith formation in this scenario?

Strategies for Bringing the Four Faith Formation Scenarios to Life (Act)

Part Four in this book presents sixteen strategies with practical ideas and resources for addressing the challenges and opportunities in each scenario over the next ten years. The sixteen strategies are not just "good ideas." Each one is grounded in practices that are already being implemented in one form or another in congregations and religious organizations today. The good news is that there are proven strategies, ideas, and resources that can bring the four scenarios to life in a congregation.

The sixteen strategies are offered as a starting point for designing the future of faith formation in each scenario. They are not intended as a definitive list, but as a helpful guide. Many of the strategies can be customized for use in multiple scenarios. Every church can learn from the experience of these strategies and innovations, and adapt them to the size, geography, people, and cultures of a particular church.

Faith Formation 2020 Strategies

1. Faith Formation through the Life of the Whole Church (Scenarios 1 and 4)
2. Faith Formation using Digital Media and Web Technologies (All Scenarios)
3. Family Faith Formation (Scenarios 1, 2, and 4)
4. Intergenerational Faith Formation (Scenarios 1 and 4)

5. Generational Faith Formation (Scenarios 1, 2, and 4)
    - Faith formation with the iGeneration and Millennial Generation
    - Faith formation with Generation X
    - Faith formation with the Baby Boomer Generation
    - Faith formation with the Builder Generation
6. Milestones Faith Formation (All Scenarios)
7. Faith Formation in Christian Practices (All Scenarios)
8. Transforming the World: Engagement in and Formation for Service and Mission (All Scenarios)
9. Spiritual Formation (All Scenarios)
10. Multi-Ethnic Faith Formation (All Scenarios)
11. Faith Formation for Spiritual Seekers (Scenario 2)
12. Apprenticeships in Discipleship (Scenarios 2 and 4)
13. Pathways to Vibrant Faith and Active Engagement (Scenario 2 and 4)
14. Faith Formation in Third Place Settings (Scenarios 2 and 3)
15. Empowering the Community to Share their Faith (Scenario 1)
16. Interfaith Education and Dialogue (Scenario 1)

In chapter 2 we turn our attention to designing a comprehensive plan for Faith Formation 2020 in your church that builds on current faith formation efforts and utilizes the four scenarios and the sixteen strategies to plan for the future.

Resources Consulted for Scenario Thinking

GBN Bulletin Fall 2009. Global Business Network. (www.gbn.com/consulting/article_details.php?id=94&breadcrumb=ideas)

Global Business Network: www.gbn.com

Ogilvy, Jay and Peter Schwartz. *Plotting Your Scenarios*. Global Business Network. (www.gbn.com/consulting/article_details.php?id=24)

Scearce, Diana, Katherine Fulton, and the Global Business Network Community. *What If: The Art of Scenario Planning for Nonprofits*. Global Business Network. (www.gbn.com/consulting/article_details.php?id=27)

Swartz, Peter. *The Art of the Long View*. Peter Schwartz. New York: Currency Doubleday, 1996.

Why Scenarios? Global Business Network. (www.gbn.com/about/scenario_planning.php)

Resources Consulted for Driving Forces

American Congregations 2008. Faith Communities Today. Hartford: Hartford Institute for Religion Research, 2009. (http://faithcommunitiestoday.org/research-based-products-congregational-leadership)

American Congregations at the Beginning of the Twenty-First Century: The National Congregations Study 2008. Mark Chaves, Shawna Anderson, and Jason Byasse. (www.soc.duke.edu/natcong)

American Religious Identification Survey (ARIS 2008). March 2009. Barry A. Kosmin and Ariela Keysar. Program on Public Values. Hartford: Trinity College, 2009. (www.americanreligionsurvey-aris.org/reports/ ARIS_Report_2008.pdf)

Chaves, Mark. "We're even more spiritual; even less religious." *Faith and Leadership Blog.* July 2, 2009. (www.faithandleadership.com/blog/07-02-2009/mark-chaves-were-even-more-spiritual-even-less-religious)

Dinges, William. "Faith, Hope, and (Excessive) Individualism." *Handing on the Faith.* Edited by Robert Embelli. New York: Crossroad, 2006.

Dinges, William. "The American Cultural Context for Adolescent Catechesis." *Source Book on Adolescent Catechesis: Volume 1.* Washington, DC: NIAC, 2008. (www.adolescentcatechesis.org)

Faith in Flux: Changes in Religious Affiliation in the U.S. April 27, 2009. Pew Research Center. (http://pewresearch.org/pubs/1204/religion-changes-affiliations-survey)

"Future of the Internet." Pew Internet & American Life Project. (www.pewinternet.org/Presentations/2010/Jun/The-Future-of-the-Internet--National-Geographic.aspx)

Generation M2: Media in the Lives of 8- to 18-Year-Olds. Kaiser Family Foundation Study (January 2010). (www.kff.org/entmedia/mh012010pkg.cfm)

"Many Americans Say Other Faiths Can Lead to Eternal Life." Pew Forum on Religion & Public Life. July 31-Aug. 10, 2008. (http://pewforum.org/Many-Americans-Say-Other-Faiths-Can-Lead-to-Eternal-Life.aspx)

Olson, David T. *The American Church in Crisis.* Grand Rapids: Zondervan, 2008.

Pew Internet & American Life Project (www.pewinternet.org)

Pew Social & Demographic Trends (http://pewsocialtrends.org).

Pew Research Center (http://pewresearch.org).

Smith, Christian, with Patricia Snell. *Souls in Transition: The Religious and Spiritual Lives of Emerging Adults.* New York: Oxford University Press, 2009.

U.S. Religious Landscape Survey. June 23, 2008. Pew Forum on Religion and Public Life. (http://religions.pewforum.org)

U.S. Latino Religious Identification 1990-2008: Growth, Diversity and Transformation. Juhem Navarro-Rivera, Barry A. Kosmin and Ariela Keysar. Program on Public Values. Hartford: Trinity College, 2009. (www.americanreligionsurvey-aris.org)

Wuthnow, Robert. *After the Baby Boomers: How Twenty- and Thirty-Somethings Are Shaping the Future of American Religion.* Princeton: Princeton University Press, 2007.

Faith Formation 2020 Scenarios

Relationship with Organized Religion and Christianity

Receptive to Organized Religion

Scenario #4
Participating but Uncommitted

The fourth scenario describes a world in which people attend church activities but are not actively engaged in their church community or spiritually committed. They may participate in significant seasonal celebrations, such as Christmas and Easter, and celebrate sacraments and milestone events, such as marriage and baptism. Some may even attend worship regularly, and send their children to religious education classes. Their spiritual commitment is low and their connection to the church is more social and utilitarian than spiritual. Congregations are challenged to provide faith formation that recognizes that belonging (engagement) leads to believing (spiritual commitment) and a more vibrant faith, and develop approaches for increasing people's engagement with the church community and the Christian tradition.

Scenario #1
Vibrant Faith and Active Engagement

The first scenario describes a world in which people of all ages and generations are actively engaged in a Christian church, are spiritually committed, and are growing in their faith. People have found their spiritual home within an established Christian tradition and a local faith community that provides ways for all ages and generations to grow in faith, worship God, and live their faith in the world. Congregations are challenged to provide lifelong faith formation for all ages and generations, at home and at church, that develops vibrant faith, is continuous throughout life, and engages all people in the life and mission of the church community.

LOW ⟵—————— Hunger for God and the Spiritual Life —————⟶ **HIGH**

Scenario #3
Unaffiliated and Uninterested

The third scenario describes a world in which people experience little need for God and the spiritual life and are not affiliated with organized religion and established Christian churches. The Unaffiliated and Uninterested reject all forms of organized religion and reflect a steadily increasing percentage of the American population, especially among the 18-29-year-olds. Congregations are challenged to find ways to "plant" themselves in the midst of the cultures and worlds of the Unaffiliated and Uninterested, build relationships, and be witnesses to the Christian faith in the world today.

Scenario #2
Spiritual but Not Religious

The second scenario describes a world in which people are spiritually hungry and searching for God and the spiritual life, but mostly likely not affiliated with organized religion and an established Christian tradition. Some may join a non-denominational Christian church focused on their spiritual needs, while others may find an outlet for their spiritual hunger in small communities of like-minded spiritual seekers, in local or global acts of service—or in online spiritual resources and communities. The Spiritual but Not Religious reflect a growing minority of the American population, especially among the 18-39-year-olds. Congregations are challenged to engage people where their live (physical and virtual communities), build relationships, engage in spiritual conversations, and offer programs and activities that nourish their spiritual growth.

Resistant to Organized Religion

APPENDIX: EIGHT DRIVING FORCES AFFECTING THE FUTURE OF FAITH FORMATION

By reviewing research studies, analyzing trends, and consulting with leaders, the Faith Formation 2020 Initiative selected eight significant forces—critical uncertainties whose future direction is not known, but are already having a significant impact on faith formation today and it appears will continue to do so over the next decade. These eight trends may continue on their present course or change direction, but, in either case, it appears that they will have a significant impact on the future direction of faith formation through 2020. The eight significant uncertainties include:

- declining numbers of Christians and growing numbers of people with no religious affiliation
- increasing number of people becoming more "spiritual" and less "religious"
- declining participation in Christian churches
- increasing diversity and pluralism in American society
- increasing influence of individualism on Christian identity and community life
- changing patterns of marriage and family life
- declining family religious socialization
- increasing impact of digital media and web technologies

Declining Numbers of Christians and Growing Numbers of People with No Religious Affiliation

The population of the United States continues to show signs of becoming less religious. One of the most significant indicators of people's receptivity to organized religion is the finding from the 2009 *American Religious Identification Survey* (ARIS) which reported that 15% of Americans claimed no religious affiliation, nearly double the 1990 figure of 8%. The Pew Research study, *Faith in Flux*, confirmed this trend—finding that the number of people who say they are unaffiliated with any particular faith doubled to 16%. Among Americans ages eighteen to twenty-nine, one in four say they are not currently affiliated with any particular religion.

Similar to the general American public, Latinos have become less identified with Christianity—down from 91% in 1990 to 82% in 2008. Mirroring the overall national trend, there has been a significant jump in the number and percentage of Nones, the no-religion population. Nones increased fourfold among Latinos from nine hundred thousand or 6% in 1990 to nearly four million or 12% in 2008, making it the fastest growing segment.

At the same time the number of American adults identified as Christians dropped 10% from 86% in 1990 to 76% in 2008. The historic Mainline churches and denominations have experienced the steepest declines while the non-denominational Christian identity has been trending upward particularly since 2001.

It appears that the challenge to Christianity in the United States does not come from other religions but rather from a rejection of all forms of organized religion. The two studies confirm that Americans are slowly becoming less Christian and that in recent decades the challenge to Christianity in American society does not come from other world religions or new religious movements but rather from a rejection of all organized religions. This growing non-religious minority reduces the traditional societal role of congregations and places of worship in family celebrations of lifecycle events. Forestalling of religious rites of passage, such as marriage and baptism, and the lowering expectations on religious funeral services, could have long lasting consequences for religious institutions.

Sources

American Religious Identification Survey (ARIS 2008). March 2009. Barry A. Kosmin and Ariela Keysar. Program on Public Values. Hartford: Trinity College, 2009. (www.americanreligionsurvey-aris.org/reports/ARIS_Report_2008.pdf)

Faith in Flux: Changes in Religious Affiliation in the U.S. April 27, 2009. Pew Research Center. (http://pewresearch.org/pubs/1204/religion-changes-affiliations-survey)

U.S. Latino Religious Identification 1990-2008: Growth, Diversity & Transformation. Juhem Navarro-Rivera, Barry A. Kosmin and Ariela Keysar. Program on Public Values. Hartford: Trinity College, 2009. (www.americanreligionsurvey-aris.org)

Increasing Number of People Becoming More "Spiritual" and Less "Religious"

The vast majority of Americans—approximately 80%—describe themselves as both spiritual and religious. Still, a small but growing minority describe themselves as Spiritual but Not Religious (meaning not connected to organized religion). If we define the Spiritual but Not Religious as people who say that they are at least moderately spiritual but not more than slightly religious, then 9% of respondents were Spiritual but Not Religious in 1998, rising to 14% in 2008. Today, 18% of eighteen- to thirty-nine-year-olds say they are Spiritual but Not Religious, compared to only 11% a decade ago.

What does the growth of this Spiritual but Not Religious segment of the population mean for organized religion in the United States? If what people mean when they say they are Spiritual but Not Religious is that they are generally concerned with spiritual matters but are not interested in organized religion, then this trend indicates a growing minority of the population whose spiritual inclinations do not lead them to become involved in churches, synagogues, or mosques. In our increasingly pluralistic society, to be "spiritual" is more likely to represent an eclectic spirituality, drawing not only from the various streams of Christian theology—Catholic, Orthodox, Episcopal, Protestant, and Pentecostal—but including elements of other religious insights—Buddhism, Jewish mysticism, Hinduism, and Islam. Individuals mix their own spiritual potpourri.

Sources

American Congregations at the Beginning of the Twenty-First Century: The National Congregations Study 2008. Mark Chaves, Shawna Anderson, and Jason Byasse. (www.soc.duke.edu/natcong)

Chaves, Mark. "We're even more spiritual; even less religious." *Faith and Leadership Blog*. July 2, 2009. (www.faithandleadership.com/blog/07-02-2009/mark-chaves-were-even-more-spiritual-even-less-religious)

Declining Participation in Christian Churches

By all measures of participation, the trends point toward declining participation in church life in mainline Protestant and Catholic churches, including worship attendance, marriages and baptisms in the church, and children and youth participation in faith formation programming. Combined with the trend toward fewer Christians and the growing numbers of the religiously unaffiliated, it appears that succeeding generations of Christians are less likely to be exposed to formation in the Christian faith because worship attendance is down, and therefore participation in church life, education, and activities is down. This means less exposure to the Christian tradition and teachings, reduced opportunities to experience the Christian way of life, and far less reinforcement of the Christian faith in church settings.

Worship

For twenty years, the American Research Project (TACRP) has been accumulating church statistical data and compiling the yearly attendance average of more that two hundred thousand churches. As reported in *The American Church in Crisis*, research shows that from 1990 to 2006 attendance at Christian churches has remained constant, with about fifty-two million people attending church services on any given weekend. During those sixteen years, however, the population of the United States has grown by an equivalent number, fifty-two million people. Church attendance has not come anywhere close to keeping up with population

growth. This means that while in 1990 about 20.6% of the United States population was in church on any given weekend, today only 17.3% are in worship. *If current trends continue, by 2020 that 17.3% of Americans attending worship today will drop to
14.7% of Americans—meaning that more than 85% of Americans will be staying away from
worshipping God at church.*

On this basis it is likely that the evangelical church will not keep up with population
growth between 2005 and 2020. The weekend attendance percentage at evangelical
churches will fall below 9% of the population by 2010 and will be at 8.5% in 2020. All
mainline denominations are projected to continue to decline, continuing a downward
slide that started in 1965. Established churches in mainline denominations are declining at a rate of 2% per year, meaning that they will shrink by almost 30% in attendance
from 2005 to 2020. The Roman Catholic Church will grow in membership because
of immigration, but Mass attendance will continue to decline. The drop-off in attendance will continue to be most pronounced in the Northeast and the Midwest. Mass
attendance will decline from 7.1% of the United States population attending a Roman
Catholic parish each weekend in 1990 to 4% in 2020. The growing priest shortage is
already causing consolidation and retrenchment in many parishes, and this will escalate.

Generational Differences

Worship numbers don't account for the generational differences in worship attendance between those in their twenties and thirties and those sixty-five and older.
Over the next ten years the age groups with highest participation in church life will
be replaced by age groups that participate at a much lower rate. This trend will be
most prominent among Mainline and Catholic churches. These generational trends
point to lower rates of participation over the next ten years.

Percentage Who Attend at Least Weekly

(U.S. Religious Landscape Survey 2007, Pew Forum on Religion & Public Life)

	18-29	30-49	50-64	65+
Total Population	33%	36%	40%	54%
Protestant - Evangelical Churches	54%	57%	59%	65%
Protestant - Mainline Churches	32%	27%	34%	48%
Protestant - Historically Black Churches	55%	53%	65%	68%
Catholic Church	34%	36%	42%	62%

Re-enforcing the generational trends in worship attendance is the profile of
emerging adult faith and spirituality from the National Study on Youth and Religion

(NSYR). Christian Smith believes that most emerging adults (twenty- to thirty-year-olds) in America today fall into one of six different types when it comes to religion and spirituality. Only 15% embrace a strong religious faith and another 30% believe and perform certain aspects of their religious traditions. At least 40% have no connection to a religious tradition.

- Type 1. Committed Traditionalists (no more than 15% of the emerging adults). Committed Traditionalists embrace a strong religious faith, whose beliefs they can reasonably well articulate and which they actively practice.
- Type 2. Selected Adherents (about 30% of all emerging adults). Selected Adherents believe and perform certain aspects of their religious traditions but neglect and ignore others.
- Type 3. Spiritually Open (about 15% of emerging adults). Spiritually Open emerging adults are not personally very committed to a religious faith but are nonetheless receptive to and at least mildly interested in some spiritual or religious matters.
- Type 4. Religiously Indifferent (at least 25% of emerging adults). Religiously Indifferent emerging adults neither care to practice religion nor oppose it. They are simply not invested in religious either way; it really doesn't count for that much.
- Type 5. Religiously Disconnected (no more than 5%). Religiously Disconnected emerging adults have little to no exposure or connection to religious people, ideas, or organizations.
- Type 6. Irreligious (no more than 10%). Irreligious emerging adults hold skeptical attitudes about and make critical arguments against religion generally, rejecting the idea of personal faith. (Smith and Snell, 166–68)

Hispanic Trends

Hispanics are very similar to the overall population of the United States in their frequency of attending religious services. Overall, 37% of Hispanics and 37% of the adult United States population say they attend a church or other house of worship at least weekly. Among youths, 36% of Hispanics ages sixteen to twenty-five and 33% of all youths ages eighteen to twenty-five say they attend religious services weekly.

Among young Hispanics, immigrants attend church services more regularly than do the native born. Four in ten (40%) young immigrants say they attend church weekly, while one-third (33%) of second-generation and 31% of third-generation young Hispanics say the same. Church attendance falls off most steeply among the third generation, nearly one in five (19%) of whom say they never attend. A majority (60%) of Hispanics identify as Catholic. Among young Hispanics, this figure falls to 56%, and among second- and third-generation young Latinos, just under half (49%) say they are Catholic. Language usage is related to religious identity. Two-thirds (67%) of Spanish-dominant young Latinos say they are Catholic, while only 57% of bilingual and only 47% of English-dominant young Latinos say the same.

Sources
Olson, David T. *The American Church in Crisis*. Grand Rapids: Zondervan, 2008.
Faith in Flux: Changes in Religious Affiliation in the U.S. April 27, 2009. Pew Research Center. (http://pewresearch.org/pubs/1204/religion-changes-affiliations-survey)
Smith, Christian, with Patricia Snell. *Souls in Transition: The Religious and Spiritual Lives of Emerging Adults*. New York: Oxford University Press, 2009.
U.S. Latino Religious Identification 1990-2008: Growth, Diversity and Transformation. Juhem Navarro-Rivera, Barry A. Kosmin and Ariela Keysar. Program on Public Values. Hartford: Trinity College, 2009. (www.americanreligionsurvey-aris.org)

Increasing Diversity and Pluralism in American Society

The Merriam-Webster dictionary defines pluralism in two ways, the first being as "a state of society in which members of diverse ethnic, racial, religious, or social groups maintain an autonomous participation in and development of their traditional culture or special interest within the confines of a common civilization." We can see this definition reflected in the diversity of ethnic cultures and nationalities and their traditions, customs, foods, and languages, and also in the diversity of religious traditions from the East and the West. Pluralism creates both richness and tensions. We live next door to other nations; we're engaged in conversation with people from all parts of the world, with customs and expectations vastly different from our own.

The dictionary also defines pluralism as "a theory that there are more than one or more than two kinds of ultimate reality." In this case pluralism is a world in which no single authority exercises supremacy and no single belief or ideology dominates. A country or nation becomes a tapestry of alternatives and choices. Christian culture is no longer at the center of American life; it has been replaced by a tapestry of religious and spiritual alternatives and choices. The range of religious practice and belief in American society today is enormous, and it is all around us.

Such pluralism of belief and practice undermines the plausibility and truth-claims of any single religious tradition. The diversity of religious choice and openness to everything religious results in people crisscrossing religious boundaries as they construct their own personal spiritualities. As one example of the impact of pluralism, a research study by the Pew Forum on Religion and Public Life found that roughly two-thirds (65%) of religiously affiliated Americans say that many religions can lead to eternal life. White Catholics and white mainline Protestants are the groups most likely to say that many religions can lead to eternal life, with 84% and 82%, respectively, expressing this point of view. A majority of all American Christians (52%) think that at least some non-Christian faiths can lead to eternal life. Most American Christians are not thinking only of other Christian denominations when they say many religions can lead to eternal life. To the contrary, among those who say many religions provide a path to eternal life, strong majorities believe that both Christian and non-Christian faiths can lead to eternal life.

Sources

"Many Americans Say Other Faiths Can Lead to Eternal Life." Pew Forum on Religion and Public Life. July 31–Aug 10, 2008 (http://pewforum.org/Many-Americans-Say-Other-Faiths-Can-Lead-to-Eternal-Life.aspx).

Increasing Influence of Individualism on Christian Identity and Community Life

Individualism is a pre-eminent American cultural code that is increasing due to American pluralism. It touches virtually every aspect of American life. For many Americans, the ultimate criterion of identity and lifestyle validity is individual choice. Privatized religiosity—which easily accommodates the utilitarian and expressive individualism of American culture—makes it difficult to articulate and sustain religious commitments. Specifically, religious individualism has been linked with autonomy in the moral realm; with the diminution or rejection of ecclesial authority; with more direct access to the sacred; with a higher priority for personal spiritual fulfillment; and with a privatized spirituality only loosely connected with established traditions.

It is not simply that (excessive) religious individualism means that religious identity is more autonomous and deliberate today; it is that this individualism signals a loss of how religion is anchored in a sense of belonging. The issue is the decline in connectedness: a weakening or severing of the *social* basis of religion in family, marriage, ethnicity, and community; and a decline in the perceived *necessity of communal or institutional structures as constituent of religious identity*. Religious identity today is not only less bounded by doctrine or creed; it is also less nurtured and reinforced by community.

The increasing influence of individualism has serious implications:

- Religious identities and practices in contemporary American culture are increasingly viewed as individual projects. They express the preeminent norm of "choice."
- The number of Americans wholly uninvolved with a church has gradually increased as religious institutions have lost much of their monopoly over the quest for the sacred.
- There has been a steady decline in the legitimacy of institutional authority of any kind. The loss of legitimacy by religious institutions is part of the broader problem of widespread alienation from all authoritative institutions that has occurred in American society.
- A highly significant marker of the de-institutionalization of religion is its uncoupling from "spirituality." Significant numbers of Americans see little necessary connection between being spiritual and being part of a historic

tradition, or part of a disciplined community of faith. This is reinforced by the mass media's not so subtle message that you don't need a religious community to engage "God issues."

As the level of individualism has risen, many in the religious mainstream have come to believe that church going and church authority are optional. Nominal membership increasingly replaces active involvement, a development paralleling national civic trends. Fewer Americans are spending time in church-related endeavors. Religion is less perceived as an inherited phenomenon, or as a binding community of discipleship and obligation. Religious leaders and institutions, which traditionally provided the framework within which religious meaning was constructed, have become increasingly peripheral to the spirituality and "lived religion" of private personal enterprise.

Although new forms of community and Christian movements are emerging (for example, small faith communities), the prevailing trend is toward weakened communal and institutional arrangements and lower levels of commitment and participation. For many today, the Christian tradition is not so much a binding community of discipleship and obligation as a toolkit of sacred wares for selectively constructing a personal spiritual identity.

The task is a profoundly sociological one. It means addressing the atrophy of communal participation and the need for a socially embedded Christianity. It includes the creative (re)construction and intensification of the Christian faith as a *communal* reality of habit, prayer, reflection, dialogue, and debate. It necessitates the (re)creation of more cohesive social bonds, shared memories, mutual responsibilities, permanent relationships, and other experiences of connectedness. The problem today is not only that the young have not had passed on to them a good synthesis of the Christian faith so that they might discerningly engage the culture, it is that they (and many others) see less connection between "faith" and church or community.

The increasing influence of individualism on Christian identity and community life can be seen in young adults' approach to religion and spirituality—and all of life. Sociologist Robert Wuthnow calls this approach *tinkering*—putting together a life from whatever skills, ideas, and resources that are readily at hand. He writes,

> Spiritual tinkering is quite common among young adults of today and probably will remain so among young adults of tomorrow. . . . Spiritual tinkering is a reflection of the pluralistic religious society in which we live, the freedom we permit ourselves in making choices about faith, and the necessity of making those choices in the face of the uprootedness and change that most young adults experience. It involves piecing together ideas about spirituality from many sources, especially through conversations with one's friends. . . . Spiritual tinkering involves a large minority of young adults in church shopping and church hopping. It also takes the

form of searching for answers to the perennial existential questions in venues that go beyond religious traditions, and in expressing spiritual interests through music and art as well as through prayer and devotional reading. (Wuthnow, 134–35)

Tinkering is evident among the large number of young adults who believe in God, life after death, and the divinity of Jesus, for instance, but who seldom attend religious services. Their beliefs blend continuity with the past—with the Bible stories they probably learned as children—and their behavior lets them adapt to the demands of the present. Tinkering is equally evident in the quest to update one's beliefs about spirituality. The core holds steady, persuading one that the Bible is still a valuable source of moral insight, for example, but the core is amended almost continuously through conversations with friends, reflections about unusual experiences or at work or from a popular song. (Wuthnow, 215)

Sources
Dinges, William. "Faith, Hope, and (Excessive) Individualism." *Handing on the Faith*. Edited by Robert Embelli. New York: Crossroad, 2006.
Dinges, William. "The American Cultural Context for Adolescent Catechesis." *Source Book on Adolescent Catechesis: Volume 1*. Washington, DC: NIAC, 2008. (www.adolescentcatechesis.org)
Wuthnow, Robert. *After the Baby Boomers: How Twenty- and Thirty-Somethings Are Shaping the Future of American Religion*. Princeton: Princeton University Press, 2007.

Changing Patterns of Marriage and Family Life

A number of significant trends in family life are influencing faith formation today and will have increasing impact on faith formation over the next decade. It appears from the following trends that one of the reasons for the decline in church participation is that younger Americans are marrying later, having fewer children, and having them later—all of which means that far more younger Americans are single and childless than was true a generation ago and that the same younger Americans are not settling into religious congregations at the same rate as their parents did in the 1970s.

Religious practice is especially influenced by marrying, settling down, having children, and raising them. Since individuals who marry are more likely to attend religious services than are those who delay marriage, the postponement of marriage and childbearing has contributed to the decline in church attendance.

Delayed Marriage

The first trend is delaying marriage: the average age of first marriage for men today is almost twenty-eight years old and for women it is twenty-six years old (U.S. Bureau of the Census). For people in their twenties, it has become the norm to remain unmarried. Among men in their early twenties, only 12% are married, and among women in their early twenties, only 22% are married. By their late twenties, 38% of men and 48% of women are married. By the late thirties 65% of men and 66% of women are married. At this point, the proportions have nearly reached their peak. Also, for people in their thirties and early forties, there is a much more sizable minority (a third) who are now single or divorced.

Because many other aspects of young adult life are affected by marital status—including children and the timing of children, housing needs, jobs and economic demands, and relationships with parents and friends—the importance of this shift in marital patterns can hardly be overstated. Religious practice is especially influenced by marrying, settling down, and having children and raising them. Since individuals who marry are more likely to attend religious services regularly than those who delay marriage, the postponement of marriage and childbearing has contributed to the decline in church attendance.

Living Together
The second trend is the increasing number of unmarried couples living together. In 1960, less that a half-million heterosexual unmarried couples were living together. In 1980, it was over one million. In 2007, 6.4 million unmarried couples were living together—an increase of over 600% since 1980. Cohabiting couples now make up almost 10% of all opposite-sex American couples, married and unmarried. Almost half of cohabiting women (46.8%) and 39.6% of cohabiting men were under age thirty.

Fewer Children
The third trend is married couples having fewer children and having them later—a result of the increase in the average age of marriage. The average number of births per woman is about two, and 19% of women end their childbearing years with no children. The median age at which mothers give birth to their first child is about 24.5 years old, with the birth rate increasing for women age thirty-five to thirty-nine and forty to forty-four. A century ago, women in these age groups might have been raising teenagers while giving birth to their fourth or fifth child. Currently, it is more likely that they are giving birth to their first or second child.

Decrease in Two-Parent Households
The fourth trend is a decreasing number of children living in two-parent households. In 2008, 67% of children were living with two parents, down from 77% in 1980; and 23% of children lived with only their mothers, 4% with only their fathers, and 4% with neither of their parents (U.S. Bureau of the Census).

Increase in Religiously Mixed Marriages and Partnerships
The *U.S. Religious Landscape Survey* found that more than one in four (27%) American adults who are married or living with a partner are in religiously mixed relationships.

If people from different Protestant denominational families are included, for example a marriage between a Methodist and a Lutheran, nearly four-in-ten (37%) are religiously mixed. The composition of religiously mixed marriages and partnerships in the United States is as follows:

25%   Protestant – Protestant (different denominational families)
23%   Protestant – Catholic
20%   Protestant – Unaffiliated
12%   Catholic – Unaffiliated
7%   Protestant – Other Faith (other than Protestant, Catholic, or unaffiliated)
6%   Other Faith – Unaffiliated
4%   Other mixed marriages
4%   Catholic – Other Faith

Sources
Pew Social & Demographic Trends (http://pewsocialtrends.org).
Pew Research Center (http://pewresearch.org).
U.S. Religious Landscape Survey. June 23, 2008. Pew Forum on Religion and Public Life. (http://religions.pewforum.org)
Wuthnow, Robert. "The Changing Life Worlds of Young Adults." *After the Baby Boomers: How Twenty- and Thirty-Somethings Are Shaping the Future of American Religion.* Princeton: Princeton University Press, 2007.

Declining Family Religious Socialization

Family religious socialization has always been the foundation for the development of faith and faith practices, and for participation in church life and worship. As Christian Smith observes,

> And since most of broader American society is not in the business of direct religious socialization, this task inevitably falls almost entirely to two main social entities. First are individual family households, where parents predictably do the primary socializing. Second are individual religious congregations, where other adults can exert socializing influences on youth. . . . for better or worse, these are the two critical contexts of youth religious formation in the United States. If formation in faith does not happen there, it will—with rare exceptions—not happen anywhere. (Smith, 286)

> Teenagers with seriously religious parents are more likely than those without such parents to have been trained in their lives to think, feel, believe, and act as serious religious believers, and that training "sticks" with them even when they leave home and enter emerging adulthood. Emerging adults

who grew up with seriously religious parents are through socialization more likely (1) to have internalized their parents' religious worldview, (2) to possess the practical religious know-how needed to live more highly religious lives, and (3) to embody the identity orientations and behavioral tendencies toward continuing to practice what they have been taught religiously. At the heart of this social causal mechanism stands the elementary process of teaching—both formal and informal, verbal and nonverbal, oral and behavioral, intentional and unconscious, through both instruction and role modeling. We believe that one of the main ways by which empirically observed strong parental religion produced strong emerging adult religion in offspring is through the teaching involved in socialization. (Smith, 232)

Significant indicators, such as religious identification as Christian, worship attendance, marriages and baptisms in the church, and changing generational patterns, point to a decline in family religious socialization across all denominations, but especially among Catholic and Mainline traditions. Religious practice among the next generation of parents (young adults in their twenties and thirties) is especially influenced by marrying, settling down, and having children and raising them. Since individuals who marry are more likely to attend religious services than are those who delay marriage, the postponement of marriage and childbearing has contributed to the decline in church attendance. Complicating this picture is the fact that an ever-growing percentage of Christians (at least 30%) are not getting married in a religious ceremony. The less contact that young adults have with the Christian tradition through participation in a local church, the less family religious socialization that is likely to take place when they marry and have children.

In addition, the *American Congregations 2008* study, a random sample research survey of three thousand congregations, reported that 40% of the congregations did not have parenting or marriage enrichment activities and only 18% of the congregations indicated that this was a specialty (2%) or given a lot of emphasis (16%).

Sources

American Congregations 2008. Faith Communities Today. Hartford: Hartford Institute for Religion Research, 2009. (http://faithcommunitiestoday.org/research-based-products-congregational-leadership)

Smith, Christian, with Patricia Snell. *Souls in Transition: The Religious and Spiritual Lives of Emerging Adults*. New York: Oxford University Press, 2009.

Increasing Impact of Digital Media and Web Technologies

Technology and digital media is transforming the ways we live. Think of the impact the following innovations are having on individuals, families, social groups, organizations, and society as a whole: the personal computer, iPod, iPhone, iPad, iTunes, e-mail, Web 2.0, Google, Twitter, Facebook, YouTube, Wikipedia, Skype, social networking, webinars, blogs, wikis, video- and photo-sharing, and so much more. Globalization and pluralism are driven by this unprecedented technological change. People meet on Facebook and share their inspirations on YouTube all the while Twittering to an assortment of friends. Groups of people at opposite ends of a continent or around the globe don't need to leave their own contexts in order to meet in real time and in video on Skype or some Webinar format. Telephones are no longer connected by wires in the ground, but satellites in the sky that make them usable at all times, everywhere. Social connectivity is being leveraged globally online. People's use of the internet's capabilities for communication—for creating, cultivating, and continuing social relationships—is undeniable. However, time spent online often takes time away from important face-to-face relationships.

Increasing Internet Usage

While it may be hard to believe, the web is about five thousand days old (in 2010). Everything we all take for granted was published online in the last five thousand days. The internet is increasingly embedded in our daily lives. Most of us find it impossible to function without the Internet. Virtually all of those twenty-nine and younger in the United States today are online (as of 2010): 93% of teens (12–17) and young adults (18–29), 81% of adults thirty to forty-nine years old, 70% of adults fifty to sixty-four years old, and 38% of adults sixty-five and over.

Increasing Mobile Phone Usage

Increasingly people are accessing the internet on smart phones like the iPhone. In a Pew Internet and American Life Project study, adults were asked about ten different non-voice data activities they might do on their cell phones: sending or receiving text messages, taking a picture, playing a game, checking email, accessing the internet, recording video, instant messaging, playing music, getting maps or directions, and watching video. In 2009, 69% of all adult Americans said they had at some time done at least one of the ten activities versus 58% in late 2007. In 2009, 44% of all adult Americans said they had done at least one of the non-voice data activities on a typical day, up from 32% in 2007.

When mobile users are away from home or the office, they like mobile access to stay in touch with others, but also to access information on the go. For example: 50% say it is very important to them to have mobile access in order to stay in touch with other people; 46% say that mobile access is very important for getting online information on the go; and 17% say mobile access is very important to them so they can share or post online content while away from home or work.

Increasing Media Use

Media are among the most powerful forces in young people's lives today. Eight- to eighteen-year-olds spend more time with media than in any other activity besides (maybe) sleeping—an average of more than seven hours a day, seven days a week. The television shows they watch, video games they play, songs they listen to, books they read, and websites they visit are an enormous part of their lives, offering a constant stream of messages about families, peers, relationships, gender roles, sex, violence, food, values, clothes, and an abundance of other topics too long to list.

Over the past five years (2004–2009), young people have increased the amount of time they spend consuming media (television, music/audio, computer, video games, print, movies) by one hour and seventeen minutes daily, from 6:21 to 7:38—almost the amount of time most adults spend at work each day, except that young people use media seven days a week instead of five. Moreover, given the amount of time they spend using more than one medium at a time, today's youth pack a total of ten hours and forty-five minutes worth of media content into those daily seven hours—an increase of almost two hours of media exposure per day over the past five years.

An explosion in mobile and online media has fueled the increase in media use among young people. The story of media in young people's lives today is primarily a story of technology facilitating increased consumption. The mobile and online media revolutions have arrived in the lives—and the pockets—of American youth. Today (2010), 20% of media consumption occurs on mobile devices—cell phones, iPods, or handheld video game players. Moreover, almost another hour consists of "old" content—television or music—delivered through "new" pathways on a computer (such as Hulu or iTunes). Over the past five years, the proportion of eight- to eighteen-year-olds who own their own cell phone has grown from about four in ten (39%) to about two-thirds (66%). The proportion with iPods or other MP3 players increased even more dramatically, jumping from 18% to 76% among all eight- to eighteen-year-olds.

We can be sure that over the next ten years new, breakthrough digital technologies will transform our lives even further. What will be the impact of this technological revolution on education, business, politics, social life, or religious congregations?

Sources

"Future of the Internet." Pew Internet and American Life Project. (www.pewinternet.org/Presentations/2010/Jun/The-Future-of-the-Internet-National-Geographic.aspx)

Generation M2: Media in the Lives of 8- to 18-Year-Olds. Kaiser Family Foundation Study (January 2010). (www.kff.org/entmedia/mh012010pkg.cfm)

Pew Internet & American Life Project (www.pewinternet.org)

TWO

Designing the Shape of Faith Formation 2020

▶ *How can congregations design the future of faith formation using the four scenarios as a guide for addressing the life situations and spiritual and religious needs of a wide diversity of people?* The future of faith formation will, in large part, be determined by how well churches provide comprehensive, lifelong faith formation that is inclusive of all ages and generations and responsive to the diverse life situations, and spiritual and religious needs of people in all four scenarios: people of vibrant faith and active engagement in a church, people who participate in church life but are not spiritually committed, people who are spiritual but not engaged in a church community, and people who are uninterested in the spiritual life and not affiliated with a church community.

The processes and tools in chapter 2 will assist your church in finding practical ways to expand the scope of faith formation to reach and engage people in all four scenarios. One way to provide comprehensive faith formation for everyone, anytime, anywhere, 24/7/365 is by developing a *Lifelong Faith Formation Network* of programs, activities, and resources that incorporate a variety of ways to learn in a blended approach to faith formation integrating physical face-to-face settings and virtual online settings and utilizing utilizes a wide variety of faith formation resources and programs, people and communities. The design process integrates your church's current faith formation programs, activities, and resources with the creation of new initiatives—strategies, programs, activities, resources—specifically designed to address new spiritual and religious needs of people in each scenario.

Key Features of a Lifelong Faith Formation Network

A Lifelong Faith Formation Network is a way to provide faith formation for everyone, anytime, anywhere, 24/7/365. The Network approach to lifelong faith formation has six key features:

1. A *Lifelong Faith Formation Network* addresses the diverse life tasks and situations, spiritual and religious needs, and interests of all ages and generations in the four scenarios by offering a variety of content, programs, activities, and resources.

2. A *Lifelong Faith Formation Network* guides individuals and families in discerning their spiritual and religious needs and creating personal learning pathways—a seasonal or annual plan for faith growth and learning.

3. A *Lifelong Faith Formation Network* incorporates informal learning as well as formal learning in faith formation.

4. A *Lifelong Faith Formation Network* utilizes a variety of faith formation models to address the diverse life tasks and situations, religious and spiritual needs, and interests of people: learning on your own, in small groups, in large groups, in the congregation, and in the community and world.

5. A *Lifelong Faith Formation Network* blends face-to-face, interactive faith formation programs and activities with virtual, online faith formation programs, activities, and resources.

6. A *Lifelong Faith Formation Network* incorporates communities of practice to connect individuals and groups throughout the congregation.

FEATURE I

A Lifelong Faith Formation Network addresses the diverse life tasks and situations, spiritual and religious needs, and interests of all ages and generations in the four scenarios by offering a variety of content, programs, activities, and resources.

To address the diversity of people in each of the four scenarios, churches need to offer a wider variety of faith formation options in physical and virtual settings. Today churches have available to them the resources and tools to provide lifelong faith formation for *all* ages and generations and to address the religious and spiritual needs of people in each of the four scenarios. Churches can utilize the life of their faith community; the variety of excellent print, audio, and visual resources in faith formation; the new digital media and online technologies; and the innovations and resources of other Christian churches to develop faith formation that varies in content, expectations, depth, involvement, and timing.

In the past churches have often chosen the "one size fits all" mentality for programming. The culture of our day is all about personalization and customization. Several decades ago the typical bookstore at the mall featured several dozen books on the *New York Times* best seller lists, books by popular bestselling authors, and a very limited variety of specialized titles. In the early 1990s Borders and Barnes and Noble opened megastores with one hundred thousand titles that addressed a wide diversity of customers' needs and interests. In 1995 Amazon.com opened for business online with millions of titles, addressing an even greater diversity of readers' needs and interests. Amazon.com will even recommend books to you based on the interests expressed in your previous book purchases.

The same personalization and customization can be seen in music and in films. More than 99% of music albums on the market today are not available in Wal-Mart. However, iTunes offers millions of songs online available for download 24/7 and is constantly adding music, both old and new. Of the more than two hundred thousand films, television shows, documentaries, and other videos that have been released commercially, the average Blockbuster store carries just three thousand titles. However, Netflix has over one hundred thousand DVDs available for rental online and delivered to your home in about one business day. By offering such great diversity Amazon.com, iTunes, and Netflix not only make money on the "blockbusters" they sell and rent but also on every title in their vast storehouse, even if they only sell or rent one copy a month. (Amazon.com, iTunes, and Netflix are only three examples of the transformation taking place in business and culture today.)

Faith formation is no longer about finding *the* program for a particular age group or generation. Churches can now meet people at the point of their spiritual, religious, and learning needs and offer personalized pathways for faith growth. Today, as never before, church have access to faith formation programming, activities, and resources that can be personalized and customized to address the diversity of people's religious and spiritual needs. Resources for learning abound in every environment (at home, in the church, in the community, online). A primary task of a Lifelong Faith Formation Network is to identify these resources and link individuals, families, and communities with them effectively. The new reality of faith formation programming is that churches can offer activities that cater to niches— individuals, families, and small groups with a particular spiritual or religious need, interest, passion, concern, or life issue. They no longer have to worry about reaching a "mass audience" with "one size fits all" programming.

FEATURE 2

A Lifelong Faith Formation Network guides individuals and families in discerning their spiritual and religious needs and creating personal learning pathways—a seasonal or annual plan for faith growth and learning.

Expanding the options for faith formation by offering "something for everyone," means that churches can engage more people in faith formation, even if some of the offerings involve only one person. This respects the principle that *learning is a process of active inquiry with initiative residing in the learner.* Increasingly today, due in part to the web and social media, people are searching out what they want to know, when they want and need to know it. People are becoming more and more self-directed in their learning, and they have almost unlimited access to information through the Internet and the wide variety of print and media learning resources available in our society today. Giving power to individuals and families to shape their own learning does not mean abandoning them to their own devices. Rather, it creates a new role and responsibility for faith formation leaders—to serve as guides and facilitators helping people identify growth needs, finding resources and settings for faith formation, identifying next steps on their journey, and so on.

A Lifelong Faith Formation Network, rich in a diversity of content and a variety of ways to learn, can guide people in creating their own personal learning pathways. Churches can develop processes for helping individuals and families diagnose their religious and spiritual learning needs (online and in-person) and create their own annual or season plan for faith growth and learning. A "faith growth learning plan" helps people identify where they are on their spiritual journey, what they need for continuing their growth, who else might share that need, and the resources that could help them meet that need. Churches can provide mentors or guides to assist people in developing their spiritual growth plan and accessing the programs and resources that fit their plan. Mentors or guides can be available for one-on-one conversations as people move through their growth plan.

> We invite you to join us on the greatest journey of your life—the Journey of Knowing, Loving and Serving God—as we strive to become a community of deeply committed Christians. We know that sometimes getting started can be daunting, especially in such a large church, but we want to travel this journey with you. Our Adult Discipleship Ministry offers you a navigation system that provides directions, routes and traveling companions to support and encourage you along the way. We believe that nothing in the world will bring you greater joy, greater challenge, and greater meaning than the journey into life as God intended us to live it. To help encourage and equip you for your Journey, we've created the Journey assessment tool. The "next steps" chart offers recommendations for spiritual growth. Go online to: www.cor.org/next steps

or the Connection Point in the Narthex of Resurrection Church to view detailed listing of classes and service opportunities and to register.

The Sojourn Community Church uses a similar approach in the personal renewal plan (http://sojournchurch.com/blog/2009/07/22/personal-renewal-plan). These approaches can be applied to all ages and generations

Churches can engage families more consciously, actively, and experientially in learning, growing in faith, and participating in church life through an annual, multi-dimensional faith growth plan. The annual plan can be a blend of whole family activities and individual parent-child activities. Families can be organized into groups, each with a leader who meets with the family group regularly to facilitate learning and reflection. Churches set expectations for learning and participation. Families create their annual plan around a menu of offerings designed to help them fulfill the church's expectations, for example: (1) participating in Sunday worship (regularly, but at least twice monthly); (2) participating in important church year feasts and celebrations, such as Advent, Christmas, Lent, Holy Week; (3) participating in monthly family learning programs on religious themes; (4) participating in at least six mission/service projects during the year, (5) participating in an annual spiritual formation retreat experience, and (6) engaging in family home practices, such as reading the Bible, celebrating rituals and traditions, and praying.

FEATURE 3

A Lifelong Faith Formation Network incorporates informal learning, as well as formal learning in faith formation.

Learning is a lifelong process and people need access to a wide variety of learning activities throughout life. We are a society of lifelong learners. Learning in adulthood is now taken as normative. Over the twelve-month period from Spring 2004–2005 (the latest year statistics are available), 44% of adults in the United States reported having participated in *formal* adult educational activities, excluding full-time only enrollments in college/university or vocational/technical credential programs. The 44% of adults who participated in formal adult educational activities were divided almost equally between work-related courses (27% of all adults in the U.S.) and personal interest courses (21% of all adults in the United States).

By most estimates *informal learning* accounts for more than 70% of adult learning taking place today. In what is known as the 70/20/10 learning concept. Robert Eichinger and Michael Lombardo, in collaboration with Morgan McCall of the Center for Creative Leadership, explain that 70% of learning and development takes place from real-life and on-the-job experiences, tasks, and problem solving; 20% of the time learning and development comes from other people through information and formal feedback, mentoring, or coaching; and 10% of learning and development comes from formal training.

Informal learning describes a lifelong process whereby individuals acquire attitudes, values, skills and knowledge from daily experience and the educational influences and resources in his or her environment, from family and neighbors, from work and play, from the marketplace, the library, the mass media, and the Internet. Informal learning can be intentional or not. There might be a teacher, but that teacher is probably a colleague or friend. We might read an article or book, visit a website, listen to a podcast, or watch a video online. We might visit Home Depot or Lowe's for a clinic on home repair or gardening or stop by our local bookstore or library for a reading group or special program. On television many channels are devoted to informal learning. The programs of *The Food Network*, while not formal education, promote learning as shows teach people how to cook, try new recipes, and so on. The variety of home improvement shows, such as the "This Old House" on PBS, or the home makeover shows on the TLC and HGTV networks, promote learning, even though they are not formal educational TV programs.

Formal and informal learning can be *intentional*—when an individual aims to learn something and goes about achieving that objective, or *unexpected*—when in the course of everyday activities an individual learns something that he or she had not intended or expected.

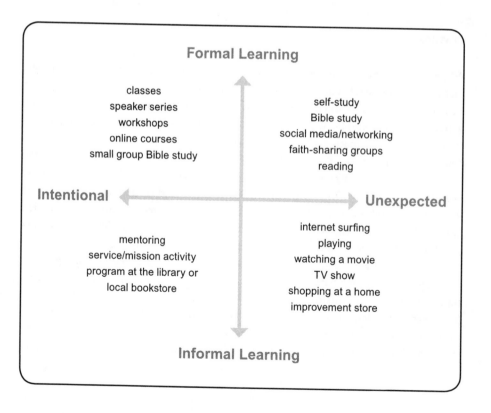

Applying the four types of learning to faith formation, we can visualize the relationship among these four types of learning in the following way.

Most of faith formation efforts in churches are *formal* and *intentional* learning through organized programs. Churches can expand their faith formation efforts by promoting all four types of learning. For example, Sunday worship is *informal* and *intentional* learning. A church can help people learn from their participation in worship through a weekly journal or activities booklet (online and in print) with reflection questions on the Scripture readings and the sermon. The readings and sermon can also be available in print or audio for further study on the church's website. The journal or activities booklet could also be used in a weekly faith sharing group or in table discussion after Sunday worship. These are all examples of informal and intentional learning activities. Where are the *informal* learning opportunities for people of all ages and for families in your congregation and community?

FEATURE 4

A Lifelong Faith Formation Network utilizes a variety of faith formation models to address the diverse life tasks and situations, religious and spiritual needs, and interests of people. With such a wide diversity of people and needs, a Lifelong Faith Formation Network provides a diversity of content and activities, *and* a variety of ways for people to engage the content and activities. A Lifelong Faith Formation Network incorporates six faith formation models—on your own, at home, in small groups, in large groups, in the congregation, and in the community and world—providing a variety of faith formation models for people to learn and growth in faith that respects their preferred styles of learning, their life situations, and their time constraints. Churches can use the six faith formation models to (1) inventory their current faith formation programs, activities, and resources, (2) uncover new faith formation opportunities, and (3) design faith formation that offers the same "content" in six different models, giving people six ways to learn and grow in faith. The six faith formation models include:

- **Faith Formation on Your Own**: through reading, online courses, audio and video programs, movies, television programs
- **Faith Formation at Home**: through Bible reading, storytelling and caring conversation, prayer and devotions, rituals and traditions, service
- **Faith Formation in Small Groups:** through Bible and theology study groups, social issues study groups, faith sharing groups, lectionary-based groups, service/mission action groups, support groups, special interest groups
- **Faith Formation in Large Groups**; through courses, speaker series, workshops, film festivals, retreats, conferences, intergenerational programs
- **Faith Formation in the Congregation:** through Sunday worship, church year events and celebrations, service/mission activities, ministry and leadership in the church and community

- **Faith Formation in the Community and World**: through programs, courses, clinics, workshops, and presentations at universities, retreat centers, YMCAs, libraries, bookstores, regional church programs; through engagement in community/political action, local and global service and justice projects

Every faith formation activity plan for an age group or family can offer a variety of faith formation models with differing levels of depth and commitment, in online and face-to-face settings, and at a variety of times and locations that are convenient for people. This approach means that people can have a variety of ways to learn and grow in faith, removing many of the more common obstacles to participating in faith formation.

The six faith formation models expand the ways a church can address a particular spiritual or religious need, a church event or church year season, the Bible and biblical teachings, and the religious tradition and teachings. For example, a faith formation activity plan for adults during Lent could include the following activities:

- providing a book of Scripture readings, reflections, and prayers for each day of Lent (print and online)
- making all the sermons/homilies during Lent available online in mp3 files with a personal and small group study guide
- providing daily Bible readings, reflections, and prayers emailed to adults and available online
- offering a Bible study on the Lenten lectionary readings after the Sunday worship service, and an online small group meeting during the week to study and reflect on the readings
- presenting a guest speaker for a two-evening program on Lenten themes during the first two weeks of Lent; making the video of the two presentations available online in a podcast with a study guide
- promoting a retreat day on a Lenten theme sponsored by the local retreat house the week prior to Holy Week
- providing resources for Lenten study and reflection online
- celebrating a reconciliation service during the third week of Lent

Feature 5

A Lifelong Faith Formation Network blends face-to-face, interactive faith formation programs and activities with virtual, online faith formation programs, activities, and resources.

Faith formation includes learning activities in physical places and virtual spaces, blending face-to-face, interactive learning with virtual, online learning. Online websites, social networking services, and digital technologies (an iPod Touch, smart cell phones, iPad) mean that churches can deliver faith formation experiences and resources anytime and anywhere, reaching people wherever they go online (at home, work, school, on vacation, and at the coffee house). The interplay between learning in physical places and virtual online spaces can revolutionize faith formation in a church.

There are two ways to envision the relationship between the physical and virtual. The first approach begins with people's participation in face-to-face learning activities (small group, large group, congregation, community/world) and then uses virtual online spaces (learning activities, print/audio/video, social networking) to extend, deepen, and support the learning that began in the physical program. For example, a church sponsors a three-session program or intergenerational program on the coming year's lectionary cycle of readings, such as the Gospel of Luke. The learning from this short program is then extended and deepened with (1) online weekly commentaries and activities on the Sunday readings from the Gospel of Luke, (2) an online Bible study program (independent or with a small group) on the Gospel of Luke, (3) a university course on the Gospel of Luke on iTunes U, and 4) an online blog that allows people to post their reflections on each Sunday's reading and invites discussion online.

The second approach integrates faith formation in virtual spaces (online) with faith formation in physical spaces using the six faith formation models. For example, a church can use its website to develop an online spiritual formation center focusing on spiritual disciplines and practices and using a variety of already existing resources. (See Strategy #9 Spiritual Formation in chapter 4 for additional ideas and resources.)

On Your Own
- Daily prayer delivered to people's computers and mobile devices: www.sacredspace.ie, www.taize.fr, www.upperroom.org, www.loyolapress.com
- Fixed hour prayer online: www.explorefaith.org/prayer/fixed/hours.php
- Spiritual guides and mentoring available for people
- Spiritual reading: list recommended books on the church website
- Online retreat: *A Thirty-Four week retreat for Everyday Life* from Creighton University, (http://onlineministries.creighton.edu/CollaborativeMinistry/cmo-retreat.html)
- Online spirituality course: forty-day retreats with spiritual guides like Thomas Merton, Joyce Rupp, Henri Nouwen, and Joan Chittister from Spirituality and Practice (www.SpiritualityandPractice.com)

At Home
- Weekly and seasonal prayer resources: online and in booklets

In Small Groups
- Spiritual formation course: *Companions in Christ: A Small-Group Experience in Spiritual Formation* for adults, *The Way of Pilgrimage* for youth, and *Companions in Christ: The Way of the Child* for children (Upper Room, www.companionsinchrist.org)

- Spiritual book clubs: monthly meetings to discuss the book-of-the-month
- Prayer groups

In Large Groups
- Intergenerational learning programs on prayer: monthly sessions for all ages on prayer practices
- Retreat experiences at church or a retreat center
- Workshop series on the spiritual disciplines: *lectio divina*, silence, contemplation, the *Examen*, meditation, spiritual reading, fixed hour prayer
- Monastery trip to experience monastic life and prayer

In the Congregation
- Church-wide retreat experience
- Prayer room with resources about prayer and spiritual practices
- Advent and Lent prayer services

Feature 6

A Lifelong Faith Formation Network incorporates communities of practice to connect individuals and groups throughout the congregation.

One ways to keep individuals and groups engaged in faith formation connected to each other in the Lifelong Faith Formation Network is through communities of practice—groups of people who have a shared interest who come together to learn from each other. Communities of practice have three dimensions: the domain (what it's about); the topic (the issues that they are facing); and the community (the people who are involved). Communities of practice use a variety of approaches to connect, such as face-to-face meetings, teleconferences, video conferencing, social networking, and working on projects together. It is a mix of formal and informal methods. Some of them are online; some of them are face-to-face. Some of them happen weekly; some of them happen monthly or yearly.

A congregation is a community of practice. Practices like worship, liturgy, pastoral care, outreach, and social justice are important to the congregation's vitality. What you want are people who are passionate about those practices to develop them so that they are thriving in the congregation. An example would be people in a congregation who are engaged in justice and service projects—in the church and in the world—who could regularly connect, and even meet, to share their reflections and insights, communicate their insights to the whole congregation, and continue to support each other in their efforts. They can also invite new people to join their efforts. A community of practice around social justice could include not only church members, but also people in the wider community who have similar interests.

Another example might be people engaged in reading and studying the Bible. They may do this on their own or in small groups, but they are engaged in a large community of practice focused on reading and studying the book. A Lifelong Faith Formation Network connects these people, face-to-face or online, to share what they are learning and how they read and apply the Bible to daily life, to explore common issues in reading the Bible, review new resources, and educate new members (apprentices) in reading the Bible. The community of practice around reading and studying the Bible disseminates their learning throughout the congregation, providing a learning opportunity for all church members to grow in their understanding of the Bible.

Most of the skills and expertise we learn, we learn from others in practice, rather than in a course or from a book. It's helpful to have those, but the way we really learn is in practice with other practitioners. If you have a community of practice, someone can say, "I'm calling you about what I saw on your website or on Facebook. I heard that you tried this, and I'd love to talk to you about it." Communities of practice can connect people and diffuse learning and Christian practices across the congregation. There are opportunities through the Lifelong Faith Formation Network to cultivate and support communities of practices around particular topics or issues or Christian practices.

Designing a Lifelong Faith Formation Network

The goal of the design process is to guide your church in developing and implementing a plan for a Lifelong Faith Formation Network, utilizing a wide variety of programs, activities and resources, that *builds* on the current faith formation offerings of your church and *expands* faith formation to address the religious and spiritual needs of people in the four scenarios of Faith Formation 2020. The design process includes nine planning tasks. Customize the process for your church's context and priorities. (All of the Tools listed in the design process can be found at the end of Part 2 and can also be downloaded from www.FaithFormation2020.com for use in your church.)

1. Form a Lifelong Faith Formation Network Task Force.

2. Prepare a statement of your church's vision and goals for lifelong faith formation.

3. Develop an inventory of your church's current faith formation programs, activities, and resources using the four scenarios.

4. Describe the diverse life tasks and situations, spiritual and religious needs, and interests of age groups and families in each of the four scenarios; and develop a profile of the most important needs.

5. Research people, programs, activities, and resources to address the priority life issues and spiritual/religious needs.

6. Design new initiatives to address the new spiritual and religious needs in each of the four Faith Formation 2020 scenarios.

7. Develop an Integrated plan for the Lifelong Faith Formation Network with all of the programs, activities, and resources organized according to the four scenarios and the six faith formation models.

8. Develop an online faith formation center for connecting people to each other and to the resources of the Lifelong Faith Formation Network.

9. Develop a marketing/promotion plan to promote the Lifelong Faith Formation Network.

Task I

Leadership: Form a Lifelong Faith Formation Network Task Force.
Develop a task force that reflects the scope of lifelong faith formation (ages, generations, families) and brings together people with experience in face-to-face and online faith formation. The task force should include church staff, current faith

formation leaders, and new members who bring new perspectives and experiences to the design work (for example, young adults in their twenties and thirties). The primary responsibility of the task force is to design the Network: (1) research the religious and spiritual needs of the community; (2) research face-to-face and online faith formation resources, programs, and activities (content aggregating); (3) select (curate) the most appropriate resources, programs, and activities to address the needs; 4) design the Network with all of its offerings; and 5) "publish" the Network offers through a website and/or in print (catalog). There will also be other planning work such as organizing implementation logistics, finding leaders and resources where needed, promoting the Network, monitoring progress, and conducting evaluations. The task force needs a coordinator/convener who facilitates the work of the group.

Task 2

Visioning: Prepare a statement of your church's vision and goals for lifelong faith formation.
Work together as a task force to prepare a short statement of your church's vision and goals for the Lifelong Faith Formation Network. (See **Tool #1** for the *Charter on Lifelong Faith Formation* from the Episcopal Church, an excellent example of a lifelong vision.) Together as a team review the important documents on the vision and goals for lifelong faith formation in your denomination or faith tradition. You might want to invite a guest speaker to present a workshop on the goals and vision of lifelong faith formation or find a video presentation. You can contact your diocese/ synod/ regional church body for suggestions.

Task 3

Assessing: Develop an inventory of your church's current faith formation programs, activities, and resources using the four scenarios.
Develop an inventory of your church's current faith formation activities and programs for all ages and generations for each of the four scenarios. Use **Tool #2** at the end of this chapter to organize your inventory. After completing the inventory, discuss how well your church's faith formation is addressing the four scenarios using the following questions:

- What are the strengths of your congregation's faith formation programs, activities, and resources viewed through the lens of the four scenarios?
- What is most effective in your current programs, resources, and activities?
- Who is being served by current faith formation programming? Who is not?

- What are the weaknesses of your congregation's faith formation programs viewed through the lens of the four scenarios?
- Where are the greatest needs or gaps? What are the priority areas for growth and improvement?

Use **Tool #8** to add your current faith formation programs, activities, and resources to your *Lifelong Faith Formation Network*. Identify the following information for each activity. Develop a profile for each of the four scenarios. Record your results on large sheets of paper using the format on **Tool #8**.

- People: age group, family, or generation
- Life tasks, religious and spiritual needs addressed
- Faith formation program, activity, or resource
- Faith formation model (on your own, at home, small group, large group, congregation, community, and world)
- Dates and times
- Location (physical/facility and/or online/website)

(For an example of an integrated learning plan for all ages and generations review the HI-Life Faith Formation Annual Learning Plan of Holy Infant Catholic Parish, Durham, North Carolina (www.holyinfantchurch.org). Download a copy of their Faith Formation Handbook at: http://images.acswebnetworks.com/1/443/FaithFormationHandbook.pdf.)

Task 4

Researching: Describe the diverse life tasks and situations, spiritual and religious needs, and interests of age groups and families in each of the four scenarios; and develop a profile of the most important unmet needs.

People in each of the four scenarios have distinct spiritual and religious needs, interests, and life situations that are directly related to the particulars of the scenario. By consulting research findings and listening carefully to people in your community, you can determine foundational spiritual and religious needs, interests, and life tasks that faith formation still needs to address. Using this knowledge, your church can expand faith formation programs, activities, and resources to offer enough variety to reach every person and household with faith formation experience that address their spiritual and religious needs, life tasks, and/or interests.

1. Consult research and experience.

Using research and the experience of your task force, describe the foundational spiritual and religious needs, interests, and life tasks of age groups and families in your church for each scenario. For each scenario, discuss the questions: Who are the people in this scenario? What are the religious and spiritual needs of people (age groups and families) in this scenario? What are their religious and spiritual hopes or desires? Your profile for each scenario can include: (1) life issues, (2) life cycle tasks and generational characteristics, (3) milestones and transitions, (4) religious needs, (5) spiritual needs, and (6) ethnic/cultural needs. Use **Tool #3** to guide you in researching the people in each scenario.

- **Life Issues**: What's happening in the lives and world of people (age group or family) today—the myriad dimensions of human life today: family, work, leisure, relationships, sexuality, suffering and grief, social and political issues, community issues?
- **Life Cycle Tasks and Generational Characteristics**: What are the developmental life tasks facing people in the decades of life from childhood through old adulthood? What are the unique generational characteristics of the iGeneration (2000 and later), the Millennial Generation (1980–1999), Generation X (1964–1979), Baby Boom Generation (1946–1964), and the Builder Generation (1945 and earlier)? (See Strategy 5 in chapter 4 for brief descriptions of each generation.)
- **Milestones and Transitions:** What are the significant milestones/transitions throughout life, such as marriages, births, graduations, geographic relocations, family formation and re-formation, career changes, empty nests, retirement, unanticipated illness, divorce, and the loss of loved ones?
- **Religious Needs:** What are the significant religious and learning needs of people at each stage of life?
- **Spiritual Needs:** What are the significant spiritual needs of individuals and families at each stage of life?
- **Ethnic/Cultural Needs**: Who are the ethnic/cultural communities in your church? What are the unique lived experiences, needs, and aspirations of people from each ethnic/cultural community in your church?

2. Conduct focus groups for each scenario.
An excellent way to gather information about people in your community is through focus groups. Organize focus groups of six to twelve people for each of the four scenarios. You might do several focus groups for each scenario to involve a wider spectrum of age groups and families. Select a diversity of people in each focus group, reflecting the ethnic/cultural and socioeconomic character of your church, and the various lifestyles (single, married, families, divorced, and so one). Use the following questions, also found on **Tool #4**, as a guide for developing your own focus group interviews.

- How would you describe your age group in key words or phrases?
- What are some of the key life tasks that your age group is experiencing?
- What are some of the important life issues that your age group is experiencing today?
- What are the most meaningful experiences you have in life? What makes these experiences meaningful to you?
- How important is your relationship with God? Why?
- Where do you experience God most?
- What are the significant spiritual issues that your age group is experiencing today?
- What is most important to you about being a Christian (or a member of a particular denomination or faith tradition) today?
- How do you live your Christian faith? Name some of the ways you put your faith into practice.
- How can the church help you to continue growing as a Christian? Be specific.
- Name some of the things you would like to see your church offer for your age group?

3. Conduct research out in the community.

Engage your team in becoming anthropologists by observing the people in your community. Develop an observation checklist and ask team members to spend a week simply observing people at work, at school, at play, at stores, and so on. Segment your audience by age groups for observation and analysis: families with children, teens, young adults, midlife adults, older adults, etc. Consider questions such as:

- What are some of the most popular activities for (your group) in the community?
- Where does (your group) gather outside of work and school—coffee shop, gym, mall, park, community center, YMCA/YWCA, and so on? What are they doing there?
- Where do people work? Do most people work in your community or do they commute to another area? What types of jobs do people have?
- What are the most popular or well attended churches in your community?
- Where are (your group) on Sunday morning, if they are not at worship?

4. Find Patterns in the Research Findings.

Identify patterns or recurring themes of life tasks and spiritual/religious needs for each scenario. Begin by discussing the results of the research on individuals, age groups, families, and generations that applies to that scenario and then name themes that emerge from your research and discussion.

5. Develop a Profile of Most Important Needs.

Based on your analysis of the research, take each of the four scenarios and identify *the most important* life issues and spiritual/religious needs of each people (age groups, families, generations) that your church needs to address in the coming years. For each scenario answer the question: *What would people in this scenario like to see the church offer them through faith formation?* Use **Tool #5** to develop your profile and select your top priorities.

Task 5

Discovering: Research people, programs, activities, and resources to address the priority life issues and spiritual/religious needs.

Today, as never before, a local church has access to an abundance of adult faith formation programming, resources, and networks that can address the diversity of adult learning needs. Resources for learning abound in every environment; a primary task of a Lifelong Faith Formation Network is to identify these resources and link learners with them effectively. Using the list of the priority life issues and spiritual/religious needs as a guide, research the resources available to address these issues and needs. Eventually, many of these resources will become part of your *Lifelong Faith Formation Network*. Use **Tool #6** to conduct your research. Consider the following categories:

- **People Resources**: Conduct a gifts/talents/skills/knowledge survey of the people resources in your church, the wider community, the wider church (diocese/synod/regional church body), colleges and seminaries, church-related organizations, and so on, who can be invited to take a leadership role in a Lifelong Faith Formation Network. Consider people who teach courses or specialized programs, guest presenters on specialized topics, leaders for small groups and Bible studies, prayer guides/spiritual directors, leaders for service/mission programs, and so on.

- **Physical, Face-to-Face Faith Formation Programs and Activities:** Identify face-to-face faith formation activities that you can use to address priority issues and spiritual/religious needs. There are a variety of options: (1) programs that your church is already sponsoring, (2) an opportunity that you are not utilizing (for example, design reflection activities around Sunday worship), (3) a new program that your church can design or adopt, and (4) a program sponsored by another organization that you can promote as part of your plan. Consider programs in your church, the wider community, the diocese/synod/regional church body, retreat and conference centers, colleges and universities, religious organizations, and so on. Indicate the faith formation model(s) used in the program: Faith Formation on Your Own,

Faith Formation at Home, Faith Formation in Small Group, Faith Forming in Large Group, Faith Formation in the Congregation, and/or Faith Formation in the Community and World.

- **Print and Media Faith Formation Resources:** Identify print and media resources from publishers and religious organizations that you can use to address the priority issues and spiritual/religious needs.

- **Online Faith Formation Programs, Activities, and Resources:** Identify online faith formation programs, activities, social networks, and resources that you can use to address priority issues and spiritual/religious needs. Churches can utilize the ever increasing "library" of online resources: *books* (see Google Books), *courses* and *podcasts* (see iTunes University), *videos* (see YouTube and God Tube), *age-specific* sites (see Disciples Now, Busted Halo, Kids Spirit Online), *small group studies* (see The Thoughtful Christian), *multi-faceted religious content* (see Patheos), and so much more. These types of online programs, activities, and resources can become an integral element of learning programs and faith formation offerings for all ages and for families. Research the online resources of your own denomination or religious tradition, and online courses and webinars offered by colleges, universities, seminaries, and religious organizations. (See Strategy #2. Faith Formation using Digital Media and Web Technologies for more ideas about using digital and online resources.)

Task 6

Designing: Design new initiatives to address the new priority spiritual and religious needs in each of the four Faith Formation 2020 scenarios.
There are three elements in the design process: (1) *inspiration*—the need or opportunity that motivates the search for solutions; (2) *ideation*—the process of generating, developing, and testing ideas; and (3) *implementation*—the path that leads from the project stage into people's lives.

Select the *most important* life issues and spiritual/religious needs of individuals, age groups, families, generations in each scenario that you want to target for the development of new initiatives in faith formation. You can target one or two scenarios that need the most attention. Use the following process as a guide for designing each new initiative. Repeat this process for each priority need that you have selected.

Step 1. Select a priority need.
Select a priority need for a scenario and group of people for your new initiative.

Step 2. Consult the Faith Formation 2020 Strategies.
Consult the description of sixteen strategies for Faith Formation 2020 in Part

Four of this book for ideas and resources that might apply to the scenario and people you have targeted.

1. Faith Formation through the Life of the Whole Church (Scenarios 1 and 4)
2. Faith Formation using Digital Media and Web Technologies (All Scenarios)
3. Family Faith Formation (Scenarios 1, 2, and 4)
4. Intergenerational Faith Formation (Scenarios 1 and 4)
5. Generational Faith Formation (Scenarios 1, 2, and 4)
   - Faith formation with the iGeneration and the Millennial Generation
   - Faith formation with Generation X
   - Faith formation with the Baby Boomer Generation
   - Faith formation with the Builder Generation
6. Milestones Faith Formation (All Scenarios)
7. Faith Formation in Christian Practices (All Scenarios)
8. Transforming the World: Engagement in and Formation for Service and Mission (All Scenarios)
9. Spiritual Formation (All Scenarios)
10. Multi-Ethnic Faith Formation (All Scenarios)
11. Faith Formation for Spiritual Seekers (Scenario 2)
12. Apprenticeships in Discipleship (Scenarios 2 and 4)
13. Pathways to Vibrant Faith and Active Engagement (Scenario 2 and 4)
14. Faith Formation in Third Place Settings (Scenarios 2 and 3)
15. Empowering the Community to Share their Faith (Scenario 1)
16. Interfaith Education and Dialogue (Scenario 1)

Step 3. Generate creative ideas.
Generate ideas for innovative programs, activities, and/or strategies to provide faith formation. Use one or more of the following creative thinking activities to generate ideas. Before you begin generating ideas, it might be helpful to remind people of the rules of brainstorming:

- Defer judgment.
- Encourage wild ideas.
- Build on the ideas of others.
- Stay focused on one topic.
- Pursue one conversation at a time.
- Go for quantity.

Activity: "What If" You Used Your Imagination

Use imagination to generate ideas. The easiest way to begin is by saying: "I need fresh and novel ideas to solve my challenge. I will suspend all judgment and see what free and easy ideas I can think up. It doesn't matter how weird or offbeat they are." Allow your team the freedom to conceptualize without judging ideas in terms of the real world. Ask team members to list as many "what if" statements as they can on sticky notes (for example, "What if we developed a community café to reach people who are spiritual, but not involved in the church community?"). Ask them to complete the "What if . . ." statement personally, writing one statement per sticky note. After several minutes, ask people to place their sticky notes on a sheet of easel paper. Then cluster similar ideas together. When ideas are grouped based on common characteristics or themes, an organization and structure begins to arise from the information. More ideas are generated as people begin to see the structure and fill in the gaps. A sense of priority is often revealed as one or more of the clusters claim the energy and interest of the group. Move on to evaluation.

Activity: Perfect World

In "Perfect World" a group can visualize what the perfect situation would be in five years and then work backwards from that point, identifying where they would need to be at the end of each year. Think about what it would look like if you had the perfect solution to your challenge. In a perfect world what would your idea, program, activity, or resource look like? In a perfect world, cars would never break down, never get dirty, never need gas or oil, never go out of style, and so on. Look at each "perfect" criteria and generate ideas about how to achieve it or use it. One of the benefits of Perfect World is the consensus that is generated when people think about the future. Looking at the possibilities generates excitement and enthusiasm. Generate as many ideas in the time allotted, cluster similar ideas together. Move on to evaluation.

Activity: Brainwriting Sheets

Brainwriting is a simple technique that can be used to break through the group participation barrier in brainstorming and to stimulate the power of divergent thinking. It is basically a way to brainstorm on paper while allowing the anonymous contribution of ideas. Speed and quantity are emphasized and the fear of being judged is reduced by the anonymous input.

The brainwriting form is a sheet of paper divided into twenty-one squares (three across and seven down). There should be one more sheet than the number of group members. In a few minutes of brainwriting, a group of six people can easily generate 147 ideas (twenty-one ideas per sheet, seven sheets).

1. One sheet per person plus one. Each person receives a brainwriting sheet and one additional sheet is placed in the center of the table where everyone can reach it.

2. Three ideas then switch. Each person writes an idea in the three top-most empty boxes and then places the sheet in the center and

takes an available sheet and writes three more ideas on that sheet, again in the three top empty boxes.

3. List ideas once. The process is continued until all the sheets are filled or until everyone is out of ideas. Have enough blank sheets on hand to keep the process going if there are lots of ideas being generated.

4. Bounce. When ideas begin to slow, people should scan the previous ideas and try to bounce off of them or create variations and new directions.

The sheets can be cut into the idea squares for clustering. The individual ideas are laid out on a table and people can walk around the table looking at the ideas, moving them into categories and removing redundancies. This process generally generates new ideas or variations, so someone should be prepared to capture new ideas. Once a structure begins to emerge from the ideas, the idea squares could be taped to sticky notes and placed on a large piece of paper for selecting the one or more priority ideas. Move on to evaluation.

Activity: "How Might We?"
Brainstorm responses to the question: "How Might We?" Distribute sticky notes and pens/markers to everyone on the team. Ask them to start their opportunity statements with "How Might We . . ." and abbreviate on sticky notes to "HMW." Go for quantity, not quality at this point. Post all of the ideas on sheets of easel paper. Together as a group select three to five HMW opportunity statements through discussion or the use of voting (see below). You might want to cluster HMW statements before discussion and voting. After selecting the three to five HMW statements, write each of the selected statements on a separate sheet of easel paper and brainstorm ideas for turning the opportunity into a practical project. Cluster similar ideas and select the best ideas for each HMW statement. Move on to evaluation.

Step 4. Evaluate the ideas.
Evaluate your ideas and select one or more innovative programs, activities, and/ or strategies for your target audience. The group can discuss the ideas to see which one(s) surface(s) as the best choice(s) or you can use a voting strategy to select ideas. In "dot voting" each person receives a colored sticky dot (usually five) to use in indicating their preference for an idea. The ideas are listed on a sheet of easel paper. People can distribute their dots however they choose—from giving the five best ideas one dot each or using all five votes on the one idea they strongly endorse. Tally the votes and discuss and confirm the one or more ideas that have emerged as priorities that you want to translate into projects.

Step 5. Design an implementation plan.

Describe, in detail, each of your new initiatives (strategy, program, activity, or resource). Develop a plan for each initiative by developing the actions that you will need to take to move from idea to implementation. Use the design worksheet on **Tool #7.**

- How many of the six faith formation models will be utilized?
- What are the dates and times?
- What is the location: physical/facility and/or online/website?
- What are the implementation steps and target dates (timeline) for completing each step?
- What resources will you need to implement the initiative?
- How much will the initiative cost?
- How many leaders will you need to implement the initiative, how you will find them, and how you will prepare them?

Step 6. Implement the initiative through small scale prototyping.

Consider a version 1.0 pilot effort (prototyping) of the program, activity, strategy, or resource with a small group of your target audience before scaling-up the initiative to reach a wider audience. Through prototyping, you can test the initiative and the implementation plan, get feedback from your target audience, improve the initiative, and then develop plans to reach a wide audience.

Step 7. Implement the initiative with a wider audience and continue evaluation and improvements.

After making adjustments based on the pilot, develop version 2.0 and implement the plan with a wider audience. Use the marketing suggestions on **Tool #9** to assist you in promoting the initiative to a wider audience.

Continue to improve the initiative. Communicate the stories and examples of the benefits and blessings that are coming to individuals, groups, families, and to your whole church community. Continue to reach new audiences.

Task 7

Integrating: Develop an integrated plan for the Lifelong Faith Formation Network with all of the programs, activities, and resources organized according to the four scenarios and the six faith formation models.

1. Add New Initiatives to the Lifelong Faith Formation Network.

Use **Tool #8** to add your new faith formation programs, activities, and resources to your *Lifelong Faith Formation Network.* Identify the following information for each activity.

- People: age group, family, or generation
- Life tasks, religious and spiritual needs addressed
- Faith formation program, activity, or resource
- Faith formation model (on your own, at home, small group, large group, congregation, community and world)
- Dates and times
- Location (physical/facility and/or online/website)

Add your new information to the large sheets of paper listing your current faith formation programs, activities, and resources for each scenario.

2. Consider adding "whole church" faith formation experiences to the Network.
One of the strengths of a "network" approach is the ability to personalize and customize faith formation experiences for the spiritual, religious, and learning needs of people. To balance these personalized faith formation experiences, consider providing faith formation programs and activities that provide a common focus, theme, or experience for all ages and generations. This can be accomplished in at least two ways.

One way to provide whole church faith formation is to utilize intergenerational programs and activities which provide a common faith formation experience for all ages and generations. This can be done through intergenerational learning experiences which bring all generations together at the same time for a learning program. Church-wide themes can include: church year feasts and seasons (Advent, Christmas Lent, Holy Week, Easter, Pentecost), the Creed and Christian beliefs, morality and the Ten Commandments, transforming the world (service, social justice, peace, care for creation), prayer and spiritual practices, and the Sunday lectionary readings. A church can also provide intergenerational faith formation through a church-wide service project that involves all ages, such as World Vision's "Your Faith in Action Sunday" project. A third example of intergenerational faith formation is through a whole church spiritual formation experience, such as a church-wide retreat day for all ages. (See Strategy #1. Faith Formation through the Life of the Whole Church and Strategy #4. Intergenerational Faith Formation for more details, examples, and resources.)

A second way to provide whole church faith formation is by using common themes in age group and family programming, aligning faith themes across all age-group learning programs in the parish: children (or family programs), teens, and adults, so that everyone is studying the same theme at the same time. Many curriculum resources already provide this common-theme approach for all ages, for example: *Akaloo* (www.akaloo.org), *FaithWeaver* (http://sundayschool.group.com/faithweaver), *Gather Round* (www.gatherround.org), *Living the Good News* (www.morehouseeducation.org/living-the-good-news), and *Seasons of the Spirit* (www.spiritseasons.com).

3. Review the Network Plan.

Review the final version of your Lifelong Faith Formation Network plan.

- What are the strengths of your Network plan viewed through the lens of the four scenarios?
- Who is being served by the Network plan when viewed through the lens of the four scenarios? Who is now being served that was not served in prior faith formation efforts?
- Which scenarios still need further development? How do you envision development of the Network over the next several years?

Task 8

Connecting: Develop an online faith formation center for connecting people to each other and to the resources of the Lifelong Faith Formation Network.

The best way to implement the Lifelong Faith Formation Network is through an online center at your church's website or on a new website or social networking platform. The capacity of web technology to connect us immediately and transparently to both people and content means that the constraints of the physical world need no longer limit our formational imaginations. Thanks to technology, the old notion of the "world as our classroom" has now become a practically possibility.

Even if your church website is not able to incorporate an online faith formation center, you can create a new, dedicated website for the *Network* using a service such as Weebly which even provides free hosting (see www.weebly.com) or a social networking platform like Ning (www.ning.com) which has a low annual fee. To see an example of a network using Ning go to the Book of Faith Initiative of the Evangelical Lutheran Church in America (http://bookoffaith.ning.com). The purpose of the Book of Faith Initiative is to increase biblical literacy and fluency. The Book of Faith Network on Ning includes (1) stories of churches implementing the Book of Faith Initiative, (2) a blog, (3) conversations, (4) interest groups, (5) videos and photos, (6) event listings, and (7) resources.

Another example of an online "network" approach to education is Glow, the world's first national intranet for education, that is transforming the way the curriculum is delivered in Scotland (see www.ltscotland.org.uk/usingglowandict). Glow provides a trusted and safe environment for pupils, practitioners and parents, a space to create personalized programs of work and share thinking and curricular resources, a variety of online tools to enhance learning experiences, virtual learning to share information and take part in a lesson, tools to communicate and collaborate across the network, communities of practice that offer practitioners rich opportunities to share and collaborate, innovations in learning and teaching approaches by engaging and immersing young people in powerful and relevant learning experiences, and motivation and support for individualized learning, personalization, and choice.

Glow includes a variety of features, such as: (1) the *Glow Directory*, an index of all the users throughout Scotland, where users can find others with similar areas of interest or expertise, collaborate across the country, and make connections with others to improve learning and teaching; (2) *Glow Group*, an area that connects people and ideas through communities of interest using tools such as discussion boards, chat rooms, document stores, image galleries, and web conferencing; (3) *Glow Meet*, a web conferencing tool allowing people to interact using video, audio, and a shared whiteboard space; (4) *Glow Learn*, the virtual learning environment (VLE) that includes tools to share, organize, and search for digital resources and courses, and provide access to structured content; (5) *Glow Messenger*, an electronic messaging service allowing users to exchange text messages with others online immediately; and (6) *Glow Chat*, a moderated chat room that sits inside the secure online environment.

An online Lifelong Faith Formation Network would present all of the faith formation offerings of the church, organized in a similar format to **Tool #8**, and searchable by each of the categories.

- People: age group, family, or generation
- Life tasks, religious and spiritual needs addressed
- Faith formation program, activity or resource
- Faith formation model (on your own, at home small group, large group, congregation, community and world)
- Dates and times
- Location (physical/facility and/or online/website)

The online Lifelong Faith Formation Network could incorporate the following features to help people develop their own individualized learning and faith growth plans. All of these features would be developed in response to the faith formation programs, activities, and resources identified in the Network.

- a calendar of all Network offerings
- registration procedures for face-to-face programs and activities
- resources recommended in the Network for people to use online or download
- links to recommended Network faith formation programs on other websites
- ways for people to connect with each other (social networking) and share their reflections, stories, faith practices, and so on.
- ways to extend relationships and learning initiated in church events and gathered faith formation programs
- ways for people to upload content to the site: articles, reflections, stories, audio files, and videos
- blogs organized by age groups or families or scenario or Network program/ activity

- discussion threads and groups for kindred groups or connected to a Network program or activity
- online courses, Bible studies, and webinars for Network programs developed by the church or accessed online through seminaries, universities, publishers, iTunes University, and other online course providers
- audio and video podcasts recommended by the Network that could be accessed through the website or with links to recommended sites such as iTunes and YouTube
- audio and video podcasts of gathered learning programs at the church
- links to free e-book libraries, such as Google Books and Internet Archive, and online Bibles, such as Bible Gateway and Biblica
- daily, weekly, and seasonal resources for all ages and families, including faith conversation activities, devotions and prayer, Bible reading activities and Bible studies, service projects, and rituals and traditions
- a milestones and life transitions center with sections for each milestone that include rituals, blessings, commentaries, personal stories, a "gathering space" for sharing stories and ideas
- themed "gathering spaces" for synchronous and asynchronous interaction, including live text-based chat and live audio/video conferences, threaded discussions, collected blog links, self-paced tutorials on a range of topics, and so on
- a mission/service opportunity clearinghouse for local, national, and international internships, volunteer opportunities, and jobs

Many churches have begun to use their website as a faith formation network, reflecting many of the features that could be incorporated into a Lifelong Faith Formation Network. Explore Willowcreek Church: www.willowcreek.org; and http://classes.willowcreek.org; and The United Methodist Church of the Resurrection: www.cor.org; and www.cor.org/programs-ministries.

A Network Catalog

A church can also create a Lifelong Faith Formation Network catalog with annual or seasonal offerings (a "course catalog" and calendar) in print format and publish it in an online format with a calendar of events. The catalog includes descriptions for every faith formation activity (face-to-face and online), indicating clearly the content or focus of the program and the particulars, such as date, location, cost, time, website location, and so on. Explore the following examples of a catalog approach at these churches and download a sample of their catalogs: Ginghamsburg Church (http://ginghamsburg.org, for children, youth, adult, and service/mission catalogs); and Holy Infant Catholic Parish (www.holyinfantchurch.org, for their faith formation handbook: http://images.acswebnetworks.com/1/443/FaithFormationHandbook.pdf.).

Task 9

Promoting: Develop a marketing/promotion plan to promote the Lifelong Faith Formation Network.

Generate ideas as a team for marketing/promoting the Lifelong Faith Formation Network to members of the church and to those not participating in the church. Develop church-wide strategies and targeted strategies for particular groups. **Tool #9** includes ideas for creating your message and ideas for your marketing plan. United Methodist Communications has produced an excellent online guide for developing a marketing plan in churches. Go to their website to explore ideas and strategies and download the guide: www.umcom.org/site/c.mrLZJ9PFKmG/b.5160951/k.54F3/Church_Marketing_Plan.htm.

Resources Consulted

Bonk, Curtis J. *The World is Open: How Web Technology Is Revolutionizing Education*. San Francisco: Jossey-Bass, 2009.

Brown, John Seely, and Richard P. Adler. "Minds on Fire: Open Education, the Long Tail, and Learning 2.0." *Educause*. January/February 2008.

Davidson, Cathy N. and David Theo Goldberg with the assistance of Zoë Marie Jones. *The Future of Learning Institutions in a Digital Age,* Cambridge: MIT Press, 2009. (Free download: http://mitpress.mit.edu/books/chapters/Future_of_Learning.pdf)

Glow. www.ltscotland.org.uk/usingglowandict (Glow is the world's first national intranet for education that is transforming the way the curriculum is delivered in Scotland.)

Redesigning Jewish Education for the Twenty-First Century. A Lippman Kanfer Institute Working Paper. New York: JESNA. (www.Jesna.org)

Roberto, John. *Becoming a Church of Lifelong Learners*. New London: Twenty-Third, 2006.

Scearge, Diana, Gabriel Kasper, and Heather McLeod Grant. "Working Wikily." *Stanford Social Innovation Review*. Summer 2010.

Stone, Thomas. "Blending Web 2.0 Technologies with Traditional Formal Learning: A Guide for CLOs and Training Managers." Rochester: Element K Corporation, 2009. www.elementk.com.

Synder, William. "Cultivating Communities." *Faith and Leadership*. (www.faithandleadership.com/multimedia/willliam-snyder-cultivating-communities)

Transforming Congregational Education: Lessons Learned and Questions for the Future. A Lippman Kanfer Institute Working Paper. New York: JESNA. (www.Jesna.org)

Wenger, Etienne, Richard McDermott, and William N. Synder. *Cultivating Communities of Practice*. Cambridge: Harvard Business School Press, 2002.

TOOL #1

A Vision of Lifelong Faith Formation

Most Christian churches have similar goals for faith formation. Churches want faith formation that helps all ages and generations to grow in their relationship with God, develop a deeper understanding of the Bible and their faith tradition, relate the Christian faith to life today, participate in the life and ministries of the faith community, and live as disciples of Jesus Christ in their daily life at home, in the workplace, in the community and the world. Churches want faith formation that touches the head, the heart, and actions of adults. They want faith formation that informs, forms, and transforms.

The Charter for Lifelong Christian Formation of the Episcopal Church, adopted at the Episcopal Church's General Convention in July 2009, captures so many of the elements of a lifelong vision that can shape the future of faith formation in Christian churches. The *Charter*, slightly adapted here to include all Christian churches, provides a comprehensive vision for developing a congregation's vision and practice of lifelong faith formation.

Christian formation is a lifelong journey with Christ, in Christ, and to Christ. Lifelong Christian faith formation is lifelong growth in the knowledge, service and love of God as followers of Christ and is informed by scripture, tradition and reason.

Through the Christian Church God **invites** all people:

- To enter into a prayerful life of worship, continuous learning, intentional outreach, advocacy and service.
- To hear the Word of God through scripture, to honor church teachings, and continually to embrace the joy of Baptism and Eucharist, spreading the Good News of the risen Christ and ministering to all.
- To respond to the needs of our constantly changing communities, as Jesus calls us, in ways that reflect our diversity and cultures, as we seek, wonder and discover together.

- To hear what the Spirit is saying to God's people, placing ourselves in the stories of our faith, thereby empowering us to proclaim the Gospel message.

Through the Christian Church, God **inspires** all people:

- To experience liturgy and worship, which draws us closer to God, helps us discern God's will, and encourages us to share our faith journeys.
- To study Scripture, mindful of the context of our societies and cultures, calling us to seek truth anew while remaining fully present in the community of faith.
- To develop new learning experiences, equipping disciples for life in a world of secular challenges, and carefully listening for the words of modern sages who embody the teachings of Christ.
- To prepare for a sustainable future by calling the community to become guardians of God's creation.

Through the Christian Church, God **transforms** all people:

- By doing the work Jesus Christ calls us to do, living into the reality that we are all created in the image of God and carrying out God's work of reconciliation, love, forgiveness, healing, justice and peace.
- By striving to be a loving and witnessing community, which faithfully confronts the tensions in the church and the world as we struggle to live God's will.
- By seeking out diverse and expansive ways to empower prophetic action, evangelism, advocacy and collaboration in our contemporary global context.
- By holding all accountable to lift every voice in order to reconcile oppressed and oppressor to the love of God in Jesus Christ our Lord.

(See *Charter for Lifelong Faith Formation* at www.formationcharter.com.)

TOOL #2

Faith Formation 2020 Inventory

Scenario #I. Vibrant Faith and Active Engagement

The first scenario describes a world in which people of all ages and generations are actively engaged in a Christian church, are spiritually committed, and are growing in their faith. People have found their spiritual home within an established Christian tradition and a local faith community that provides ways for all ages and generations to grow in faith, worship God, and live their faith in the world.

Who we are addressing	Ways we are addressing this through faith formation

Scenario #2. Spiritual but Not Religious

The second scenario describes a world in which people are spiritually hungry and searching for God and the spiritual life, but mostly likely not affiliated with organized religion and an established Christian tradition. Some may join a nondenominational Christian church focused on their spiritual needs, while others may find an outlet for their spiritual hunger in small communities of like-minded spiritual seekers, in acts of service—locally or globally, or in online spiritual resources and communities.

Who we are addressing	Ways we are addressing this through faith formation

Scenario #3. Unaffiliated and Uninterested

The third scenario describes a world in which people experience little need for God and the spiritual life and are not affiliated with organized religion and established Christian churches. The Unaffiliated and Uninterested reject all forms of organized religion and reflect a steadily increasing percentage of the American population.

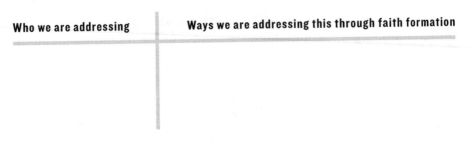

Who we are addressing	Ways we are addressing this through faith formation

Scenario #4. Participating but Uncommitted

The fourth scenario describes a world in which people attend church activities, but are not actively engaged in their church community or spiritually committed. They may participate in significant seasonal celebrations, such as Christmas and Easter, and celebrate sacraments and milestone events, such as marriage and baptism. Some may even attend worship regularly, and send their children to religious education classes. Their spiritual commitment is low and their connection to the church is more social and utilitarian than spiritual.

Who we are addressing	Ways we are addressing this through faith formation

TOOL #3

Life Issues and Spiritual/Religious Needs

Develop a profile of the spiritual and religious needs, interests, and life situations of people in each of the four scenarios.

1. Scenario #1. Vibrant Faith and Active Engagement
2. Scenario #2. Spiritual but Not Religious
3. Scenario #3. Unaffiliated and Uninterested
4. Scenario #4. Participating but Uncommitted

For each scenario answer the questions:

- Who are the people in your community in this scenario? How would you describe them?
- What are the religious and spiritual needs of people (age groups and families) in this scenario? How would you describe one or two aspects of each group's religious and spiritual hopes or desires?

Consider the following areas in your research:

1. **Life Issues**: What's happening in the lives and world of people (age group or family) today—the myriad dimensions of human life today: family, work, leisure, relationships, sexuality, suffering and grief, social and political issues, community issues?

2. **Life Cycle Tasks and Generational Characteristics**: What are the developmental life tasks facing people in the decades of life from childhood through old adulthood? What are the unique generational characteristics of the iGeneration (2000 and later), the Millennial Generation (1980–1999), Generation X (1964–1979), Baby Boom Generation (1946–1964), and the Builder Generation (1945 and earlier)?

3. **Milestones and Transitions:** What are the significant milestones/transitions throughout life, such as marriages, births, graduations, geographic relocations, family formation and re-formation, career changes, empty nests, retirement, unanticipated illness, divorce, and the loss of loved ones?

4. **Religious Needs:** What are the significant religious and learning needs of people at each stage of life?

5. **Spiritual Needs:** What are the significant spiritual needs of individuals and families at each stage of life?

6. **Ethnic/Cultural Needs**: Who are the ethnic/cultural communities in your church? What are the unique lived experiences, needs, and aspirations of people from each ethnic/cultural community in your church?

TOOL #4

Focus Group Interviews

Organize focus groups of six to twelve people for each age group from young teens (middle school) through older adults, for parents of children, for parents of teens, and for people who represent each of the four scenarios. Be sure to select a diversity of people in each focus group, reflecting the ethnic/cultural and socio-economic character of your church, and the various states in life (single, married, divorced, and so on).

Use the following questions as a guide for developing your own focus group interviews.

1. How would you describe your age group in key words or phrases?

2. What are some of the key life tasks that your age group is experiencing?

3. What are some of the important life issues that your age group is experiencing today?

4. What are the most meaningful experiences you have in life? What makes these experiences meaningful to you?

5. How important is your relationship with God? Why?

6. Where do you experience God most?

7. What are the significant spiritual issues that your age group is experiencing today?

8. What is most important to you about being a Christian (or a member of a particular denomination or faith tradition) today?

9. How do you live your Christian faith? Name some of the ways you put your faith into practice.

10. How can the church help you to continue growing as a Christian? Be specific. Name some of the things you would like to see your church offer for your age group.

TOOL #5

A Profile of Spiritual and Religious Needs
in Each Scenario

Based on the results of your research, discussion, and focus group interviews, identify *the most important* life issues and spiritual/religious needs of each group (individuals, age groups, families, generations) that your church needs to address in each of the four scenarios. For each scenario answer the question: *What would people in this scenario like to see the church offer them through faith formation?*

Scenario #1. Vibrant Faith and Active Engagement

People	What are their priority spiritual and religious needs?	What would they like to see the church offer them through faith formation?

Scenario #2. Spiritual but Not Religious

People	What are their priority spiritual and religious needs?	What would they like to see the church offer them through faith formation?

Scenario #3. Unaffiliated and Uninterested

People	What are their priority spiritual and religious needs?	What would they like to see the church offer them through faith formation?

Scenario #4. Participating but Uncommitted

People	What are their priority spiritual and religious needs?	What would they like to see the church offer them through faith formation?

TOOL #6

Resources for the Lifelong Faith Formation Network

1. People Resources

Using your priority issues and learning needs as guide, conduct a gifts/skills/knowledge survey of the people resources in your church, the wider community, the wider church, colleges and seminaries, and church-related organizations who can be invited to take a leadership role in the Network plan. Consider people who teach courses or specialized programs, guest presenters on specialized topics, leaders for small groups and Bible studies, prayer guides/spiritual directors, and leaders for service/mission programs .

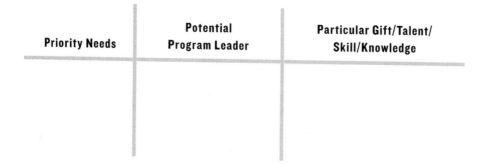

Priority Needs	Potential Program Leader	Particular Gift/Talent/ Skill/Knowledge

2. Face-to-Face Faith Formation Programs and Activities

Identify face-to-face faith formation activities that you can use to address priority issues and spiritual/religious needs. There are a variety of options: (1) programs that your church is already sponsoring, (2) an opportunity that you are not utilizing (for example, design reflection activities around Sunday worship), (3) a new program that your church can design or adopt, and (4) a program sponsored by another organization that you can promote as part of your plan. Consider programs in your church, the wider community, the wider church, retreat and conference centers, colleges and universities, and religious organizations. Indicate the faith formation model(s) used in the program: Faith Formation on Your Own, Faith Formation at Home, Faith

Formation in Small Groups, Faith Formation in Large Groups, Faith Formation in the Congregation, and/or Faith Formation in the Community and World.

Priority Needs	Program	Faith Formation Model	Location	Date/ Timing	Cost

3. Print and Media Faith Formation Resources

Identify print and media resources from publishers and religious organizations that you can use to address the priority issues and spiritual/religious needs. Indicate which of the six faith formation model(s) are used in the resource.

Priority Needs	Resource	Publisher	Faith Formation Model	Cost

4. Online Faith Formation Programs, Activities, and Resources

Identify online faith formation programs, activities, social networks, and resources that you can use to address priority issues and spiritual/religious needs. Indicate which of the six faith formation model(s) are used in the activity.

Priority Needs	Website	Activity	Faith Formation Model	Website Address	Cost

TOOL #7

Designing New Initiatives
for Faith Formation 2020

There are three elements in the design process: (1) *inspiration*—the need or opportunity that motivates the search for solutions; (2) *ideation*—the process of generating, developing, and testing ideas; and (3) *implementation*—the path that leads from the project stage into people's lives.

Step I. Select a priority need.
Select a priority need for a scenario and group of people for your new initiative.

Step 2. Consult the Faith Formation 2020 Strategies.
1. Faith Formation through the Life of the Whole Church (Scenarios 1 and 4)
2. Faith Formation using Digital Media and Web Technologies (All Scenarios)
3. Family Faith Formation (Scenarios 1, 2, and 4)
4. Intergenerational Faith Formation (Scenarios 1 and 4)
5. Generational Faith Formation (Scenarios 1, 2, and 4)
    •   Faith formation with the iGeneration and the Millennial Generation
    •   Faith formation with Generation X
    •   Faith formation with the Baby Boomer Generation
    •   Faith formation with the Builder Generation
6. Milestones Faith Formation (All Scenarios)
7. Faith Formation in Christian Practices (All Scenarios)
8. Transforming the World: Engagement in and Formation for Service and Mission (All Scenarios)
9. Spiritual Formation (All Scenarios)
10. Multi-Ethnic Faith Formation (All Scenarios)

11. Faith Formation for Spiritual Seekers (Scenario 2)
12. Apprenticeships in Discipleship (Scenarios 2 and 4)
13. Pathways to Vibrant Faith and Active Engagement (Scenario 2 and 4)
14. Faith Formation in Third Place Settings (Scenarios 2 and 3)
15. Empowering the Community to Share their Faith (Scenario 1)
16. Interfaith Education and Dialogue (Scenario 1)

Step 3. Generate creative ideas.

Generate ideas for innovative programs, activities, and/or strategies to provide faith formation. Remember the rules of effective brainstorming:

- Defer judgment.
- Encourage wild ideas.
- Build on the ideas of others.
- Stay focused on one topic.
- Pursue one conversation at a time.
- Go for quantity.

Step 4. Evaluate the ideas.

Evaluate your ideas and select one or more innovative programs, activities, and/or strategies for your target audience. The group can discuss the ideas to see which one(s) surface(s) as the best choice(s) or you can use a voting strategy to select ideas.

Step 5. Design an implementation plan.

Describe, in detail, each of your new initiatives (strategy, program, activity, or resource). Develop a plan for each initiative by developing the actions that you will need to take to move from idea to implementation. Use the "Design Worksheet."

- How many of the six faith formation models will be utilized?
- What are the dates and times?
- What is the location: physical/facility and/or online/website?
- What are the implementation steps and target dates (timeline) for completing each step?
- What resources will you need to implement the initiative?
- How much will the initiative cost?
- How many leaders will you need to implement the initiative, how you will find them, and how you will prepare them?

Step 6. Implement the initiative through small scale prototyping.

Consider a version 1.0 pilot effort (prototyping) of the program, activity, strategy, or resource with a small group of your target audience before scaling-up the initiative to reach a wider audience. Through prototyping, you can test the initiative and the implementation plan, get feedback from your target audience, improve the initiative, and then develop plans to reach a wider audience.

Step 7. Implement the initiative with a wider audience and continue evaluation and improvements.

After making adjustments based on the pilot, develop version 2.0 and implement the plan with wider audience. Use the marketing suggestions on **Tool #9** to assist you in promoting the initiative to a wider audience. Continue to improve the initiative. Communicate the stories and examples of the benefits and blessings that are coming to individuals, groups, families and to your whole church community. Continue to reach new audiences.

Designing Worksheet for a New Initiative

Scenario # _____

Priority Spiritual/Religious Need: _____

Target Participants: _____

Faith Formation Models

☐   on your own   ☐   large group
☐   at home   ☐   congregation
☐   small group   ☐   community and world

Dates and Times: _____

Location (physical/facility and/or online/website): _____

Implementation Steps and Timeline

	What	When	Who
1.			
2.			
3.			
4.			
5.			
6.			
7.			
8.			
9.			
10.			

Resources Needed to Implement the Initiative:

Leaders Needed to Implement the Initiative:

Costs to Implement the Initiative:

TOOL #8

Lifelong Faith Formation Network Plan

Scenario # _____

People *	Life Task, Religious and Spiritual Need	Faith Formation Program, Activity or Resource	Faith Formation Model **	Dates and Time	Location ***

*   age, family, generation
**   on your own, at home, small group, large group, congregation, community, and work
***   physical/facility, online/website

TOOL #9

Marketing Suggestions

Create Your Message

1. **Find the inherent drama within your offering**: What's interesting in your project? How does it respond to something within the lives of people?

2. **Translate that inherent drama into a meaningful benefit**: What are the major benefits in participating? Why should people respond? The benefit should come directly from the inherently dramatic feature. And even though you have four or five benefits, stick with one or two—three at most.

3. **Get people's attention**: How will you interest people? People do not pay attention to advertising. They pay attention only to things that interest them. So you've just got to interest them.

4. **Motivate your audience to do something**: What do you want people to do once you've introduced the Network? You must tell people exactly what you want them to do. Tell them to go online to register for a program, send in a registration form, call someone, and so on.

5. **Be sure you are communicating clearly**: Do people understand what you're talking about? Make sure you are putting your message across. Show your promotion or booklet or website or advertising to ten people and ask them what the main point is. If one person misunderstands, that means 10% of the audience will misunderstand. Make revisions so your message is clear.

You may need to develop several "messages" for each target audience. Be sure to pay careful attention to the titles of your programs so that they capture people's interests. Develop descriptions that are positive in tone, indicate clearly the content or focus of the program, and include the particulars (date, location, cost, and time).

Develop Marketing Strategies
for the Lifelong Faith Formation Network

1. Brainstorm marketing/promotion strategies: print catalog of the Network, website, online ads, e-newsletter, email, Facebook page, Twitter messages, and so on.

2. Use your church's website to promote the Network, post regular announcements, new program offerings, calendar, and so on.

3. Establish a Facebook site for your project and include a calendar of events with descriptions, locations, times, a link to your church's website, current news, stories from people who are participating, and so on.

4. Send email or regular mail invitations targeted to particular groups or ages.

5. Have the pastor share the benefits of the Network at Sunday worship.

6. Host information sessions to describe the Network, for example, after Sunday worship.

7. Promote the Network in the community: coffee shops, YMCA/YWCA, gyms, bookstores, theaters, schools/colleges, and so on.

8. Include information about the Network in new member packets. Send a personalized invitation to new members.

9. Promote the Network at all gathered programs and events in the church.

THREE

Leading Faith Formation 2020

▶ Faith Formation 2020 presents new challenges for leaders and requires particular knowledge and skill for effective leadership. Chapter 3 presents six of the most important competencies necessary for leading a congregation's Faith Formation 2020 plan and implementation. Chapter 3 is not intended as a presentation of contemporary leadership thinking and its application to Christian leadership. These six competencies have been selected because of their relevance to the designing, implementing, and leading Faith Formation 2020 in a church. The six leadership competencies include:

1. Becoming an Adaptive Leader
2. Becoming an Innovative Leader
3. Becoming a "Blue Ocean" Leader
4. Becoming a Change Leader
5. Becoming a Culturally Intelligent Leader
6. Becoming a Curator of Content

There are tools for the first five leadership competencies at the end of Chapter 3 that can help you apply the content and processes to your church community.

Becoming an Adaptive Leader

Leadership experts Ronald Heifetz and Marty Linsky define leadership as *"the activity of mobilizing people to tackle the toughest problems and do the adaptive work necessary to achieve progress."* Leadership would be an easy and safe undertaking if organizations and communities only faced problems for which they already knew the solutions. Everyday, people have problems for which they do, in fact, have the necessary know-how and procedures—what leadership experts Ronald Heifetz and Marty Linsky call *technical problems*. But there are also a whole host of problems that are not amenable to authoritative expertise or standard operating procedures. They cannot be solved by someone who provides answers from on high. Heifetz and Linsky refer to these problems as *adaptive challenges* because they require experiments, new discoveries, and adjustments from numerous places in the organization or community. Without learning new ways—changing attitudes, values, and deep-seated behaviors—people cannot make the adaptive leap necessary to thrive in the new environment. The sustainability of real change depends on having the people with the problem internalize the change itself.

Sharon Daloz Parks, in *Leadership Can Be Taught*, describes the distinction between technical and adaptive issues:

> *Technical problems* (even though they may be complex) can be solved with knowledge and procedures already in hand. In contrast, *adaptive challenges* require new learning, innovation, and new patterns of behavior. In this view, leadership is the activity of mobilizing people to address adaptive challenges—those challenges that cannot be resolved by expert knowledge and routine management alone. Adaptive challenges often appear as swamp issues—tangled, complex problems composed of multiple systems that resist technical analysis and thus stand in contrast to the high, hard ground issues that are easier to address but where less is at stake for the organization or the society. They ask for more than changes in routine or mere performance. They call for changes of heart and mind—the transformation of long-standing habits and deeply held assumptions and values. (Parks, 10)

Technical problems are well defined: their solutions are known and those with adequate expertise and organizational capacity can solve them. For example, a church that sees the participation of children and their families decline in the summer can develop a multi-week Vacation Bible School program that engages children and their parents during the summer months. It is a technical problem because the resources are available for purchase and the implementation tasks, while requiring plenty of work, are well known and within the existing skill-set of the church's faith formation leadership.

Adaptive challenges are entirely different. The challenge is complex and not so well defined, and the answers are not known in advance. Adaptive challenges require innovation and learning. For example, developing a plan for the faith formation of Baby Boomers in a church is an adaptive challenge today. People in this generation present a whole new set of challenges and opportunities for churches. They bring new spiritual and religious needs, and are creating a new "stage of life" that combines work, retirement, volunteerism, and family. There are few established models or resources for faith formation with this generation. This adaptive challenge will require creating new models and approaches, experimenting, evaluating, redesigning, and continuous learning.

Adaptive leadership is an iterative process that involves three key activities: (1) *observing* events and patterns around you; (2) *interpreting* what you are observing (developing multiple hypotheses about what is really going on; and (3) *designing* interventions based on the observations and interpretations to address the adaptive challenge you have identified. Each of these activities builds on the ones that come before it; and the process overall is iterative: you repeatedly refine your observations, interpretations, and interventions. The process for developing a Lifelong Faith Formation Network and creating innovations described in chapter 2 of this book reflects this adaptive leadership process of observing, interpreting, and designing.

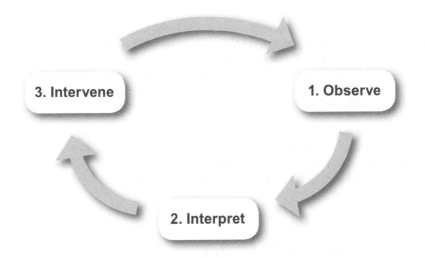

In the view of Heifetz and Linsky, leadership is about mobilizing a congregation to engage its own most pressing problems and deepest challenges. Leadership builds capacity and sustainability within a congregation as it mobilizes a congregation to engage and make progress on its deepest challenges. Leaders help people understand the changed nature of their situation, and develop new ways of doing faith formation and being church. Mobilizing people for adaptive work is to help them enter into that zone of risk where new learning and new self-understanding, as well as new ways of acting, can be discerned.

"What Heifetz describes as adaptive work is, at its heart, spiritual work. It involves the central dynamics of the spiritual life and of transformation, which includes loss, risk and trust, even death and resurrection. Our sacred Scriptures, sacraments and our symbols are all powerful resources for adaptive challenges and adaptive work that we face at this time. No program, effort at restructuring, or 'right' pastor alone will meet this challenge. It involves our own changes of minds and hearts" (Robinson, 45).

The driving forces affecting the future of faith formation and the response to the challenges of the four scenarios will, for most churches, demand a response outside of their current "toolkit." In many churches there exists a gap between the vision of the scenarios and the church's current practices and operational capacity that cannot be closed by the expertise and procedures currently in place. Faith Formation 2020 represents an adaptive challenge that calls for innovation, experimentation, and continuous learning.

Resources on Adaptive Leadership

Ford, Kevin G. *Transforming Church: Bringing Out the Good to Get to Great*. Carol Stream: Tyndale, 2007.

Heifetz, Ronald. *Leadership without Easy Answers*. Cambridge: Harvard University Press, 1995.

Heifetz, Ronald, and Marty Linsky. *Leadership on the Line: Staying Alive through the Dangers of Leading*. Cambridge: Harvard Business School Press, 2002.

Heifetz, Ronald, Marty Linsky, and Alexander Groshow. *The Practice of Adaptive Leadership*. Cambridge: Harvard Business School Press, 2009.

Parks, Sharon Daloz. *Leadership Can Be Taught: A Bold Approach for a Complex World*. Cambridge: Harvard Business School Press, 2005.

Robinson, Anthony B. *Leadership for Vital Congregations*. Cleveland: Pilgrim, 2006.

Video Presentations by Ronald Heifetz on Adaptive Leadership

Faith & Leadership (Duke University): www.faithandleadership.com/multimedia/ronald-heifetz-the-nature-adaptive-leadership

Institute for Educational Leadership (Ontario, Canada): www.education-leadership-ontario.ca/videos06-07.shtml

Vimeo Video Presentation: http://vimeo.com/13117695

Becoming an Innovative Leader

Innovation can be defined as people creating value through the implementation of new ideas. The challenge of the four scenarios and the unmet spiritual and religious needs of people in our communities call out for innovation and leaders who practice innovative processes and skills. In *The Ten Faces of Innovation* Tom Kelley describes ten people-centric tools developed at IDEO, an international design firm, that define some of the innovation roles that teams can use to express different points of view and create a broader range of innovative solutions. Innovation is all about people. It is about the roles people can play, the hats they can put on, the personas they can adopt.

These ten faces of innovation provide methods and techniques that a team can use to infuse a continuous spirit of innovation in a congregation.

The Three Learning Roles

Churches need constantly to gather new sources of information in order to expand their knowledge and grow. These three learning roles help keep your team from becoming too internally focused, and remind everyone not to be so smug about what you "know." People who adopt the learning roles are humble enough to question their own worldview, and in doing so they remain open to new insights every day.

1. *The Anthropologist* is the person who ventures into the field to observe how people interact with daily life and experiences in order to come up with new innovations. The Anthropologist is extremely good at reframing a problem in a new way, applying it to daily life. Anthropologists share such distinguishing characteristics as the wisdom to observe with a truly open mind, empathy, intuition, the ability to "see" things that have gone unnoticed, a tendency to keep running lists of innovative concepts worth emulating and problems that need solving, and a way of seeking inspiration in unusual places.

    Faith Formation 2020 Examples: conducting focus groups, interviewing people, observing people's everyday life (school, work, shopping, recreation, and so on), identifying where and how people spend their time and money

2. *The Experimenter* celebrates the process, not the tool, testing and retesting potential ways to make ideas tangible. A calculated risk-taker, this person models everything from programs to activities to resources in order to efficiently reach a solution. To share the fun of discovery, the Experimenter invites others to collaborate.

    Faith Formation 2020 Example: piloting a program and receiving feedback from the participants that can be used to improve and expand the program

3. *The Cross-Pollinator* draws associations and connections between seemingly unrelated ideas or concepts to break new ground. Armed with a wide set of interests, an avid curiosity, and an aptitude for learning and teaching, the Cross-Pollinator brings in big ideas from the outside world to enliven their organization. People in this role can often be identified by their open mindedness, diligent note-taking, tendency to think in metaphors, and ability to reap inspiration from constraints.

    Faith Formation 2020 Example: bringing ideas from a variety of sources and locations (books, websites, other churches) into the design process; exploring how other organizations and businesses reach people (for example, museums, community centers, gyms, coffee shops, arts and music performances) and the types of activities they sponsor to engage people; investigating what is working at other churches and synagogues

The Three Organizing Roles

Organizing roles are played by individuals who are savvy about the often counter-intuitive process of how organizations move ideas forward. Many believe that good ideas should speak for themselves. The Hurdler, the Collaborator, and the Director know that even the best ideas must continuously compete for time, attention, and resources. Those who adopt these organizing roles don't dismiss the process of budget and resource allocation.

4. *The Hurdler* is a tireless problem-solver who gets a charge out of tackling something that's never been done before. When confronted with a challenge, the Hurdler gracefully sidesteps the obstacle while maintaining a quiet, positive determination. This optimism and perseverance can help big ideas upend the status quo as well as turn setbacks into an organization's greatest successes.

    Faith Formation 2020 Examples: leading problem-solving and finding alternative ways to doing things, finding discounts and low-cost ways to implement an innovation, connecting with people who can contribute services for free or at cost to move a project ahead

5. *The Collaborator* is the rare person who truly values the team over the individual. In the interest of getting things done, the Collaborator coaxes people out of their work silos to form multidisciplinary teams. In doing so, the person in this role dissolves traditional boundaries within the church and creates opportunities for team members to assume new roles. More of a coach, the Collaborator instills the team with the confidence and skills needed to complete the shared journey.

    Faith Formation 2020 Examples: facilitating teamwork through the planning and design work, involving people outside of the team (in the church or community) to partner in the development of new initiatives, expanding the people and resources available to the team for designing and implementing initiatives by going outside the church community

6. *The Director* has an acute understanding of the bigger picture, with a firm grasp on the pulse of their church. Consequently, the Director is talented

at setting the stage, targeting opportunities, bringing out the best in their players, and getting things done. Through empowerment and inspiration, the person in this role motivates those around them to take center stage and embrace the unexpected. Five traits of successful directors include: (1) they give center stage to others, (2) they love finding new projects, (3) they rise to tough challenges, (4) they shoot for the moon, and (5) they wield a large toolbox for solving problems and improvising.

> Faith Formation 2020 Examples: seeing the big picture of the four scenarios and keeping this vision in front of people at all times; equipping people for their roles and responsibilities in faith formation; uncovering new opportunities and projects for implementing the vision of faith formation; engaging the team in problem-solving and improvising

The Four Building Roles

The building roles apply insights from the learning roles and channel the empowerment from the organizing roles to make innovation happen. When people adopt the building personas, they stamp their mark on your organization. People in these roles are highly visible, so you'll often find them right at the heart of the action.

7. *The Experience Architect* is that person relentlessly focused on creating remarkable experiences for people. This person facilitates positive experiences through programs, activities, digital interactions, spaces, and events. Whether an architect or a sushi chef, the Experience Architect maps out how to turn something ordinary into something distinctive—even delightful—every chance they get.

    > Faith Formation 2020 Example: designing and conducting new faith formation experiences that connect deeply with people's spiritual and religious needs and that are engaging, exciting, multi-sensory, and experiential

8. *The Set Designer* transforms physical environments into powerful tools to influence behavior and attitude and provide the optimal setting for learning and formation. They create spaces for work and planning that stimulate creativity. They design, redesign, and/or re-purpose spaces to make them conducive to learning and formation.

    > Faith Formation 2020 Examples: creating engaging and multi-sensory spaces for faith formation at home, church, and in the community; creating and utilizing art to communicate the Christian faith; exploring new settings and venues for groups to gather for faith formation

9. *The Caregiver* is the foundation of human-powered innovation. Through empathy, Caregivers work to understand each individual and family and create relationships. Good Caregivers anticipate people's needs and are ready to respond. They keep the needs of people front and center in planning and implementation.

    Faith Formation 2020 Examples: attending to the needs and life situation of people in planning and implementation; personalizing and customizing the faith formation experience to address the spiritual and religious needs of people in all four scenarios; reaching out to people not engaged in faith formation and building relationships

10. *The Storyteller* builds both internal morale and external awareness through compelling narratives that communicate the vision and goals of faith formation, and real life stories of people in the four scenarios. The Storyteller goes beyond oral tradition to work in whatever medium best fits the message: video, narrative, animation. The Storyteller presents the stories of those who have benefited from faith formation. The Storyteller can spark emotion and urgency, transmit vision and goals, and lead people to action and involvement.

    Faith Formation 2020 Examples: producing audio and video stories of people's spiritual and religious needs in each of the four scenarios and explaining why the church needs to respond; producing audio and video accounts of people's participation in faith formation; telling the story of Faith Formation 2020 in a church and the many faith formation offerings in a church through print and video presentations

---

Resources on Innovation

Brown, Tim. Change by Design: *How Design Thinking Transforms Organizations and Inspires Innovation*. New York: HarperBusiness, 2009.

Horth, David and Dan Buchner. *Innovation Leadership*. Center for Creative Leadership, 2009 (Download at: www.ccl.org)

Kelley, Tom. *The Ten Faces of Innovation*. New York: Doubleday, 2005.

Websites

IDEO website: www.ideo.com

OpenIDEO website: http://openideo.com

Ten Faces of Innovation website: www.tenfacesofinnovation.com

Becoming a Blue Ocean Leader

In *Blue Ocean Strategy*, W. Chan Kim and Renee Mauborgne present the concept of a "Blue Ocean Strategy" as a way for an organization (your congregation) to enter a market or audience that's open and undisturbed (think of people not involved in church, new married couples, families with young children, people in their twenties and thirties).

When it comes to defining what Blue Ocean Strategy is, it helps to start by picturing a vast ocean. Most businesses are located in what the authors call a red ocean. The red ocean is jam-packed with other businesses, all offering similar products and services, and competing with each. Blue oceans are the exact opposite. Blue oceans are open and empty, with plenty of space to expand and sail where you want. In blue oceans there is often no competition, or, if there is any, it is effectively irrelevant to you because it can't touch you. Here demand, customers, and growth are yours for the taking. You and your organization stop using the competition as your benchmark, and go your own way.

Understanding Blue Ocean Strategy is easiest when you look at how an existing company has applied the concept successfully. For this example, let's look at Netflix, the online and rent-by-mail movie rental organization. Stop and think about how you borrowed movies in the late 1990s. You probably got them from a bricks and mortar store, at a fairly high price. And you had to return them promptly or face outrageously high late fees. This usually meant driving back to the store by 11:00 am. Until 1997, this was simply the way movies were rented. No one questioned it—at least until Netflix appeared. Netflix's approach was 100% consumer-focused, and its business model tore down the existing walls of the industry. Netflix created its blue ocean by being completely different from its competition:

- It had no store. Movies were chosen by customers online. This kept costs down for Netflix, and for its consumers.
- Since movies were mailed out, people no longer had to drive to drop them off.
- Postage was taken care of by Netflix, getting rid of another source of customer annoyance.
- Late fees were eliminated. You could keep a movie as long as you wanted.
- Movies could also be watched online. This eliminated waiting, and added considerable value for customers.
- Pricing was set using a flat-fee monthly membership structure, instead of on a "per movie" basis. This gave members more value for their money.

Netflix completely changed the way people rented movies, and changed how movie rental companies delivered those movies. As a result, they had complete control of the online and rent-by-mail market for almost a decade. Competition has now crept in, but Netflix has had such a big head start in the industry and has such a strong brand name that it's going to be hard for the competition to shake them.

It is important to realize that organizations don't have to completely redefine their industry or organization in order for Blue Ocean Strategy to work. Most of the time, blue oceans are created from within existing organizations. It's usually about designing one new product or service and linking it to what buyers really want, even if they don't realize they want it.

Peirce College is another example of a Blue Ocean Strategy. To break out of the red ocean of competition in the market of post-secondary education, Peirce has endeavored to offer unprecedented value to learners on the one hand and build a more efficient and cost effective business model on the other. The College has three interchangeable delivery systems: on-campus (land-based in Philadelphia); on-site (land-based corporate and community cluster locations); and online (Internet-mediated distance learning). They have produced educational options that are interchangeable: offering the same curricula and course syllabi; taught by the same professors; and yielding the same educational outcomes. Students have moved seamlessly among the three systems. This design has fostered quality assurance, convenience, and flexibility. Students have received the same highly relevant education regardless of whether they are in Philadelphia, Chicago, San Francisco, or Barcelona. Moreover, students around the country and across the globe receive high-quality and tailor-made customer services. They may register on a year-round basis and graduate from Peirce obtaining bachelor's degrees and relevant professional certifications. In the meantime, Peirce has managed to achieve all these breakthroughs in value for learners at the lowest possible costs. To fund the needed technological growth and development for delivering an unprecedented learning experience, Peirce diverted resources from those taken-for-granted areas of expenditure into areas that are central to learner's academic experience.

Peirce College started their journey of value innovation by looking at unmet needs of noncustomers. Whereas most colleges were focusing on serving traditional-age students, a vast pool of learners was overlooked or underserved. Working adults, for example, found it hard to complete an on-campus degree program while fulfilling their duties at work. Moreover, as adult learners mostly sought to improve their career prospect through enhancing their academic credentials, community and regional colleges that only offered associate degrees were less attractive to them. Next came military personal as well as those who worked in employment sectors that required constant relocation. Traditional campus-based learning models obviously did not suit their needs. Finally, there existed a vast number of learners residing in other regions or even in foreign countries that Peirce never considered as its potential customers. They found that, despite their differences, all these people wanted to pursue higher learning in a credible and high-quality program with a practical, career-oriented curriculum and flexibility in terms of registration, completion time, and learning location. Exploring the commonalities across these people provided Peirce with important insights for market reconstruction to pull in all-new demand.

Positive results emerged quickly. Online enrollment forecasts were exceeded by 300% in the first year alone. The market penetration moved across the country. Degree-seeking students have enrolled from forty-three of the fifty states, the District of Columbia, the U.S. Virgin Islands, and thirty other countries. The College has achieved a national scope with international reach in less than a decade. Beyond having access to vastly greater numbers of prospective students, the College unlocked markets among military personnel (active, reserves, and retired) as well as other employment sectors where relocation, and related disruptions to the educational process, are a significant challenge. Learners residing in more remote locations, with limited land-based educational options, emerged as an important constituency as have online community college students seeking a bachelor's degree while continuing to use the Internet platform in harmony with work/career responsibilities. The average age of a Peirce student shifted from 21.5 to 34.5 years.

Total enrollments nearly tripled. The College has enjoyed strong financial performance with a string of annual operating surpluses. This has enabled the College to properly resource further expansion; increase scholarship funds; avoid borrowing; improve employee compensation; and maintain one of the lowest private college tuition rates. About 65% of total annual tuition revenue comes from Peirce Online— a delivery system and source which did not exist ten years ago!

What would this concept mean for churches and Faith Formation 2020? A Blue Ocean Strategy is way to expand or grow faith formation—to re-imagine current faith formation offerings and design initiatives to reach new audiences (blue ocean). The four scenarios provide a way to envision the possibilities and create faith formation where there is no competition—within the church or even in the wider community. The Lifelong Faith Formation Network serves to expand faith formation to reach everyone, anytime, anywhere, 24/7/365. It opens up "blue ocean" for creating new faith formation programs, activities, and resources that do not have any internal competition and may not have any external competition. The responses to the Faith Formation 2020 scenarios can present a "blue ocean" opportunity for churches.

How can a church create a blue ocean in faith formation? Here are several factors to consider, translated from the business world into the church world:

1. How can we create high *quality* and exceptional experiences in faith formation for people that will change the lives of the target audience? Be sure to specify a target audience, such as young families or emerging adults or the Spiritual but Not Religious.

2. What are the strategic *factors* (time, cost, availability, location, and so on) that will unlock the target audience so that they will engage in a faith formation program, activity, or resource? Which are the most important factors? Once the most important strategic factors are establish to

reach the target audience, the value proposition of the strategic move is established.

3. What are the projected *outcomes* (number of people served, quality of participation, increased participation, and so on) that would describe the effectiveness of the initiative? (In the business world this would be the profit proposition. In churches it could be called the results proposition.)

4. What are the adoption hurdles in executing a blue ocean strategic move and how will you overcome these? This is the people proposition of blue ocean strategy.

In summary, to create a blue ocean successfully, a church should address quality, strategic factors, outcomes, and adoption sequentially and formulate and execute its strategic move by aligning value, results, and people propositions. To assess whether a blue ocean idea will be successful or not, consider the following: (1) if there is high quality and exceptional experiences in the idea; (2) if the strategic factors will make the idea accessible to the target audience; (3) if the projected results can be attained to ensure the effectiveness of the idea; and (4) if the adoption hurdles in actualizing the idea have been addressed. It is a simple but robust test that allows people to evaluate the success potential of blue ocean ideas and sheds light on how the idea may need to be improved to unlock a blue ocean of new audiences.

Resources

Kim, W. Chan and Renee Mauborgne. "Blue Ocean Strategy." *Harvard Business Review.* October 2004. Reprint #R0410D. (Also available at: http://mindsetandattractionmarketing.com/Blue_Ocean_Strategy.pdf)

Kim, W. Chan and Renee Mauborgne. *Blue Ocean Strategy: How to Create Uncontested Market Space and Make the Competition Irrelevant.* Cambridge: Harvard Business School Press, 2005.

Lendo, Dr. Arthur J. "The Strategic Move of Peirce College." www.blueoceanstrategy.com/abo/peirce.html

Website

Blue Ocean Strategy website: www.blueoceanstrategy.com

Becoming a Change Leader

In their book *Switch: How to Change Things When Change Is Hard*, Chip and Dan Heath, authors and professors, ask why it's so hard to make lasting changes in our companies, in our communities, and in our own lives. The primary obstacle, say the Heaths, is a conflict that's built into our brains. Psychologists have discovered that our minds are ruled by two different systems—the rational mind and the emotional mind—that compete for control. The rational mind wants a great beach body; the emotional mind wants that Oreo cookie. The rational mind wants to change something at work; the emotional mind loves the comfort of the existing routine. This tension can doom a change effort—but if it is overcome, change can come quickly.

They propose a framework that sets out three ways change happens. (For practical checklists for each step of the process download *Switch Your Organization: A Workbook* by Chip and Dan Heath at http://heathbrothers.com/resources.)

1. *Direct the Rider* (the conscious mind), eliminating what looks like resistance but is more often a lack of clarity by providing crystal-clear direction.
    *   Follow the bright spots: investigate what's working and clone it.
    *   Script the critical moves: don't think big picture, think in terms of specific behaviors.
    *   Point to the destination: change is easier when you know where you're going and why it's worth it.

2. *Motivate the Elephant* (the subconscious), eliminating what looks like laziness but is more often exhaustion by engaging emotions to get people on the same path as you.
    *   Find the feeling: knowing something isn't enough to cause change. Make people feel something.
    *   Shrink the change: break down the change until it no longer spooks the Elephant.
    *   Grow your people: cultivate a sense of identity and instill the growth mindset.

3. *Shape the Path* (the situation), eliminating what looks like a people problem but is more often a situation problem, by making the environment more conducive to the change you seek.
    *   Tweak the environment: when the situation changes, the behavior changes. So change the situation.
    *   Build habits: when behavior is habitual, it's "free"—it doesn't tax the Rider. Look for ways to encourage habits.
    *   Rally the herd: behavior is contagious. Help it spread.
    (Heath and Heath, 259)

A story in their book about hospitals and change illustrates the three elements of their approach.

> In 2004, Donald Berwick, a doctor and the CEO of the Institute for Health-care Improvement (IHI), had some ideas about how to save lives—massive numbers of lives. Researchers at the IHI had analyzed patient care with the kinds of analytical tools used to assess the quality of cars coming off a production line. They discovered that the "defect" rate in health care was as high as 1 in 10—meaning, for example, that 10% of patients did not receive their antibiotics in the specified time. This was a shockingly high defect rate—many other industries had managed to achieve performance at levels of 1 error in 1,000 cases (and often far better). Berwick knew that the high medical defect rate meant that tens of thousands of patients were dying every year, unnecessarily.

> Berwick's insight was that hospitals could benefit from the same kinds of rigorous process improvements that had worked in other industries. Couldn't a transplant operation be "produced" as consistently and flawlessly as a Toyota Camry?

> Berwick's ideas were so well supported by research that they were essentially indisputable, yet little was happening. He certainly had no ability to force any changes on the industry. IHI had only seventy-five employees. But Berwick wasn't deterred.

> On December 14, 2004, he gave a speech to a room full of hospital administrators at a large industry convention. He said, "Here is what I think we should do. I think we should save 100,000 lives. And I think we should do that by June 14, 2006—18 months from today. Some is not a number; soon is not a time. Here's the number: 100,000. Here's the time: June 14, 2006—9 a.m."

> The crowd was astonished. The goal was daunting. But Berwick was quite serious about his intentions. He and his tiny team set out to do the impossible.

> IHI proposed six very specific interventions to save lives. For instance, one asked hospitals to adopt a set of proven procedures for managing patients on ventilators, to prevent them from getting pneumonia, a common cause of unnecessary death. (One of the procedures called for a patient's head to be elevated between 30 and 45 degrees, so that oral secretions couldn't get into the windpipe.)

> Of course, all hospital administrators agreed with the goal to save lives, but the road to that goal was filled with obstacles. For one thing, for a hospital to reduce its "defect rate," it had to acknowledge having a defect rate. In other words, it had to admit that some patients were dying needless deaths. Hospital lawyers were not keen to put this admission on record.

Berwick knew he had to address the hospitals' squeamishness about admitting error. At his December 14 speech, he was joined by the mother of a girl who'd been killed by a medical error. She said, "I'm a little speechless, and I'm a little sad, because I know that if this campaign had been in place four or five years ago, that Josie would be fine. . . . But, I'm happy, I'm thrilled to be part of this, because I know you can do it, because you have to do it." Another guest on stage, the chair of the North Carolina State Hospital Association, said: "An awful lot of people for a long time have had their heads in the sand on this issue, and it's time to do the right thing. It's as simple as that."

IHI made joining the campaign easy: It required only a one-page form signed by a hospital CEO. By two months after Berwick's speech, over a thousand hospitals had enrolled. Once a hospital enrolled, the IHI team helped the hospital embrace the new interventions. Team members provided research, step-by-step instruction guides, and training. They arranged conference calls for hospital leaders to share their victories and struggles with one another. They encouraged hospitals with early successes to become "mentors" to hospitals just joining the campaign.

The friction in the system was substantial. Adopting the IHI interventions required hospitals to overcome decades' worth of habits and routines. Many doctors were irritated by the new procedures, which they perceived as constricting. But the adopting hospitals were seeing dramatic results, and their visible successes attracted more hospitals to join the campaign.

Eighteen months later, at the exact moment he'd promised to return—June 14, 2006, at 9 a.m.—Berwick took the stage again to announce the results: "Hospitals enrolled in the 100,000 Lives Campaign have collectively prevented an estimated 122,300 avoidable deaths and, as importantly, have begun to institutionalize new standards of care that will continue to save lives and improve health outcomes into the future."

The crowd was euphoric. Don Berwick, with his 75-person team at IHI, had convinced thousands of hospitals to change their behavior, and collectively, they'd saved 122,300 lives—the equivalent of throwing a life preserver to every man, woman, and child in Ann Arbor, Michigan.

This outcome was the fulfillment of the vision Berwick had articulated as he closed his speech eighteen months earlier, about how the world would look when hospitals achieved the 100,000 lives goal: "And, we will celebrate. Starting with pizza, and ending with champagne. We will celebrate the importance of what we have undertaken to do, the courage of honesty, the joy of companionship, the cleverness of a field operation, and the results we will achieve. We will celebrate ourselves, because the patients whose lives we save cannot join us, because their names can never be known. Our contribution will be what did not happen to them. And, though they are unknown, we will know that mothers and fathers are at graduations and weddings they would have missed, and that grandchildren will know grandparents they might never have known, and holidays will be taken, and work completed, and books read, and symphonies heard, and gardens tended that, without our work, would have been only beds of weeds."

Don Berwick and his team catalyzed a change that saved 100,000 lives, yet Berwick himself wielded no power. He couldn't change the law. He couldn't fire hospital leaders who didn't agree with him. He couldn't pay bonuses to hospitals that accepted his proposals.

Berwick had the same tools the rest of us have. First, he directed his audience's Riders. The destination was crystal clear: Some is not a number; soon is not a time. Here's the number: 100,000. Here's the time: June 14, 2006—9 a.m. But that wasn't enough. He had to help hospitals figure out how to get there. So he proposed six specific interventions, such as elevating the heads of patients on ventilators, that were known to save lives. By staying laser-focused on these six interventions, Berwick made sure not to exhaust the Riders of his audience with endless behavioral changes.

Second, he motivated his audience's Elephants. He made them feel the need for change. Many of the people in the audience already knew the facts, but knowing was not enough. Berwick had to get beyond knowing, so he brought his audience face-to-face with the mother of the girl who'd been killed by a medical error: "I know that if this campaign had been in place four or five years ago, that Josie would be fine." Berwick was also careful to motivate the people who hadn't been in the room for his presentation. He didn't challenge people to "overhaul medicine" or "bring TQM to health care." He challenged them to save 100,000 lives. That speaks to anyone's Elephant.

Third, he shaped the Path. He made it easier for the hospitals to embrace the change. Think of the one-page enrollment form, the step-by-step instructions, the training, the support groups, the mentors. He was designing an environment that made it more likely for hospital administrators to reform. Berwick also knew that behavior was contagious. He used peer pressure to persuade hospitals to join the campaign. (Your rival hospital across town just signed on to help save 100,000 lives. Do you really want them to have the moral high ground?) He also connected people—he matched up people who were struggling to implement the changes with people who had mastered them, almost like the "mentors" found in Alcoholics Anonymous. Berwick was creating a support group for health care reform. (Heath and Heath, 19-23)

Resources

Heath, Chip and Dan Heath. *Switch: How to Change Things When Change Is Hard.* New York: Broadway, 2010.

Heath, Chip and Dan Heath. *Switch Your Organization: A Workbook.* Download from http://heathbrothers.com/resources.

Website
Heath Brothers: http://heathbrothers.com/
Podcast Series (http://heathbrothers.com/resources)
Switch for Managers
Switch for Marketers
Switch for the Social Sector
Switch for Personal Change

Becoming a Culturally Intelligent Leader

We move in and out of socioethnic cultures, generational cultures, and organizational cultures in our daily lives. Numerous other cultural contexts exist in our lives as well, including cultures organized by professional careers, gender-oriented cultures, and cultures characterized by sexual preference and socioeconomic difference. One of the essentials for leadership in the twenty-first century is the ability to develop cultural intelligence, that is a person's capability to function effectively in situations characterized by cultural diversity—ethnic, religious, generational, and organizational to name only four.

As the world becomes more connected than ever, cross-cultural interactions are becoming the critical issue of our day. Cultural intelligence is needed by ministry leaders all across the United States. The flattened world is bringing us more and more encounters with people who aren't like us. We cannot hope to become experts on every cultural context in which we find ourselves. But through cultural intelligence, we can enhance our ability to interact with one another in ways that are respectful, loving, and dignifying.

David Livermore illustrates the challenge of living in a culturally diverse world with this example of a youth leader in a congregation:

> Let's use a youth leader to think about the reasons a twenty-first century ministry leader needs cultural intelligence. In addition to serving youth from various ethnic backgrounds, a youth worker also deals with the generational divides between the youth, their parents, and the seniors in the church. On top of that, the youth pastor must learn the culture of the particular church and possibly the denomination of which it is a part. Who holds the power, how is conflict handled, and what are the sacred rituals? But then add to these differences the subcultures among the youth themselves, whether they be jocks, goths, rave enthusiasts, techies, or preppies. Increasingly youth base their cultural identity on issues such as sexual preference, social class, and musical genre. And then the youth leader must deal with the upcoming missions trip to Mexico. And the invitation to partner with an urban youth ministry nearby. And the overriding tension felt by youth pastors to engage students with the gospel while struggling to relate the church culture from

which they operate to the all-pervasive popular culture and Internet-linked world in which students feel most at home. Get the picture? Cultural intelligence relates to the everyday realities of life in the twenty-first century. (Livermore, 30)

Think about the five to ten different cultural contexts you most regularly encounter. What ethnic cultures are represented in your church, community, and work life? Where do you travel and who do you encounter? What organizational cultures do you engage week by week? What generational dynamics do you face among your family and friends, and in your church community?

David Livermore, in his books *Cultural Intelligence: Improving Your CQ to Engage Our Multicultural World* and *Leading with Cultural Intelligence*, describes four dimensions of cultural intelligence (CQ).

1. *CQ Knowledge* is understanding cross-cultural issues and differences. It is a person's knowledge of how cultures are similar and how cultures are different. It includes knowledge about cultural universals (for example, all cultures have language, values, symbols, rituals) and about unique cultural characteristics (for example, unique values, social interaction norms, religious beliefs, economic and legal systems, aesthetic values). The point is not to be an expert on every culture but to understand core cultural differences and their effects on everyday business.

2. *CQ Strategy (Interpretive)* is the degree to which people are mindful and aware when they interpret cross-culturally and make sense of culturally diverse experiences. Strategy CQ is awareness that individuals have different cultural value orientations and these different orientations influence perceptions, sense-making, motivation, and behavior. It includes thinking and strategizing before an encounter, checking assumptions during an encounter, and adjusting mental maps when actual experiences differ from expectations.

3. *CQ Drive (Motivation, Perseverance)* is the person's level of interest, drive, and motivation to adapt cross-culturally. Drive CQ involves interest in experiencing other cultures and the extent to which you think you are capable of interacting effectively with people who have different cultural backgrounds. It includes the intrinsic value that you place on diverse interactions—the enjoyment and sense of satisfaction (intangible benefits) people get personally when interacting with those who are different culturally from yourself. It includes the extrinsic value (tangible benefits) that you derive from diverse interactions—the instrumental benefits you get when interacting with those who are different culturally from yourself. Lastly, it includes a people's sense

of confidence that they can function effectively in different cultural settings or in diverse cultural settings where people have cultural backgrounds that are different from your own.

4. *CQ Action (Behavioral)* is the extent to which people appropriately change their verbal and nonverbal actions when they interact cross-culturally. It is the capability to change behavior to fit other cultures. This requires having a flexible repertoire of responses to suit various situations while still remaining true to one's self. Action CQ includes having and using a flexible range of non-verbal behaviors (that is, body language, physical gestures, facial expressions); having and using a flexible range of verbal behaviors (that is, accent, tone, expressiveness); modifying typical behavior, based on cultural differences, to put others at ease; and changing both verbal and nonverbal actions to fit the specifics of particular cultural interactions or settings.

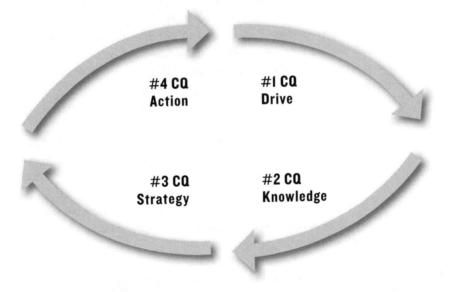

#4 CQ Action   **#1 CQ Drive**

#3 CQ Strategy   **#2 CQ Knowledge**

These four dimensions can be used by leaders as a four-step cycle for developing cultural intelligence both over the long haul and in case-by-case situations. Imagine using this process as a leader preparing to work with one cultural group (ethnic, social group, generational) in your church.

- *Step 1. CQ Drive* (motivational dimension): gives us the energy and self-confidence to pursue the needed understanding and planning necessary for a particular cross-cultural assignment. Leaders with high CQ drive are motivated to learn and adapt to new and diverse cultural settings. Their confidence in their adaptive abilities is likely to influence the way they perform in multicultural situations.

> *What's my level of confidence and motivation for this cross-cultural situation? If it's lacking, what can I do to increase it?*

- *Step 2. CQ Knowledge* (cognitive dimension) provides us with an understanding of basic cultural issues that are relevant to this assignment. Leaders high in CQ knowledge have a rich, well-organized understanding of culture and how it affects the way people think and behave. They possess a repertoire of knowledge in knowing how cultures are alike and different. They understand how culture shapes behavior.

> *What cultural understanding do I need for this cross-cultural situation?*

- *Step 3. CQ Strategy* (metacognitive dimension) allows us to draw on our cultural understanding so we can plan and interpret what's going on in this situation. Leaders with a high CQ strategy develop ways to use cultural understanding to develop a plan for cross-cultural situations. These leaders are better able to monitor, analyze, and adjust their behaviors in different cultural settings. They are conscious of what they need to know about an unfamiliar culture.

> *What do I need to plan in order to work cross-culturally effectively?*

- *Step 4. CQ Action* (behavioral dimension) provides us with the ability to engage in effective, flexible leadership for a task. Leaders with high CQ action can draw on the other three dimensions to translate their enhanced motivation, understanding, and planning into action. They possess a broad repertoire of behaviors, which they can use depending on the context.

> *What behaviors, such as verbal and nonverbal communication, should I adapt for this cross-cultural situation?*

The four step cycle offers a promising way to move CQ from theory to practice. We can continually move through the four steps at a macro level in thinking about our overall leadership across a diversity of situations. And we can work through the loop even on the fly while engaging in cross-cultural conversations. (Adapted from *Leading with Cultural Intelligence* by David Livermore.)

Cultural intelligence is an essential skill for twenty-first century ministry leaders. It is what we need when we work with people from different cultural contexts, whether they're across the street or multiple time zones away. Cultural intelligence is needed when pastoring a church or leading faith formation in multicultural America, leading a ministry that serves various generational cultures, participating in short-term mission trips, or figuring out the organization dynamics of ministry where we serve.

Resources
Livermore, David A. *Cultural Intelligence: Improving Your CQ to Engage our Multicultural World.*
    Grand Rapids: Baker Academic, 2009. (Includes a cultural intelligence self-assessment.)
Livermore, David A. *Leading with Cultural Intelligence: The New Secret to Success.* New York:
    American Management Association, 2010.

Websites
Cultural Intelligence Center Website: http://culturalq.com
David Livermore Website: http://davidlivermore.com/cq

Video Presentations
David Livermore video: video: http://www.youtube.com/watch?v=SMi7yhHjASQ

Becoming a Curator of Content

Leading Faith Formation 2020 and the Lifelong Faith Formation Network with its diversity of programs, activities, and resources for all ages and generations will require a new role for leaders—to become *curators* of the faith formation content and experiences available to people in your congregation. The term "content curation" stems from traditional museum curation: museum curators collect art and artifacts and identify the most relevant or important to be displayed in an exhibit for the public. Museum curators are subject-matter experts that guide an organization's overall art collection.

The role of content curators is now being applied to online content. In the near future, experts predict that content on the web will double every seventy-two hours. This dramatic increase in information requires content curators who continually find, group, organize, and share the best and most relevant content on a specific issue or topic. Content curators can provide a personalized, qualified selection of the best and most relevant content and resources available. They do not create more content, but make sense of all the content that others are creating.

A curator is an individual or organization who excels at helping others make sense. A good curator must be skilled at:

- locating and evaluating valuable content
- organizing and connecting content so that it is as accessible as possible
- creating and re-purposing content when it adds to the underlying value
- capitalizing on the Social Web to build connections and context
- building trusted relationships with learners and other curators
- designing learning experiences

So how does content curation work? Just as librarians help us make sense of the overwhelming number of books and periodicals available in a library, content curators identify, organize, and share information that will be most relevant to their prospects.

1. *Identify*: The best librarians have access to hundreds, if not thousands, of information resources that deliver ongoing, real-time information on specific topics of interest to information patrons.

2. *Organize*: Librarians must consume and curate information in order to interpret and best understand how it addresses their patrons' information needs. Expert librarians can quickly process hundreds of documents daily, using tools that organize and automatically tag content, deliver summaries, and rank content as needed.

3. *Share*: This may be the easiest aspect of the curating role. Sharing requires that information is easily available for patrons to acquire and use on a recurring schedule. The internet—and a number of tools—makes it very easy to publish resources online. However, the best librarians are able to deliver relevant information, while also highlighting the relationships between that information so patrons can understand how all the content fits together.

Consider these three examples of content curation at work. The *NYTimes.com Topics* employs content managers who sift through *The Times'* archive to create new meaning by grouping articles and resources that were filed away (or distributed to library databases). The site also produces exceptional multimedia pieces akin to "special exhibitions," which offer a documentary and reflective aspect to news content. NBC Universal's video site *Hulu* takes videos sourced from multiple networks and then rearranges them into collections that give a new perspective to the collection as a whole. Duke University Divinity School's *Faith and Leadership* (www.faithandleadership.com) incorporates a website with print, audio, and video resources; a daily e-newsletter; and blogs with a diversity of nationally recognized bloggers (*Call and Response*) designed for Christian leaders to reflect, connect, learn, read, discuss, and imagine. The team at *Faith and Leadership* creates new content and makes available existing content from a wide variety of sources relevant for Christian leaders.

Faith formation leaders in churches will increasingly need to become *content and experience curators* as they expand faith formation into all four Faith Formation 2020 scenarios, reach new audiences with faith formation, and identify (or develop) new programs, activities, and resources to serve the expanded scope of faith formation. To address this expanded scope, faith formation leaders will need to identify and access a wider variety of content and experiences available from publishers, other churches and religious organizations, websites, and other producers of content (programs, activities, and resources). They will need to assess and evaluate its quality and appropriateness, to organize the content, and then to share (or publish) the content through the Lifelong Faith Formation Network.

Among the many roles of the twenty-first-century faith formation leader, becoming a *curator of content* will be among the most important.

Resources

Scime, Erin. "The Content Strategist as Digital Curator." *Content Strategy*. www.alistapart.com/articles/content-strategist-as-digital-curator.

Rosenbaum, Steven. "Can Curation Save Media. www.businessinsider.com/can-curation-save-media-2009-4#ixzz0xMUJYYuI

Works Cited in Chapter 3

Heath, Chip and Dan Heath. *Switch: How to Change Things When Change Is Hard*. New York: Broadway 2010.

Kelley, Tom. *The Ten Faces of Innovation*. New York: Currency/Doubleday, 2005.

Lendo, Dr. Arthur J. "The Strategic Move of Peirce College." www.blueoceanstrategy.com/abo/peirce.html

Livermore, David A. *Cultural Intelligence: Improving Your CQ to Engage our Multicultural World*. Grand Rapids: Baker Academic, 2009. (Includes a cultural intelligence self-assessment.)

Livermore, David A. *Leading with Cultural Intelligence: The New Secret to Success*. New York: American Management Association, 2010.

Parks, Sharon Daloz. *Leadership Can Be Taught: A Bold Approach for a Complex World*. Cambridge: Harvard Business School Press, 2005.

Robinson, Anthony B. *Leadership for Vital Congregations*. Cleveland: Pilgrim, 2006.

TOOL #1

Becoming an Adaptive Leader

"Leadership is the activity of mobilizing people to tackle the toughest problems and do the adaptive work necessary to achieve progress."

—Ronald Heifetz and Martin Linsky

I. Defining the Challenges Confronting Leadership

Technical Problems

- Problem is well defined.
- Answer is known.
- Implementation is clear.

Adaptive Challenges

- Challenge is complex.
- Answers are not known.
- Implementation requires innovation and learning.

Examples of Technical Problems in Your Church

Examples of Adaptive Challenges in Your Church

2. Applying the Adaptive Leadership Process

- Identify an adaptive challenge that you or your church community has addressed. What response(s) did you develop and implement? What process did you use to develop a response to the adaptive challenge? How was your process similar or different from the adaptive process described below?

- Take a new adaptive challenge and plan your approach to developing a response using the adaptive leadership process of 1) *observing* events and patterns around you; 2) *interpreting* what you are observing (developing multiple hypotheses about what is really going on; and 3) *designing* interventions based on the observations and interpretations to address the adaptive challenge you have identified.

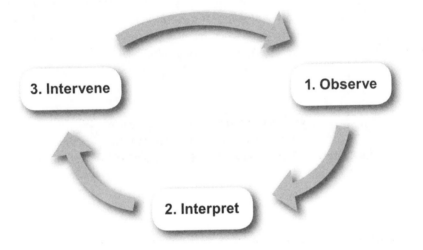

TOOL #2

Becoming an Innovative Leader

Innovation can be defined as people creating value through the implementation of new ideas. These ten faces of innovation provide methods and techniques that a team can use to infuse a continuous spirit of innovation in a congregation. *How are these ten leadership roles currently being practiced by your team? How you might use these roles in Faith Formation 2020? Which leadership roles do you need to develop on your team? Who might your invite to join the team to provide these leadership roles?*

Leadership Roles	Who demonstrates this leadership role and how?	How can you use this role in Faith Formation 2020?	Who could take this role?
O Anthropologist			
O The Experimenter			
O The Cross-Pollinator			

Leadership Roles	Who demonstrates this leadership role and how?	How can you use this role in Faith Formation 2020?	Who could take this role?
○ The Hurdler			
○ The Collaborator			
○ The Director			
○ The Experience Architect			
○ The Set Designer			
○ The Caregiver			
○ The Storyteller			

TOOL #3

Becoming a Blue Ocean Leader

To create a Blue Ocean successfully, a church should address quality, strategic factors, outcomes, and adoption sequentially and formulate and execute its strategic move by aligning value, results, and people propositions. A church can use the four elements of a Blue Ocean Strategy to develop a new initiative, evaluate a new project before it is implemented, or evaluate the implementation and effectiveness of a new project. Consider taking one new project from your Faith Formation 2020 plans and evaluating it using the four Blue Ocean Strategy elements.

- How can we create high *quality* and exceptional experiences in faith formation for people that will change the lives of the target audience? Be sure to specify a target audience, such as young families or emerging adults or the Spiritual but Not Religious.
- What are the strategic *factors* (time, cost, availability, location, and so on) that will unlock the target audience so that they will engage in a faith formation program, activity, or resource? Which are the most important factors? Once the most important strategic factors are establish to reach the target audience, the value proposition of the strategic move is completed.
- What are the projected *outcomes* (number of people served, quality of participation, increased participation, and so on) that would describe the effectiveness of the initiative? (In the business world this would be the profit proposition. In churches it could be called the results proposition.)
- What are the adoption hurdles in executing a blue ocean strategic move and how will you overcome these? This is the people proposition of blue ocean strategy.

TOOL #4

Becoming a Change Leader

Use the process developed by Chip and Dan Heath in *Switch* to develop a plan for preparing to implement a new project (how you would use each step) or to conduct an evaluation of a new project that you have already implemented (how you did or did not use each step). For practical checklists for each step of the process download *Switch Your Organization: A Workbook* by Chip and Dan Heath at http://heathbrothers.com/resources.

Direct the Rider (the conscious mind), eliminating what looks like resistance but is more often a lack of clarity, by providing crystal-clear direction.

	Ways to use this in your project
1. Follow the bright spots: investigate what's working and clone it.	
2. Script the critical moves: don't think big picture, think in terms of specific behaviors.	
3. Point to the destination: change is easier when you know where you're going and why it's worth it.	

Motivate the Elephant (the subconscious), eliminating what looks like laziness but is more often exhaustion, by engaging emotions to get people on the same path as you.

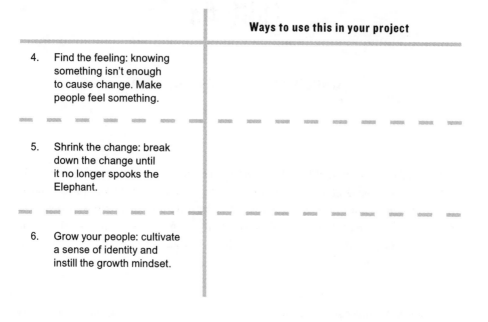

	Ways to use this in your project
4. Find the feeling: knowing something isn't enough to cause change. Make people feel something.	
5. Shrink the change: break down the change until it no longer spooks the Elephant.	
6. Grow your people: cultivate a sense of identity and instill the growth mindset.	

Shape the Path (the situation), eliminating what looks like a people problem but is more often a situation problem, by making the environment more conducive to the change you seek.

	Ways to use this in your project
7. Tweak the environment: when the situation changes, the behavior changes. So change the situation.	
8. Build habits: when behavior is habitual, it's "free"—it doesn't tax the Rider. Look for ways to encourage habits.	
9. Rally the herd: behavior is contagious. Help it spread.	

TOOL #5

Becoming a Culturally Intelligent Leader

Use the following assessment tool to starting thinking about your own CQ. Identify a particular culture in your church community as a frame of reference: ethnic, generational socio-economic, and so on. Review the description of the four dimensions of cultural intelligence before you begin. Rate yourself on the following scale:

1 – none of this fits me
2 – some of this fits me
3 – most of the description fits me
4 – all of this description fits me

CQ Drive   1 2 3 4

I am motivated to learn and adapt to new and diverse cultural settings. I enjoy meeting people of different cultural backgrounds. I am confident in my adaptive abilities to perform in multicultural situations.

CQ Knowledge   1 2 3 4

I generally understand culture and how it affects the way people think and behave. I know about the basic ways that cultures are alike and different.

CQ Strategy   1 2 3 4

I draw on my cultural understanding to plan and interpret what's going on in a situation. I am able to monitor, analyze, and adjust my behaviors in different cultural settings.

CQ Action   1   2   3   4

I have the ability to engage in effective, flexible leadership for a task. I am able to use a variety of behaviors, such as verbal and nonverbal communication, depending on the context.

Reflect
- Which of the four dimensions of cultural intelligence were strengths for you?
- Which of the four dimensions of cultural intelligence do you need to improve?
- How can you plan for improvement?

Resources
- Read one of the two books by David A. Livermore: *Cultural Intelligence: Improving Your CQ to Engage our Multicultural World* (Baker Academic, 2009) or *Leading with Cultural Intelligence: The New Secret to Success* (American Management Association, 2010).
- Review the strategies for advancing your CQ in chapter 15 of *Cultural Intelligence* and chapter 8 in *Leading with Cultural Intelligence*.

FOUR

Bringing Faith Formation 2020 Scenarios to Life

▶ *How can churches create a future for faith formation using the four scenarios as a guide to responding creatively and proactively to the religious and spiritual needs of people—today and into the future?* Part Four presents sixteen strategies with practical ideas and resources for addressing the challenges and opportunities in each scenario over the next ten years. The sixteen strategies are not just "good ideas." Each one is grounded in practices that are already being implemented in one form or another in congregations and religious organizations today. The good news is that there are proven strategies, ideas, and resources that can bring the four scenarios to life in a congregation.

The sixteen strategies are offered as a starting point for designing the future of faith formation in each scenario. They are not intended as a definitive list, but as a helpful guide. Many of the strategies can be customized for use in multiple scenarios. Every church can learn from the experience of these strategies and innovations, and adapt them to the size, geography, people, and cultures of a particular church.

The Strategies and Ideas

1. Faith Formation through the Life of the Whole Church
   - A faith formation curriculum of church life and events
   - Preparation for participation in church life
   - Immersion in the life of the church community

2.   Faith Formation using Digital Media and Web Technologies
     - Face-to-face and virtual faith formation
     - Church website
     - Online faith formation center
     - Online learning and digital learning

3.   Family Faith Formation
     - Family faith practices
     - Faith formation with young children
     - Parent formation
     - Milestones faith formation
     - Family learning programs
     - Family service
     - In-home resources
     - Increase active engagement
     - Expectations for family faith growth
     - Christian practice immersion experience

4.   Intergenerational Faith Formation
     - Intergenerational faith formation for the whole community as a core learning model
     - Intergenerational small group faith formation
     - Intergenerational Bible study or lectionary-based faith formation
     - Intergenerational version of a topic or theme in the children or youth program
     - Intergenerational faith formation before church year feasts and seasons and churchwide events
     - Intergenerational learning and relationship building through existing programs and activities

5.   Generational Faith Formation
     - Faith formation with the iGeneration and Millennial Generation
     - Faith formation with Generation X
     - Faith formation with the Baby Boomer Generation
     - Faith formation with the Builder Generation

6.   Milestones Faith Formation
     - Lifelong faith formation centered on milestones
     - Multi-faceted faith formation for each milestone
     - Moments of return

7. Faith Formation in Christian Practices
    *   Formation in Christian practices
    *   Apprenticeships
    *   Christian practice immersion experiences
    *   Christian practices infused in current faith formation programming

8. Transforming the World: Engagement in and Formation for Service and Mission
    *   Service and mission projects for all ages
    *   Education and reflection with service and mission projects
    *   Service with the wider community
    *   Study-action small groups

9. Spiritual Formation
    *   Formation in spiritual practices and disciplines
    *   Churchwide program for spiritual formation
    *   Spiritual formation infused in all faith formation programming
    *   Contemplative approach to faith formation
    *   Spiritual guides or mentors
    *   Spiritual formation for the wider community

10. Multi-Ethnic Faith Formation
    *   Culturally-specific faith formation
    *   Intercultural faith formation
    *   Culturally-inclusive faith formation

11. Faith Formation for Spiritual Seekers
    *   Spiritual formation process for spiritual seekers
    *   New expressions of Christian community for spiritual seekers

12. Apprenticeships in Discipleship

13. Pathways to Vibrant Faith and Active Engagement
    *   Multi-step formation process
    *   Catechumenal formation process

14. Faith Formation in Third-Place Settings

15. Empowering the Community to Share their Faith

16. Interfaith Education and Dialogue

Faith Formation 2020

Strategies for Each Scenario

Scenario #4
Participating but Uncommitted

- Faith formation through the life of the whole church
- Faith formation with digital media and web technologies
- Family faith formation
- Intergenerational faith formation
- Generational faith formation
- Milestones faith formation
- Faith formation in Christian practices
- Transforming the world
- Spiritual formation
- Multi-ethnic faith formation
- Pathways to vibrant faith and dialogue

Scenario #1
Vibrant Faith and Active Engagement

- Faith formation through the life of the whole church
- Faith formation with digital media and web technologies
- Family faith formation
- Intergenerational faith formation
- Generational faith formation
- Milestones faith formation
- Faith formation in Christian practices
- Transforming the world
- Spiritual formation
- Multi-ethnic faith formation
- Empowering the community to share their faith
- Interfaith education and dialogue

Scenario #3
Unaffiliated and Uninterested

- Faith formation for spiritual seekers
- Faith formation in Third-Place settings
- Faith formation with digital media and web technologies
- Milestones faith formation
- Faith formation in Christian practices
- Transforming the world

Scenario #2
Spiritual but Not Religious

- Faith formation with digital media and web technologies
- Family faith formation
- Faith formation with Millennials
- Milestones faith formation
- Faith formation in Christian practices
- Transforming the world
- Spiritual formation
- Multi-ethnic faith formation
- Faith formation for spiritual seekers
- Apprenticeships in discipleship
- Pathways to vibrant faith & active engagement
- Faith formation in Third-Place settings

Faith Formation through the Life of the Whole Church

People are formed and transformed in and through their participation (immersion) in the whole church community. Before there were curriculum, programs, activities, and resources, there was the power of the life and ministries of the congregation to "make disciples." Central to all faith formation is people's participation in a church community that forms its members in and through *koinonia* (community and communion), *leiturgia* (prayer, liturgy, and worship), *kerygma* (preaching and proclaiming the Word of God), *diakonia* (service), and *didache* (teaching). In community people can be formed and transformed by Scripture, tradition, creed, prayer, and sacrament through worship or preaching; by the tradition when it is transmitted by the community, who are the tradition in their own persons; by the sacramental life when the community takes part in baptizing, in confirming, and in coming together at the Table. The "whole church" is educating and empowering the community to engage in ministry in the midst of the world. The whole community is, by its way of living together, speaking together, praying together, and worshiping together, causing people to recognize that they are being educated by and in this community to growth in Christian faith and to lives as disciples in the world today. And when what the community believes is reflected in how the community lives, their witness invites others to join.

Bishop and scholar N.T. Wright expresses the significance and power of the church community in forming and transforming people.

> When the church is seen to move straight from worship of the God we see in Jesus to making a difference and effecting much needed change in the real world; when it becomes clear that people who feast at Jesus' table are the ones in the forefront of the work to eliminate hunger and famine, when people realize that those who pray for the Spirit to work in and through them are the people who seem to have extra resources of love and patience in caring for those whose lives are damaged, bruised, and shamed, then it is not only natural to speak of Jesus himself and to encourage others to worship him for themselves and find out what belonging to his family is all about, but it is also natural for people, however irreligious they may think of themselves as being, to recognize that something is going on that they want to be part of. In terms that the author of Acts might have used, when the church is living out the kingdom of God, the word of God will spread powerfully and do its own work. (Wright, 267)

The whole church is a center for authentic Christian learning—learning that is viewed as a lifelong endeavor, that grows out of the life of the community, and that, in turn strengthens the community. In the words of Maria Harris, "The church does not have an educational program; it is an educational program." The hallmark of a "congregation of learners" is a *culture of learning*, in which learning permeates every aspect of the congregation. Every activity is viewed as an opportunity for learning. The church, animated by the Holy Spirit, becomes the primary "teacher." The local church's embodiment of the gospel is the master communicator of the gospel. Faith formation becomes the process of transmitting the gospel, as the Christian community has received it, understands it, celebrates it, lives it, and communicates it. Robert Webber summarizes this insight well when he writes,

> In the postmodern world education will shift from the passing down of information to the passing down of wisdom through experience. Christian truth, which was regarded as propositional, intellectual, and rational will be experienced as an embodied reality. Faith will be communicated through immersion into a community of people who truly live the Christian faith. The corporate community will communicate through its depth of commitment, through hospitality, and through images such as baptism, the importance of Scripture, the significance of Eucharistic celebration, and the feasts and fasts of the Christian year. These events will shape the imagination of the believer and provide transcendent points of reference that bring meaning to the cycle of life. The meaning of the stories, symbols, cycles of time, and audiovisual experiences of faith may become the center for thoughtful discussion and application in the small group and stimulate both an intellectual and emotional knowing. (Webber, 155)

IDEAS

A faith formation curriculum of church life and events.

The events in the life of the Christian community can serve as the foundation for developing a common curriculum for all ages and generations. Charles Foster in *Educating Congregations* proposed an events-centered approach to faith formation. Church year feasts and seasons, sacraments and liturgy, justice and service, prayer and spiritual traditions, and community life events and activities can become the core of a curriculum for the whole community. This approach makes the life of church the "educational program." The goal is to develop a common curriculum which immerses everyone more deeply into the Christian faith and into the lived experience of the Christian community. The fundamental unity of the church is strengthened by establishing a core curriculum for all members of the community. The events-centered core curriculum is designed for the whole Christian community and can be supplemented by age-specific programs for children, teens, and adults.

Develop an events-centered curriculum by studying the life of your church community. Church year feasts and seasons, and Sunday worship and the lectionary readings provide an excellent starting point for developing an events-centered curriculum.

Digging deeper, the church's participation—through its ministries, community, and individual members—in serving the poor, working for justice, being peacemakers, and caring for creation provide opportunities to engage the whole community in actions for justice and in learning about the justice teachings of the Bible and Christian tradition. For example, your church's efforts to address hunger and poverty, locally and globally, can become the basis for a learning program on poverty and the needs of the poor which leads to action. Your church's involvement in caring for creation during Earth Day in April can become the basis for a learning program on the environment and stewardship.

Churches can teach the events-centered curriculum through intergenerational learning programs for the whole faith community or by integrating events-centered learning into existing faith formation programs. The learning process for events-centered faith formation involves: (1) preparing people of all ages to participate meaningfully and actively in the church event that is the focus of the curriculum; (2) engaging people in the event so that they can be formed and transformed by their participation; and (3) guiding people in reflecting on the significance and meaning of their participation in the church event, and empowering them to live their faith at home and in the world.

Preparation for participation in church life.

Faith formation can increase active engagement in the church by connecting faith formation programming to participation in church life. Churches can prepare people of all ages, but especially children and youth and their families, for participation in the life, ministry, and activities of the church community by incorporating education and resources in the language, practices, rituals, and habits that enable them to participate meaningfully in the life of the community: in worship, prayer, service, leadership, sacraments, church year feasts and seasons, and other activities and events of church life. This restores the connection between learning and practice, as well as overcoming age segregation through intergenerational experiences in community. The key is that what people are learning in their programs is aligned with hands-on participation in congregational life. For example, many churches utilize a lectionary-based model of faith formation in which the content of the learning program is the Sunday scripture readings. Here the connection is direct: what is learned in an educational program is experienced at Sunday worship. Connecting learning programs and congregational life takes many forms: liturgical seasons, Sunday lectionary readings, preparation for a congregation-wide service projects, and so on. The formation of a distinctive Christian identity is shaped by participation in the mission and practices of the faith community. Through their participation, people of all ages come to be recognized and accepted as full members of the congregation. People are not only shaped by the practices in which they participate. They also 'act back' on the community of practice, with new insights, ideas, and actions that can contribute to the transformation of those practices, and therefore, of the community.

Immersion in the life of the church community.

Faith is communicated through immersion into a community of people who truly live the Christian faith. Faith formation for all ages and generations would benefit by making hands-on participation integral to all learning experiences. "The heritage of scripture, tradition, the lives of our ancestors in the faith, creed, gospel, prayer, sacrament, and law is often taught better through worship or preaching than through classroom instruction. The tradition itself is handed on more fully when it is done in the midst of the people, the community, who are the tradition in their own persons. The life of prayer educates us most not when we read books about it but when we fall on our knees. The sacramental life nourishes us when we take part in baptizing, in confirming, and in coming together to the Table" (Harris, 44). Incorporate the actual participation in an experience of church life into the program design for age-group, family, or intergenerational learning. Instead of teaching "about" the Christian life, experience it directly as part of the overall learning program.

Works Cited

Harris, Maria. *Fashion Me A People*. Louisville: John Knox/Westminster, 1989.
Webber, Robert. *Ancient-Future Faith*, Grand Rapids: Baker, 1999.
Wright, N.T. *Surprised by Hope*. New York: HarperOne, 2008.

Resources

Roberto, John. *Becoming a Church of Lifelong Learners*. New London: Twenty-Third, 2006.
Roberto, John, with Mariette Martineau. *Generations of Faith Resource Manual*. New London: Twenty-Third, 2005.

Faith Formation with Digital Media and Web Technologies

Faith formation can utilize powerful web-based and digital technologies and resources to blend face-to-face, interactive faith formation with virtual faith formation, providing 24/7/365 faith formation for all ages and generations, anytime and anywhere. Websites, social networking services, and digital technologies (iPod Touch, iPad, smart cell phones) mean that churches can deliver faith formation experiences and resources anytime and anywhere, reaching people wherever they go online (home, work, school, vacation, coffee house). The interplay between learning in physical places and virtual online spaces can revolutionize faith formation in churches.

Web-based technologies and digital media provide the means to connect with spiritually hungry people and provide online tools and resources for them to explore faith and spirituality, engage in a spiritual conversation with others, and invite them to a faith community.

The new digital tools can empower people to connect with each other online, share their stories and faith experiences, give witness to the ways they are living their faith (practices), create faith formation content (print, audio, video) to share with others, and so many other user-generated activities.

IDEAS

Face-to-Face and Virtual Faith Formation.

There are two ways to envision the relationship between the physical and virtual.

- The **first approach** begins with people's participation in face-to-face learning activities (small group, large group, whole church, community/world) and then uses virtual online spaces with learning activities, print/audio/video resources, and social networking to extend, deepen, and support the learning that began in the physical program. For example, a church sponsors a three-session program on the Gospel of Luke in preparation for Cycle C of the upcoming liturgical year. The learning from this short program can be extended and deepened online with 1) weekly commentaries on the Sunday Gospel from Luke, 2) online Bible study program (independent or with a small group) on the Gospel of Luke, 3) a university course on the Gospel of Luke on iTunes U, and 4) an online blog that allows people to post their reflections on each Sunday's reading and invites discussion online.

- The **second approach** begins with people's involvement in online/digital learning activities and leads them to participate in face-to-face learning activities. For example, a church uses its website to develop an online spiritual formation center using a variety of already existing resources: (1) daily fixed hour prayer (liturgy of the hours), (2) weekly and seasonal prayer resources,

(3) links to prayer sites around the world (www.sacredspace.ie, www.taize.fr, www.upperroom.org), (4) an online retreat (A thirty-four week retreat for Everyday Life from Creighton University, http://onlineministries.creighton. edu/CollaborativeMinistry/cmo-retreat.html), and (5) online courses with spiritual guides like Thomas Merton, Joyce Rupp, Henri Nouwen, Joan Chittister from Spirituality and Practice (www.SpiritualityandPractice.com): Forty-day retreats with daily emails containing short readings for reflection, practice suggestions, and access to a private "Practice Circle" where people can share their wisdom and experiences with other e-course participants. The online spiritual formation center could connect people to church-based learning activities and resources, such as a relationship with a spiritual director, a spiritual formation course (such as the small group program Companions in Christ from Upper Room Books), a retreat experience at church or a retreat center, a series of workshops on the spiritual disciplines (for example, *lectio divina*, silence, contemplation, the *Examen*, meditation, spiritual reading, fixed hour prayer), and so on.

These relationships between faith formation in physical places and virtual spaces can be visualized in the following way:

One example of this integrated approach to adult faith formation is "Bible with Brian" from Ginghamsburg Church in Ohio. Brian Brown, the teaching pastor at Ginghamsburg, teaches through the entire Bible in a year, including practical application on how to live out God's truths everyday. Every Tuesday and Wednesday nights, "Bible with Brian" follows the book of the Bible featured in the daily Transformation Journal produced by the church. The journal is centered around a weekly topic and provides Bible verses about that topic, wisdom about the day's study from authors, and questions to help people apply the reading to their daily life. The Bible study begins with a meal from 5:30-6:30 p.m. and then the program from 6:30-8 p.m. or 7-8:30 p.m. Children's care and activities for birth through grade 5 are available. In addition to the gathered program, the program is available as an MP3 audio file so people can listen to it online or download it to their computer or mp3 player. Adults can also subscribe to the podcast on iTunes and listen to current and past episodes. Adults can download the "Bible with Brian" handout and use it to follow along with the audio broadcast of the program. People can also subscribe to the "Bible with Brian Spiritual Vitamins" newsletter—a daily take on the Transformation Journal from Brian Brown. (For more information go to http://ginghamsburg. org/biblewithbrian.)

Digital Media Resource in Faith Formation.

As textbooks and print resources are transformed into digital multimedia resources, faith formation in churches will increasingly use the new digital media in face-to-face programming (courses, small groups) and in providing faith formation to individuals and households via the church website, smart phone apps (iPhone), e-books, and so on. E-books and eTextbooks, which began as print resources viewed in a digital format, are being transformed into multimedia "books" when enhanced by images, web links, audio, and video when experienced on an iPad or similar devices. Packed with rich and relevant digital content, enhanced e-books expand the experience of reading a book by listening to an author read a favorite passage, watching supplementary video, or flicking through a library of photos or unpublished excerpts. One of the first digital, multimedia Bibles is the Glo Bible (www. bibleglo.com), available on DVD with support resources online. Content is accessed through Glo's five lenses: Bible (the text in its traditional form); Atlas (biblical events represented geographically); Timeline (biblical events represented chronologically); Topical (browse by subject); and Media (HD video, works of art, virtual tours and zoom-able high-resolution images). Additional content to the NIV Bible text and its study notes includes more than five hundred virtual tours with 360-degree views, 7500 encyclopedia articles, 2400 high-resolution photos, seven hundred pieces of artwork, three and a half hours of high-definition video, nearly 150 maps, and much more, allowing users to immerse themselves in the world of the Bible. All of these new digital media resources can be used in group settings, as well as individual or family settings.

Church Website.

Churches can develop a robust church website as the centerpiece of your online faith formation strategy—providing a variety of faith formation opportunities, experiences, and activities for age groups and the whole family, connecting people to recommended websites, and providing ways for people to connect with each other (social networking) and share their own reflections, stories, faith practices, and so on. Use the resources and features of your website to extend relationships and learning initiated in church events and gathered faith formation programs, and to reach people who are uninvolved in church life (Scenarios 2 and 3) or participate occasionally (Scenario 4). Incorporate a variety of features and content in your church website, such as:

- a learning center with courses and webinars on topics such as faith themes, Bible studies, life issues, and Christian practices, self-paced and facilitated by church staff and church members at scheduled times
- audio and video podcasts of gathered learning programs at the church
- links to selected online learning programs and activities from Christian churches, seminaries, universities, and publishers; links to courses on iTunes University and other online course providers
- links to selected audio and video podcasts on iTunes, YouTube, and other providers
- links to free e-book libraries, such as Google Books and Internet Archive, and online Bibles, such as Bible Gateway and Biblica
- a faith formation resource center with daily, weekly, and seasonal resources for all ages and families, including faith conversation activities, devotions and prayer, Bible reading activities and Bible studies, service projects, and rituals and traditions
- a milestones and life transitions center with sections for each milestone that include rituals, blessings, commentaries, personal stories, and a "gathering space" for sharing stories and ideas
- a worship center sharing audio and video clips of some of the sermons and other worship experiences, and extending it through the daily posting of images, songs, meditations, inspirational stories, prayers of the people, and online worship exercises
- an online parenting center with "how to" parenting articles and videos, faith enrichment resources, a "gathering space" for parents to interact, a blog staffed by parent mentors, parent-generated ideas and activities, and links to highly rated parent and family websites
- themed "gathering spaces" for synchronous and asynchronous interaction, including live text-based chat and live audio/video conferences, threaded discussions, collected blog links, self-paced tutorials on a range of topics, and so on

- a library pod with access to e-journals, e-books, archived streaming video of speakers and events, a clearinghouse-type collection of links to resources, and other Internet-mediated resources
- a mission/service opportunity clearinghouse for local, national, and international internships, volunteer opportunities, and jobs
- small group gatherings online for faith sharing, Bible study, and book discussions
- a calendar of events with locations, times, and descriptions, with Web-streamed audio and video recordings of select offerings

Several Examples of Full-Featured Church Websites
- Ginghamsburg Church: http://ginghamsburg.org
- New Hope Church: www.enewhope.org
- Newsong Church: www.newsong.net
- Northcoast Church: www.northcoastchurch.com
- Redeemer Presbyterian Church:www.redeemer.com
- St. Andrew's Presbyterian Church: www.sapres.org
- Trinity Wall Street: www.trinitywallstreet.org
- United Methodist Church of the Resurrection: www.cor.org

Online Faith Formation Center

Churches can create a virtual spiritual- or faith formation center where people can diagnose their spiritual health and growth needs, find gathered and online classes and small groups, and access resources for developing their faith and spiritual life. Incorporate in this center a spiritual assessment tool that helps people discern where they are in their spiritual journey, and a planning tool that helps people develop a spiritual growth plan for developing their personal relationship with Christ and discerning ways to live their faith in daily life. Provide mentors or guides to assist people in developing their spiritual growth plan and accessing the programs and resources that fit their plan. Mentors or guides can be available for one-on-one conversations as people move through their growth plan. (For an example of a spiritual assessment process go to the website for Church of Resurrection in Leawood, Kansas: www.cor.org/programs-ministries/the-journey/welcome-to-your-self-assessment.)

Online Learning and Digital Learning

Churches can utilize the ever increasing "library" of online learning programs and digital learning resources as an integral element of learning programs and faith formation offerings for all ages and for families.

Examples of Religious "Content" Websites
- Bible Mesh: www.biblemesh.com (learn the Bible and connect with friends)
- Book of Faith Initiative: http://bookoffaith.ning.com (Bible resources)

- Busted Halo: www. bustedhalo.com (for young adults)
- Disciples Now: www.disciplesnow.com (for youth)
- Explore Faith: www.explorefaith.org (for adults)
- Kids Spirit Online: http://kidspiritonline.com (for 11–15-year-olds)
- Odyssey Networks: www.odysseynetworks.org (multi-faith media resources)
- MethodX: www.upperroom.org/methodx (for young adults)
- Patheos: www.patheos.com (world religion and spirituality)
- Spirit and Song: http://www.spiritandsong.com (for youth)
- The Thoughtful Christian: www.thethoughtfulchristian.com (learning resources)
- Vatican Museum: http://mv.vatican.va/3_EN/pages/MV_Visite.html (all ages)
- Yfaith: http://www.yfaith.co.uk (for 10–13-year-olds)

Examples of Video Websites
- iTunes: www.apple.com/itunes
- God Tube: www.godtube.com
- Tangle: www.tangle.com
- YouTube: www.youtube.com
- Vimeo: http://vimeo.com

Examples of Course Websites
- Many universities and seminaries offer continuing education courses in theology, scripture, and the Christian life for adults, such as: C21 Online at Boston College (www.bc.edu/sites/ c21online), STEP Online Theology at University of Notre Dame (http://step.nd.edu), and The Virtual Learning Community for Faith Formation (VLCFF) at University of Dayton (http://vlc.udayton.edu).
- iTunes University (www.apple.com/itunes) has over two hundred thousand educational audio and video podcasts from top universities, museums, and learning organizations, and provides the ability to download lectures, discussions, language lessons, audiobooks, and podcasts.
- OpenCourseWare Consortium (www.ocwconsortium.org) is a free and open digital publication of high quality educational materials, organized as courses, from more than two hundred higher education institutions and associated organizations from around the world.

Resources

Baab, Lynne. *Reaching Out in a Networked World: Expressing Your Congregation's Heart and Soul.* Washington, DC: The Alban Institute, 2008.

Bailey, Brian. *The Blogging Church.* San Francisco: Jossey-Bass, 2007.

Bonk, Curtis J. *The World Is Open: How Web Technology Is Revolutionizing Education.* San Francisco: Jossey Bass, 2009.

Davidson, Cathy, and David Theo Goldberg. "The Future of Learning Institutions in a Digital Age." 2009. (http://mitpress.mit.edu/books/chapters/Future_of_Learning.pdf)

Geoghegan, Michael, and Dan Klas. *Podcast Solutions: The Complete Guide to Audio and Video Podcasting.* Berkeley: friends of Ed, 2007.

Jukes, Ian, Ted McCain, and Lee Crockett. *Understanding the Digital Generation: Teaching and Learning in the New Digital Landscape.* Kelowna: Twenty-First Century Fluency Project, 2010. (www.21stcenturyfluency.com)

Prensky, Marc. *Teaching Digital Natives: Partnering for Real Learning.* Thousand Oaks: Corwin, 2010.

Richardson, Will. Blogs, *Wikis, Podcasts, and Other Powerful Web Tools for Classrooms.* (3rd Edition) Thousand Oaks: Corwin Press, 2010.

Rosen, Larry D. *Rewired: Understanding the iGeneration and the Way They Learn.* New York: Macmillan, 2010.

Safko, Lon, and David K. Brake. *The Social Media Bible: Tactics, Tools, and Strategies.* Hoboken: John Wiley, 2009.

Shirkey, Clay. *Here Comes Everybody: The Power of Organizing without Organizations.* New York: Penguin Press, 2008. (See Clay Shirkey presentations on video at TED: http://ca.ted.com/index.php/speakers/clay_shirky.html)

Stephenson, Mark Morgan. *Web Empower Your Church.* Nashville: Abingdon, 2006.

Useem, Andrea. "The Networked Congregation: Embracing the Spirit of Experimentation." (www.congregationalresources.org/Networked/About.asp)

Welch, Tim. *Technology Tools for Your Ministry.* New London: Twenty-Third, 2008.

Zandt, Deanna. *Share This! How You Will Change the World with Social Networking.* San Francisco: Berrett-Koehler, 2010.

Websites
Twenty-First Century Fluency Project: www.21stcenturyfluency.com
Classroom 2.0: www.classroom20.com
Digital Catechesis: http://digitalcatechesis.ning.com/
Edutopia: www.edutopia.org
HASTAC (Humanities, Arts, Science, and Technology Advanced Collaboratory): www.hastac.org
Reimaging Learning in the Twenty-First Century, John D. and Catherine T. MacArthur Foundation: www.macfound.org
Joan Ganz Gooney Center at Sesame Workshop: www.joanganzcooneycenter.org

Family Faith Formation

The task of religious socialization and faith formation falls almost entirely to two communities today. First are family households where parents do the primary socializing. Family religious socialization has always been the foundation for the development of faith and faith practices, and for participation in church life and worship. Second are religious congregations where the whole community, but especially faithful adults, can exert socializing influences on children and youth. These are the two critical contexts for the faith formation of children and youth in America today.

Christian Smith observers, "If formation in faith does not happen there, it will—with rare exceptions—not happen anywhere (Smith, 286).

First, churches can strengthen *family religious socialization*, especially in the first decade of life—by nurturing a vibrant faith in parents and equipping them with the skills and tools for developing faith at home. Reflecting on the long term impact of family socialization on emerging adults (eighteen to twenty-three), researcher Christian Smith, in his book *Souls in Transition*, emphasizes the importance and impact of family socialization.

> Teenagers with seriously religious parents are more likely than those without such parents to have been trained in their lives to think, feel, believe, and act as serious religious believers, and that training "sticks" with them even when the leave home and enter emerging adulthood. Emerging adults who grew up with seriously religious parents are through socialization more likely (1) to have internalized their parents' religious worldview, (2) to possess the practical religious know-how needed to live more highly religious lives, and (3) to embody the identity orientations and behavioral tendencies toward continuing to practice what they have been taught religiously. At the heart of this social causal mechanism stands the elementary process of teaching—both formal and informal, verbal and nonverbal, oral and behavioral, intentional and unconscious, through both instruction and role modeling. We believe that one of the main ways by which empirically observed strong parental religion produced strong emerging adult religion in offspring is through the teaching involved in socialization. (Smith, 232)

Second, churches can develop the *home as a center of faith formation* by promoting foundational family faith practices: caring conversations, rituals and traditions, prayer, Bible reading, and service. Research consistently shows that effective religious socialization comes about through embedded family religious practices; that is, through specific, deliberate religious activities that are firmly intertwined with the daily habits of family routines, of eating and sleeping, of having conversations, of adorning spaces in which people live, of celebrating the holidays, and of being part of a community. The daily household routine is marked by rituals of prayer, by conversations about God, and by sacred objects. Holidays provide special occasions for experiencing the warmth of family, friends, and fellow congregants.

Third, churches can *educate and equip parents* to embed foundational faith practices into the daily experience of family life. Once again, Christian Smith and the National Study on Youth and Religion point out that the evidence clearly shows that the single most important social influence on the religious and spiritual lives of adolescents is their parents.

Fourth, churches can *engage families* more fully in the life and ministries of the church community.

Fifth, churches can *strengthen the partnership between home and congregation* to focus on empowering, resourcing, and supporting the development of the family as the center of faith formation.

IDEAS

Family faith practices.

Effective religious socialization comes about through embedded practices. Churches can equip parents, and the whole family, with the skills and resources to incorporate faith practices into family life: caring conversations, eating together—especially the power of Sunday meals and holidays, praying together—especially at meals, reading the Bible, engaging in devotions, celebrating rituals and traditions, service, providing moral instruction, and worshipping together with the church community. Guide families in recognizing the presence of God in their daily life of family practices and activities.

Demonstrate family faith practices through Sunday worship and church programs and activities to teach, model, and demonstrate family faith practices that families can incorporate into home life. Weekly worship and church events are opportunities for families to experience faith practices—prayer, Bible reading, service, and rituals and traditions—which can be extended into the home. Provide practice-related resources to help families live their faith at home.

Example: Four Keys for Practicing Faith
(Vibrant Faith Ministries, www.vibrantfaith.org)

1. **Caring Conversation.** Christian values and faith are passed on to the next generation through supportive conversation. Listening and responding to the daily concerns of children and youth makes it easier to have meaningful conversations regarding the love of God, and are ways to express God's love to others. Hearing their parents' "faith stories" is one of the most important influences on the faith of children and teenagers.

2. **Family Devotions and Prayer.** The Christian faith shapes the whole of our lives and involves a lifetime of study, reflection, and prayer. Family devotions provide a way to learn more about the Bible and Christian tradition as a family, and apply the teachings to daily life as a follower of Jesus Christ. This understanding of a devotional life includes, but is not limited to, public worship, bedtime prayers, Bible reading and study, table grace, evening and morning prayers, and praying alone at any time of the day or night.

3. **Family Rituals and Traditions.** Families identify themselves and tell their family stories through daily routines, celebrations, and rituals. Family rituals

can take many forms from daily rituals such as mealtime, bedtime, leaving and returning; celebrations such as birthdays, anniversaries, and special achievements; church year rituals at home such as Advent and Lent; milestones such as births and deaths, first day of school and graduations, and so on. Family rituals and traditions speak volumes about what the family values, believes, and promotes, and how much the family values its faith.

4. **Family Service.** Engaging in service with one's family is a powerful opportunity for growing in faith. Both youth and adults are more likely to have a growing, strong faith when their family serves others together: in the home, in the congregation, in the community and world. (Anderson and Hill)

Example: FAITH 5—Faith Acts in the Home
(Faith Inkubators, www.faithink.com)

The FAITH 5 connects church to home, faith to life, and parents to kids in a powerful way. The five steps of the FAITH 5 are:

*   *Step One: Share highs and lows.* Name something good and bad you experienced today.

*   *Step Two: Read a verse from your Bible.* Bible verses that families explore every night.

*   *Step Three: Talk about how the verse relates to highs and lows.* Unpack the verse a bit. What does it mean in your own words? How might it relate to where you are today in your highs and lows?

*   *Step Four: Pray for one another's highs and lows, for your family, and for the world.* Simply talk to God, thank Jesus for the good, and ask the Holy Spirit for guidance in specific problems.

*   *Step Five: Bless one another.* Trace the sign of the cross on one another's forehead or palm as a reminder that you belong to God and to one another.

Faith formation with young children.

Churches can begin family faith formation with new parents during pregnancy by nurturing the faith growth of the parents, preparing them for the vocation of parenting, understanding their new child, celebrating the baptism milestone, providing resources for nurturing family faith (continuing through the next several years), welcoming and engaging them in the Christian community as a new family. Begin parent education and formation before the birth of the child and continue throughout life, providing the setting for teaching, modeling, and demonstrating family faith practices that can be incorporated into home life. Establish "pregnancy and early childhood advice centers" to support parents through the pregnancy and early years of childhood. Provide parent mentors, such as parents whose children are now young adults, to provide one-on-one mentoring and support. Connect new parents by providing mall groups for encouragement, support, and learning. Utilize the church website and other websites and online resources for resourcing and social networking among parents. Parent education and faith formation will need to address the religious and spiritual needs and backgrounds of the millennial generation of parents who are in their twenties and thirties.

Parent formation.

Churches can target milestones and critical transitions during childhood, adolescence, and young adulthood, to provide opportunities for parent faith formation and parent education, in-person and online. Provide stand-alone parent faith formation and education programs and incorporate parent programs and activities into existing faith formation programs and support groups for parents, such as a mom's group. Develop a progression of parent workshops through the life cycle: (1) preparing for parenting, (2) parenting young children, (3) parenting children, (4) parenting teenagers, (5) parenting emerging adults (eighteen to thirty), and (6) parenting alone.

Milestone faith formation.

Churches can develop family faith formation around the naturally-occurring religious and lifecycle milestones in family life such as baptism, start of school, school graduations, and so on. Between milestones celebration, provide developmentally-appropriate resources—in print, audio, video, and online formats—to continue faith growth at home. (See the Milestones Faith Formation strategy for more information.)

Family learning programs.

Churches can engage families in structured learning programs for the whole family—providing opportunities to learn and grow in faith together and develop skills for sharing faith, praying, celebrating traditions, serving others, and practicing the Christian faith in daily life. Churches can utilize a variety of family learning formats such as: monthly family or intergenerational learning programs, family workshops through the year, family cluster or small group learning programs (at the church or in homes), family-centered Bible study or lectionary-based Scripture reflection, family-centered vacation Bible school, family retreats and camps, and family-centered sacramental preparation programs.

Family service.

Churches can offer a variety of developmentally-appropriate family service projects where families can choose from different levels of commitment from beginner experiences to advanced projects that are local, regional, national, and international, such as: (1) local mission projects lasting anywhere from a few hours to one day in length, (2) short-term mission trips lasting anywhere from two to five days and requiring an overnight stay on location, and (3) weeklong mission trips within the United States as well internationally, designed for families who are ready for a more intensive experience. Include a learning component for each mission/service project that focuses on understanding the issue being addressed, exploring the teachings of Scripture and tradition, developing the skills for mission and service, and then, upon completion of the project, reflecting upon the involvement. (See Transforming the World: Engagement in and Formation for Mission and Service for more information.)

In-home resources.

Churches can provide families with a variety of resources—print, audio, video, and online—to help families embed faith practices in family life at each stage of life, including resources for parents at each stage of life, for in-home celebration of church year feasts and seasons, for extending Sunday worship into the home, for celebrating milestones, for engaging in service, and so many more. Use the church website and online resources to deliver timely faith formation resources to the home, and provide social networking among families to support each other and share faith stories and practices.

Increase active engagement in church life.

Churches can connect faith formation programming to family participation in church life by designing faith formation programming to prepare families for participation in the life, ministry, and activities of the church according to their abilities. Develop learning programs and resources that provide families with the language, practices, rituals, habits that enable them to participate meaningfully in the life of the community: in worship, prayer, service, leadership, sacraments, church year feasts and seasons, and other activities and events of church life. The key is that what people are learning in their programs is aligned with hands-on participation in congregational life. For example, many churches utilize a lectionary-based model of faith formation in which the content of the learning program is the Sunday Scripture readings. Here the connection is direct: what is learned in an educational program is experienced at Sunday worship. Connecting learning programs and congregational life takes many forms: liturgical seasons, Sunday lectionary readings, preparation for a congregation-wide service projects, and so on. The formation of a distinctive Christian identity is shaped by participation in the mission and practices of the faith community. Through their participation, people of all ages come to be recognized and accepted as full members of the congregation. People are not only shaped by the practices in which they participate. They also 'act back' on the community of practice, with new insights, ideas, and actions that can contribute to the transformation of those practices, and therefore, of the community.

Expectations for family faith growth.

Churches can engage families more consciously, actively, and experientially in learning, growing in faith, and participating in church life through an annual, multidimensional faith growth plan. The annual plan can be a blend of whole family activities and individual parent-child activities. Families can be organized into groups, each with a leader who meets with the family group regularly to facilitate learning and reflection. Churches set expectations for learning and participation. Families create their annual plan around a menu of offerings designed to help them fulfill the church's expectations, for example: (1) participating in Sunday worship (regularly, but at least twice monthly); (2) participating in important church year feasts and celebrations, such as Advent, Christmas, Lent, Holy Week; (3) participating in monthly family learning programs on religious themes; (4) participating in at least six mission/service projects during the year, (5) participating in an annual spiritual formation retreat experience, and (6) engaging in family home practices, such as reading the Bible, celebrating rituals and traditions, and praying.

Christian practices immersion experiences.

Churches can offer families Christian practice immersion experiences that give them a firsthand experience of a Christian practice, such as hospitality, reading the Bible, and keeping Sabbath, and then guide them in living the practice in their daily lives. Each immersion experience begins with a direct experience of the practice—in a learning program, in the church, or in the community/world, followed by reflection on the experience, education about the practice, and resources for living the practice in daily life. Offer a variety of immersion experiences throughout the year in various program formats and timeframes. (See Faith Formation in Christian Practices for more information.)

Works Cited

Smith, Christian, with Patricia Snell. *Souls in Transition: The Religious and Spiritual Lives of Emerging Adults.* New York: Oxford University Press, 2009.

Additional Strategies

For additional ideas and resources consult the following strategies in Part Four:
- Faith Formation with Digital Media and Web Technologies
- Intergenerational Faith Formation (for a learning process for family programs)
- Milestones Faith Formation
- Faith Formation in Christian Practices
- Transforming the World: Engagement in and Formation for Service and Mission
- Spiritual Formation
- Multi-ethnic Faith Formation

Resources

Anderson, David W. *From the Great Omission to Vibrant Faith: Renewing the Role of the Home in Renewing the Church.* Bloomington: Vibrant Faith, 2009.

Anderson, David W. and Paul Hill. *Frogs without Legs Can't Hear: Nurturing Disciples in Home and Congregation*. Minneapolis: Augsburg Fortress, 2003.

Caldwell, Elizabeth. *Making a Home for Faith: Nurturing the Spiritual Life of Your Children*. Elizabeth Caldwell. Cleveland: Pilgrim, 2007.

Faith Stepping Stones. Faith Inkubators. (online resource: www.faithink.com).

Haynes, Brian. *Shift—What It Takes to Finally Reach Families Today*. Loveland: Group, 2009.

Joiner, Reggie. *Think Orange—Imagine the Impact When Church and Family Collide*. Colorado Springs: David C. Cook, 2009.

Joiner, Reggie. *The Orange Leader Handbook: A Think Orange Companion*. Colorado Springs: David C. Cook, 2010.

Keeley, Robert J. *Shaped by God: Twelve Essential Practices for Nurturing Faith in Children, Youth, and Adults*. Grand Rapids: Faith Alive, 2010.

Kehrwald, Leif, editor. *Families and Faith: A Vision and Practice for Parish Leaders*. New London: Twenty-Third, 2006.

Martineau, Mariette, Joan Weber, and Leif Kehrwald. *Intergenerational Faith Formation: All Ages Learning Together*. New London: Twenty-Third, 2008.

Milestones Ministry Manual for Home and Congregation. Bloomington: Vibrant Faith Ministries, 2007 (www.vibrantfaith.org).

Roberto, John, Editor. *Living Well: Christian Practices for Everyday Life*. Naugatuck: LifelongFaith Associates, 2009 (www.LifelongFaith.com).

Roehlkepartain, Jolene and Eugene. *Embracing Parents: How Your Congregation Can Strengthen Families*. Nashville: Abingdon, 2004.

Wigger, Bradley. *The Power of God at Home*. San Francisco: Jossey-Bass, 2003.

Websites
Faith Inkubators: www.faithink.com
Forming Faith (Center for Ministry Development): www.fashioningfaith.org
Home Word: www.homeword.com
Legacy Milestones (Brian Haynes): www.legacymilestones.com
LifelongFaith Associates: www.lifelongfaith.com
Parent Further (Search Institute): www.parentfurther.com
Search Institute: www.search-institute.org
Think Orange: www.whatisorange.org
Tumblon: http://tumblon.com
Vibrant Faith Ministries: www.vibrantfaith.org

Intergenerational Faith Formation

Most churches are intergenerational or multi-generational by membership. Some churches are *intentionally* intergenerational. They make their intergenerational character a defining feature of their community life, ministries, and programming. These churches make it a priority to foster intergenerational relationships, faith sharing, and storytelling; to incorporate all generations in worship; to develop service projects that involve all ages, and to engage all generations in learning together. For these churches, being intergenerational is a way of life. It is an integral element of their culture. It is who they are!

Bringing generations together within the church provides benefits and blessings on a variety of levels. Insights from research and pastoral experience tell us that being intentionally intergenerational:

- reclaims God's intent for faith to be shared in community and across generations
- affirms each person's value in the total community (regardless of age)
- fosters a foundation of support of each other's concerns, interests, and activities
- provides "up close and personal" formation in faith as children, teens, young adults, middle-aged adults, and older adults engage in sharing faith, teaching, learning, and praying for one another
- teaches us to care for one another
- provides role models for children and youth
- teaches us to value older adults
- allows us to pass on the traditions of family and faith
- enhances people's identification with their congregation and integration within the community
- encourages greater faith in all generations
- creates special relationships between adults and youth
- fosters leadership regardless of age or stature
- utilizes the strengths (the wisdom, experience, and knowledge) of one generation to meet the needs of another generation
- promotes understanding of shared values and respect for individuals in all stages and ages of life
- utilizes the creative talents of younger and older generations to provide service to the church and community
- overcomes the age-segregated nature of our society, taking a pro-active, counter-cultural stance in the face of the countless ways society separates and pigeon-holes into age-specific groups

Holly Catterton Allen observes, "No better place exists for the most number of people to learn Christian ways from 'more experienced members of the culture' than in intergenerational Christian communities. People of all ages and maturity levels are present actively carrying on the very essentials of Christianity. In intergenerational communities, children learn from each other, younger children, older children, teens, and adults. And adults learn from teens and children. All benefit from each other with a sense of mutuality; in essence, they grow each other up into Christ. As Lave and Wenger say, 'The *person* has been correspondingly transformed into a practitioner, a newcomer becoming an old-timer, whose changing knowledge, skills, and discourse are part of a developing identity—in short, a member of a community of practice.'"

The key to educating the whole community is intergenerational learning—bringing all ages and generations together to learn with and from each other. Intergenerational learning is a model that integrates learning, building community, sharing faith, praying, celebrating, and practicing. It is for all members of the community—young and old, single and married, families with children and empty-nest families. It involves the whole family in learning together. It equips individuals and families with the knowledge, skills, and faith-sharing activities for learning and practicing faith at home. Many churches have made intergenerational learning their primary model of learning, supported by age group learning models.

One model of intergenerational learning that is used by hundreds of churches begins with an All Ages Learning Experience (intergenerational); moves to an In-Depth Learning Experience (age-specific or intergenerational) taught in one of three formats: age group, whole group or learning activity centers; and concludes by Sharing Learning Reflections and Preparing for Home Practice (intergenerational). (For more information on this approach see the book *Intergenerational Faith Formation* in the resources.)

1.   Gathering and Opening Prayer

2.   All-Ages Learning Experience. Intergenerational learning begins with a multigenerational experience of the theme that all the generations share together.

3.   In-Depth Learning Experience. Through structured learning activities each generation—families with children, adolescents, and adults—explores the meaning of the Church event and develops the ability to participate meaningfully in the event. In-depth learning experiences are conducted in different formats:

   •   The *Age Group Format* provides parallel, age-appropriate learning for groups at the same time. Though age groups are separated, each one is focusing on the same topic—utilizing specific learning activities that are designed for their life cycle stage: families with children, adolescents, young adult, and adults.

   •   The *Whole Group Format* provides a series of facilitated learning activities for everyone at the same time using intergenerational or age-specific small groups or table groups.

   •   The *Learning Activity Center Format* provides structured intergenerational and age-specific learning activities at a variety of stations or centers in a common area.

4. Sharing Learning Reflections and Home Application. In intergenerational groups participants share what they learned and prepare for applying their learning to daily life using the Home Kit.

5. Closing Prayer Service

Example: Justice and Solidarity

Part 1. Gathering and Opening Prayer

Part 2. All Ages Learning Experience
Activity 1. Where Are You From?—tracing each individual or family journey to the U.S.
Activity 2. If the World Were a Village of 100 People

Part 3. In-Depth Learning Experience: Age Group Format
Activity 1. How Are We Connected to People around the World?
  - Family Activity: What's Inside Your House? (from around the world)
  - Adolescent and Adult Activity: What's in Your Life? (from around the world)

Activity 2. The Journey of Interdependence
  - Option 1. The Journey of the Chocolate Bar (all ages)
  - Option 2. The Journey of the Banana (all ages)
  - Option 3. The Journey of Coffee (teens or adults)

Activity 3. Presentation: Solidarity through Fair Trade
Activity 4. What do the Scriptures and Christian tradition Say about Solidarity?
  - Activity: The Good Samaritan for Today
  - Activity: Who Do We Need to Be in Solidarity With?

Activity 5. How Can We Build Solidarity among People?—Developing Action Projects

Part 4. Sharing Learning Experiences and Home Application

Part 5. Closing Prayer

(From: *Acting for Justice* by John Roberto, OSV Curriculum, 2005.)

Example: Jesus Christ, Son of God

Part 1. Gathering and Opening Prayer

Part 2. All Ages Learning Experience: Who Do You Say That I Am?

Part 3. In-Depth Learning Experience: Experiencing the Son of God through Gospel Stories

The focus of the activity centers is to discover the qualities of God by exploring a variety of gospel stories that present the words and actions of Jesus Christ, the Son of God. Each learning activity center provides an interactive and experiential way for people to explore one aspect of Jesus' divinity through gospel stories. Activity centers will engage participants in presentations, discussions, and activities. Several centers include dramatic presentations, while others engage participants in creative arts or prayer or a ritual activity. One center includes a film presentation. There is even one that includes eating. If the children get tired, there is a storytelling center just for them. Each center is staffed by a team that guides participants through the learning activities. Each center is designed for all ages, so participants can select the centers that interest them the most. Families with children stay together.

Activity Centers
- Jesus is Born (Infancy Narratives)
- Jesus is God's Beloved Son (Baptism of the Lord and Transfiguration)
- Jesus Teaches Parables of the Kingdom of God
- Jesus Heals People
- Jesus Forgives Sin
- Jesus Raises People from the Dead
- Jesus Feeds People
- Stories of Jesus (Storytelling Center)

Part 4. Sharing Learning Experiences and Home Application

Part 5. Closing Prayer

(From *Professing Our Faith* by John Roberto, OSV Curriculum, 2006)

IDEAS

Intergenerational faith formation for the whole community as a core learning model.
Churches can develop intergenerational faith formation as their core learning program for the whole Christian community, supplemented by age-specific learning for children, teens, and adults. Churches can develop a multi-year curriculum for the whole community that includes themes from the Bible, the cycle of Sunday lectionary readings, church year feasts and seasons, Christian practices, service and social justice, prayer and spiritual disciplines, core Christian beliefs, and moral teachings. When the intergenerational faith formation is the core program, churches develop

topics for a year of monthly programming for the whole faith community. Here is an example of topics for an entire year of intergenerational learning developed around the rhythm of the church year feast and seasons. This example makes clear the intimate connection between faith formation, Sunday worship (with a special focus on the lectionary), and the liturgical seasons.

Advent-Christmas	Jesus, Messiah and Son of God
January-February	Following Jesus: Called to Discipleship
Lent	Following Jesus: Praying, Fasting, and Almsgiving
Holy Week	Death of Jesus
Easter Season	Resurrection of Jesus
Pentecost	Living as the Community of Jesus Christ
Summer	Living as Disciples in the World: Serving Others

(For an additional example of an intergenerational program year, see Faith Formation in Christian Practices.)

Intergenerational small group faith formation.

Churches can form weekly (or biweekly) intergenerational small groups as a primary form of faith formation or one of the options offered people in the faith community. These groups can meet at church or in homes or in other conducive settings. They provide a setting for exploring any of the themes suggested above, but have the relational advantages of a small group and the flexibility of a small group format, for example, a group could engage in a common service project as part of their group meetings. Small groups provide an excellent way to integrate learning, praying, serving, and socializing. Many churches already offer small group faith formation, such as Bible study, which would provide an opportunity to redesign an existing age-group program into an intergenerational learning program.

Intergenerational Bible study or lectionary-based faith formation.

This approach might take a variety of forms such as an intergenerational course or workshop, a whole congregational study, intergenerational small groups, or intergenerational sessions after Sunday worship focused on the scripture readings and sermon or homily.

An intergenerational version of a topic or theme being featured in the children or youth program.

A topic that the children or youth are studying can be extended to the whole community through intergenerational learning. For example, if the children are studying about Jesus, consider offering an intergenerational program on the identity of Christ. If the young people are preparing for a service project or mission trip, use the opportunity to conduct an intergenerational session on Christian service, and get everyone engaged in supporting the teenagers. Add an intergenerational learning component to vacation Bible school by taking a theme from the program and offering an intergenerational program on that same theme for the whole community. Intergenerational learning provides a common learning experience for the whole community that can support age group learning programs.

Intergenerational faith formation before major church year feasts and seasons, and churchwide events.

The church calendar is rich with possibilities for intergenerational learning for the whole community. Conduct intergenerational programs to prepare all generations for major liturgical feasts and seasons, such as Advent, Christmas, Lent, Holy Week, and Pentecost, as well as significant events in the life of your church, such as the anniversary of the founding of the church, stewardship Sunday, or a ministries fair. There are dozens of opportunities for preparing the whole community to participate more intentionally and meaningfully in church events.

Intergenerational learning and relationship-building through existing programs and activities.

- Integrate intergenerational programming into the age-group program plan and calendar, such as quarterly intergenerational nights as part of the children's faith formation program.

- Structure age-group programs with an intergenerational connection, such as an educational program that includes interviews, a panel, and/or storytelling with people of different generations.

- Incorporate intergenerational dialogues into programming—provide opportunities for children and youth to experience the wisdom, faith, and interests of older adults through presentations, performances, and discussions. Then *reverse* the process and provide opportunities for the older adults to experience the wisdom, faith, and interests of children or teens through presentations, performances, and discussions.

- Develop mentoring relationships between youth and adults, such as prayer partners, learning-to-pray spiritual direction, service involvement, and Confirmation mentors.

- Link people of different generations (older-to-younger *or* younger-to-older) in the church who have insights and life experiences that may be helpful to the other, such as mid life and older adults helping young adults and new parents with money management and household management, or young people helping older adults navigate e-mail and the online world.

Works Cited

Allen, Holly Catterton. "Bringing the Generations Together: Support from Learning Theory." *Lifelong Faith*, Volume 3/1, Spring 2009.

Congregational Examples of Intergenerational Learning

Holy Infant Catholic Church: www.acswebnetworks.com/holyinfantchurch/hi_life

Resurrection Catholic Parish: www.gbres.org/htm/faithformation/generationsofdisciples.htm

Sacred Heart Church:www.sacredheartchurch.info/gift.html

St. Anthony on the Lake: www.stanthony.cc/CF.htm

St. Elizabeth of Hungary Parish: www.seoh.org/generations.htm

St. John the Baptist Parish: http://stjohnscatholicchurch.com/genoffaith.php

St. Ladislas Catholic Church: www.stlads.org

St. Noel Catholic Church: www.stnoel.org/ae/index.html

Resources

Across the Generations: Incorporating All Ages in Ministry (Resource Manual with CD) Minneapolis: Augsburg Fortress, 2001.

Ferguson, Nancy. *Retreats for Renewal: 5 Models for Intergenerational Weekends*. Nashville: Upper Room, 2008.

Johansson, Lois. *Hands and Hearts: Intergenerational Activities throughout the Church Year.* Harrisburg: Morehouse, 2006.

Keeeley, Robert J. *Shaped by God: Twelve Essential Practices for Nurturing Faith in Children, Youth, and Adults*. Grand Rapids: Faith Alive, 2010.

Martineau, Mariette, Joan Weber, and Leif Kehrwald. *Intergenerational Faith Formation—All Ages Learning Together*. New London: Twenty-Third, 2008.

Meyers, Patty. *Live, Learn, Pass It On!: The Practical Benefits of Generations Growing Together in Faith*. Nashville: Upper Room, 2006.

Roberto, John. *Becoming a Church of Lifelong Learners*. New London: Twenty-Third, 2006.

Roberto, John, Mariette Martineau, Joan Weber, and Leif Kehrwald. *People of Faith Intergenerational Manuals*. Orlando: OSV Curriculum, 2005-2007.

Websites

Faith Inkubators: www.faithink.com

Fashioning Faith (Center for Ministry Development): www.fashioningfaith.org

LifelongFaith Associates: www.lifelongfaith.com

Vibrant Faith Ministries: www.vibrantfaith.org

Generational Faith Formation

Faith formation for the past five or six decades has been guided by insights from developmental psychology that have shaped curriculum, program development, and educational methods. While developmental understandings will continue to shape faith formation into the future, sociological and cultural research into the "personalities" of five generations in America provides another way to shape curriculum and programs in faith formation. Generations are broader social, culture, and historical constructs, and not as precise as developmental stages of life. But each generation has distinct features that provides insights and clues for faith formation.

Today in America, and in many churches, there are five distinct generations, each with their own characteristics and worldviews and life experiences. Each generation has been shaped by unique culture, social, and religious perspectives.

- Generation 2000 or the iGeneration (2000–)
- Millennial Generation (1980–1999)
- Generation X (1965–1979)
- Baby Boom Generation (1946–1964)
- Builder Generation (1945 and earlier)

One way to develop innovative approaches and strategies to address each of the four scenarios is to become *generationally-specific*—responding to the specific religious and spiritual needs of each generation. Developing programs, activities, and resources that target specific generations and their generational characteristics. What follows are brief descriptions of the religious and spiritual needs of each generation and suggestions for faith formation that you can use to design innovative programming.

Faith Formation with the iGeneration and Millennial Generation

Twenty-First-Century Learning with the iGeneration and Millennials

The youngest generations in America—the Millennials (1980-1999) and the iGeneration (2000 and later)—reflect significant generational differences from previous generations. While still young, thirteen distinct traits of the iGeneration of children (and teenage Millennials) can already be identified: "(1) introduction to technology, literally at birth, (2) constant media diet, (3) adeptness at multitasking, (4) fervor for communication technologies, (5) love of virtual social worlds and anything internet-related, (6) ability to use technology to create a vast array of "content," (7) unique learning style, (8) need for constant motivation, (9) closeness to family, (10) confidence, (11) openness to change, (12) need for collective reflection, and (13) desire for immediacy" (Rosen, 26).

Learning experiences for Millennials and the iGeneration need to be experiential, image-rich, multi-sensory, interactive, engaging, and varied in learning style. Research is demonstrating that they learn more deeply when they apply knowledge to real-world problems and when they take part in projects that require sustained engagement and collaboration. Active learning practices have a more significant impact on learning than any other variable. The youngest generation (the "iGeneration") is a creative and multimedia generation. They think of the world as a canvas to paint with words, sights, sounds, video, music, web pages, and anything they can create. Multimedia means using multiple modalities to reach these students. They are also a generation of "content creators" who live to create, and given the chance to do so they will merge multiple media into one complex but comprehensive whole.

- Apply Howard Gardner's research on the eight **multiple intelligences** to education and provide a greater variety of ways to learn: verbal-linguistic (word smart, book smart), logical-mathematical (number smart, logic smart), visual-spatial (art smart, picture smart), bodily-kinesthetic (body smart, movement smart), musical-rhythmic (music smart, sound smart), naturalist (nature smart, environment smart), interpersonal (people smart, group smart), and intrapersonal (self smart, introspection smart).

- Apply research on **learning styles** to education by incorporating a diversity of learning activities and methods in a learning experience, recognizing that some people learn best through direct, hands-on, concrete experiences, some through reflective observation, some through an exploration and analysis of knowledge, theories, and concepts, and others through active experimentation with the new knowledge and practices.

- Engage in **active, in-depth learning** through well-designed projects, problems, and design tasks that focus learner inquiry around central questions in the disciplines and engage learners in *doing* the work of writers, scientists, mathematicians, musicians, sculptors, and critics.

- Incorporate **project-based learning** which involves completing complex tasks that typically result in a realistic product, event, or presentation. Project-based learning is (1) organized around driving questions that lead the learners to encounter central concepts or principles of a discipline; (2) focused on a constructive investigation that involves inquiry and knowledge building; (3) learner-driven, in that the learners are responsible for making choices and for designing and managing their work; (4) authentic, by posing problems that occur in the real world and that people care about.

- Have learners engage in **collaborative learning**—working in small, non-competitive groups—where they can discuss and process together what they are learning, work together on projects and activities, and practice and present what they are learning. Learning spaces are organized for learners' participation in a "learning community"—recognizing that learning takes place in a social context and relies on communication and interaction with others.

- Engage learners in **practicing** and **performing** what they are learning by incorporating real life application activities into the learning experience. Practice is a part of the learning process, not the result of it.

- Develop **visual literacy** in all learners: learning to "read" or interpret visual images and learning how to use visual images to communicate. The need to learn visual literacy arises because images were relatively rare until recently. The rise of electricity made movies, television, and the digital era possible. Visual literacy includes: (1) interpreting, understanding, and appreciating the meaning of visual images, (2) communicating more effectively by applying the basic principles and concepts of visual design, (3) producing visual images using computers and other technologies, and (4) using visual thinking to conceptualize solutions to problems.

- Utilize **digital media** to exploit the potential of the learning opportunities available through online resources and networks. We live in a digital age of a media-rich, networked world of infinite possibilities. Digital media promotes engagement, self-directed learning, creativity, and empowerment by using the Internet, computers, iPods and iPads, smart cell phones, and many other digital tools to learn and communicate in ways that were not possible in previous generations. Today's children, teens, and young adults smoothly and seamlessly dive into new Web 2.0 communication technologies. With a flick of the cell phone, they share more texts, photos, music, and video than any other demographic group on Earth. Digital media allows learners to be active creators and producers who use a wide range of digital tools to express themselves, interpret the world around them, and deepen their understanding of academic content. Their products include original music, animation, video, stories, graphics, presentations, and Web sites. They can become actively engaged in their learning processes rather than passive recipients of knowledge. They can actively collaborate in many new ways in the digital, virtual world, an environment parallel to the traditional one of face-to-face interaction. Given their fluency with digital tools, today's youth and young adults become teachers for younger and older generations. They maintain content-rich Web sites, share favorite resources, lead online workshops and classes, and develop multimedia products designed to share their knowledge with others. This teaching role enables young people to gain confidence and reinforce their own learning, because the best way to learn something is to teach it.

Works Cited

Rosen, Larry D. *Rewired: Understanding the iGeneration and the Way They Learn.* New York: Macmillan, 2010.

Resources

Chen, Milton. *Education Nation: Six Leading Edges of Innovation in Our Schools.* San Francisco: Jossey-Bass, 2010.

Curtis J. Bonk. *The World Is Open: How Web Technology is Revolutionizing Education.* San Francisco: Jossey Bass, 2009.

Darling-Hammond, Linda. *Powerful Learning: What We Know about Teaching for Understanding.* San Francisco: Jossey-Bass, 2008.

Jukes, Ian, Ted McCain, and Lee Crockett. *Understanding the Digital Generation: Teaching and Learning in the New Digital Landscape.* Kelowna: Twenty-First Century Fluency Project, 2010. (www.21stcenturyfluency.com)

McCarthy, Bernice. *About Teaching: 4MAT in the Classroom.* Bernice McCarthy. Wauconda: About Learning, 2000.

McCarthy, Bernice, and Dennis McCarthy. *About Teaching Companion: The 4MAT Implementation Workbook.* Wauconda: About Learning, 2003.

McCarthy, Bernice, and Dennis McCarthy. *Teaching Around the 4MAT Cycle—Designing Instructive for Diverse Learners with Diverse Learning Styles.* Thousand Oaks: Corwin Press, 2006.

Prensky, Marc. *Teaching Digital Natives: Partnering for Real Learning.* Thousand Oaks: Corwin, 2010.

Rosen, Larry D. *Rewired: Understanding the iGeneration and the Way They Learn.* New York: Macmillan, 2010.

Trilling, Bernie, and Charles Fadel. *Twenty-First Century Skills: Learning for Life in Our Times.* San Francisco: Jossey-Bass, 2009.

Shuler, Carol. "Pockets of Potential—Using Mobile Technologies to Promote Children's Learning." January 2009. The Joan Ganz Gooney Center at Sesame Workshop (www.joanganzcooneycenter.org/pdf/pockets_of_potential.pdf)

Websites

Twenty-First Century Fluency Project: www.21stcenturyfluency.com

Classroom 2.o: www.classroom20.com

Digital Catechesis: http://digitalcatechesis.ning.com

Edutopia: www.edutopia.org

The Joan Ganz Gooney Center at Sesame Workshop : www.joanganzcooneycenter.org

Reimaging Learning in the Twenty-First Century (John D. and Catherine T. MacArthur Foundation): www.macfound.org

Faith Formation with the Millennial Generation

In *Finding Faith: The Spiritual Quest of the Post-Boomer Generation* Richard Flory and Donald Miller report on a study of churches that are engaging emerging adults (post-boomers) and the experience of young adults in these churches. They observe that these emerging adults have embedded their lives in spiritual communities in which their desire and need for both expressive/experiential activities, whether through art, music, or service-oriented activities, and for a close-knit, physical community and communion with others are met. They are seeking to develop a balance for individualism and rational asceticism through religious experience and spiritual meaning in an embodied faith. The dominant characteristic across the young adults they interviewed was a desire for a faith that makes cognitive sense to them and that is also an expressive, embodied spiritual experience. Young adult Christians are searching for a more holistic faith than what a purely cognitive and rational approach can offer. They are seeking both a deep spiritual experience and a community experience, each of which provides them with meaning in their lives, and each of which is meaningless without the other.

Flory and Miller characterize post–Boomer faith as *expressive communalism*—reflecting an emphasis on embodiment and community: using one's body in worship; in living out, or embodying, Christian teachings, in service; and in a desire for life in a particular faith community where they can be both personally fulfilled and serve others. They desire a theologically grounded belief that makes cognitive sense to them and that is also an expressive, embodied spiritual experience. Using their research as a guide, emerging adults seek congregations and faith formation that:

- offer community and spirituality in the context of a clearly defined faith tradition
- offer worship and faith formation that is visual and experiential
- respond to their needs for empowerment, leadership opportunities, responsibility, and accountability, as well as authenticity and accessibility
- strengthen their distinctive Christian identity so that they know who they are and what they believe, and are able to honestly encounter religious differences, understand people of other faiths, and explore areas of mutuality
- provide opportunities for serving the surrounding community, "bringing the church to the community"
- study the Bible and Christian tradition, then apply it to life in an environment that promotes relationship building and encourages questioning
- engage them in creative uses of the history, traditions, and rituals of different Christian traditions for a more physically and visually oriented practice; and encouraging the development of ancient spiritual disciplines, such as silence and contemplation

In *Lost and Found: The Younger Unchurched and the Churches that Reach Them*, Ed Stetzer, Richie Stanley, and Jason Hayes, report on the findings from three LifeWay Research projects, including a large scale survey of young adults and a survey of 149 churches that were reaching an extraordinary number of young adults. Based on the responses of young adults in the research studies, the research team identified four markers of vibrant young adult ministry:

Community is vital to the emerging generations. For them, life is meant to be experienced together, and they sense a need to be involved in genuine relationships with others. They are looking for friends they can call for help when their tire is flat and people who will call and celebrate when they get a promotion. They want to walk through life with their friends. They have a need for people, and they show a deep desire for relational equity. In other words, they long to be deeply invested in others and have others deeply invested in them. They desire to be a major part of each other's lives—the day-to-day, big and small "stuff of life." They also think that others should be a part of the most important aspect of their lives—their spiritual journey.

Depth is important. Young adults want to be people of significance. Deep significance. They care about who they are and what they're becoming—"ankle deep" doesn't work for them. They told us that they'd rather be "in over their heads" in life as opposed to kicking around in the shallow end. Young adults also have interest in addressing the hard-to-talk about topics. They appreciate tough questions and despise pat answers. Their responses indicate that they like wrestling with difficult things and chewing on challenging ideas. They express a high degree of interest in processing information, and they often find the questions more important than the answers.

Responsibility is strongly valued because young adults know their choices make a difference. Decisions are everywhere: Recycle. Buy or trade fair. Sponsor a child. Respect your elders. Tithe. Love your neighbors. Respond to the crisis in Darfur. These are the type of opportunities that define this generation. They affirmed the importance of these issues, and they are committed to doing the "right" thing even as they grow in their understanding of what right means. They've concluded that all of these decisions matter, and what matters most is how they respond.

Connection is the fourth area of importance. This could be called mentoring or intergenerational ministry. They want to learn from those who have already experienced the things they are about to face. They're looking for a connection with people who will walk alongside them and advise them. They want a connection that gives them the opportunity to have someone pour their lives into them and teach them along their journey. And interestingly enough, they're willing to do that for someone else too (Stetzer, *et al.,* 67-68).

These four markers of ministry point to implications for developing faith formation and ministry with emerging adults. The young adults in the study, both churched and unchurched, expressed the following needs and interests:

- to interact with members of a group multiple times per week
- to participate in small group activities that promote relationships and belonging
- to connect with a mentor; to receive information and advice from individuals with experience
- to participate in Bible study that minimizes pat answers in the exploration of Scripture
- to participate in small group meetings to discuss life application of Scripture
- to determine their own beliefs through hands-on, practical learning experiences

- to utilize their talents and abilities through opportunities to meet needs
- to participate in hands-on outreach activities on a frequent basis that meet the needs of others
- to benefit others through global service projects

Based on its research with 149 churches that were reaching an extraordinary number of young adults, the research team found nine common characteristics in churches that are reaching young adults.

1. **Creating Deeper Community**. Churches that are effective at attracting and developing young adults place a high value on moving people into a healthy small group system. Young adults are trying to connect and will make a lasting connection wherever they can find belonging.

2. **Making a Difference through Service**. Churches that are transforming young adults value leading people to serve through volunteerism. More than being pampered, young adults want to be part of something bigger than themselves and are looking to be part of an organization where they can make a difference through acts of service.

3. **Experiencing Worship**. Churches that are engaging young adults are providing worship environments that reflect their culture while also revering and revealing God. More than looking for a good performance, young adults desire to connect with a vertical experience of worship.

4. **Conversing the Content**. Churches that are led by authentic communicators are drawing young adults into the message. Though their styles vary from topical to exegetical, authentic communicators are true to their own personal style of communication and are usually more conversational than preachy.

5. **Leveraging Technology**. Churches that are reaching young adults are willing to communicate in a language of technology familiar to young adults. Young adults sense that these churches are welcoming churches that value and understand them, engaging them where they are.

6. **Building Cross-Generational Relationships**. Churches that are linking young adults with older, mature adults are challenging young adults to move on to maturity through friendship, wisdom, and support. Young adults are drawn to churches that believe in them enough to challenge them.

7. **Moving Toward Authenticity**. Churches that are engaging young adults are reaching them not only by their excellence but by their honesty. Young

adults are looking for and connecting to churches where they see leaders that are authentic, transparent, and on a learning journey.

8. **Leading by Transparency**. Churches that are influencing young adults highly value an incarnational approach to ministry and leadership. This incarnational approach doesn't require revealing one's personal sin list so much as it requires that those in leadership must be willing to express a personal sense of humanity and vulnerability.

9. **Leading by Team**. Increasingly churches reaching young adults seem to be taking a team approach to ministry. They see ministry not as a solo venture but as a team sport—and the broader participation it creates increases the impact of the ministry. (Stetzer, *et al.,* 143–44)

Young adults are longing for community and fellowship with peers, looking for ways to reach people in need, and circling the church but not always finding a home in it. Connection is the key. Community with other young adults is extremely important in their lives. Young adults seek authentic answers in the Bible and Christian tradition, best learned through participation in small group meetings. Making a difference is essential by having the opportunity to meet the needs of others on a regular basis. Social action is cited as the major reason uninvolved young adults would consider being part of a church.

Works Cited

Flory, Richard W. and Donald E. Miller. *Finding Faith: The Spiritual Quest of the Post-Boomer Generation*. New Brunswick: Rutgers University Press, 2008.

Stetzer, Ed, and Richie Stanley, and Jason Hayes. *Lost and Found: The Younger Unchurched and the Churches that Reach Them*. Nashville: B&H, 2009.

Congregational Examples
(See also Kairos and the Bridge in the Faith Formation with Spiritual Seekers strategy.)

Example: Church of the Apostles, Seattle, WA
(www.apostleschurch.org)
Church of the Apostles is a young, emerging, Episcopal and Lutheran mission congregation—a future church with an ancient faith. The church's purpose is to *help-godchangeeverything*, by participating in God's future, within today's culture and their local zip code, living and serving in intentional, sacramental community in the way of Jesus Christ.

- **Home Groups**. At Apostles, common life in Christ starts at home and among friends. God meets us where we live and wherever two or three come together in God's name to share in Christian community. The point is not just "going to a church," but being church in our daily lives and everyday interactions with others. Home groups gather in actual houses, but also in other kinds of spaces. Some groups meet in coffeehouses, others in pubs, and some in parks or at the beach. The spaces vary, but the purpose is the same: small cells of people (followers and seekers) gathering weekly or every other week to share life, tell stories, eat meals, pray, serve and grow together in Jesus Christ. Each group has its own vibe, way of gathering, and basic path. Some groups are on a cognitive path (studying the Bible and deepening knowledge), some are on an expressive path (making music, creating art, or writing poetry), some are on a communitarian path around a lifestyle or common interest (young moms, hikers, AA recovery). Some are on a contemplative path (gathering for evening prayers or spiritual exercises), while others are on an active path (working soup kitchens, tutoring kids, building houses). Although they may take up different activities, each group is an expression of church and will therefore take time to worship, pray, reflect on scripture, and engage in a group ministry in the world.

- **Service**. Doing justice and showing mercy is core to the DNA of Christian life. What distinguished the early Christians from the surrounding society (and fueled the growth of the church) was just and merciful living, steeped in love for Jesus Christ. People took notice of how Christians cared for "orphans and widows in their distress" and kept themselves from being jaded by the ways of the world. This same love of justice and kindness is Christian spiritual formation of the highest order. Christians are called to actively serve poor, oppressed, hungry, sick and needy people; to live into and share with others the justice and mercy that God continues to rain upon the world in Christ. Apostles' Missio Dei Group coordinates a different local service project each month, as well as coordinating out of state or country projects once or twice per year.

- **Sunday Mass.** Smaller groups that meet at various times during the week for community groups, prayer, scripture reflection and service, come together each week for Mass. Apostles' worship is neither "traditional" nor "contemporary" but ancient-future. Ancient-future liturgy speaks across generations and draws equally upon ancient (hymns, chant, candles, communion) and techno-modern (alt. rock, art, ambient, projection, video) sources.

- **Events**. A variety of other activities include a Supper Club, a Theology Pub every other Tuesday night, Soul Café, and Film Nights.

Example: Generation Axis, Willow Creek Community Church, South Barrington, IL (www.generationaxis.com)

- **Missional Community Hubs** are the epicenter of Willow Creek Church's ministry with emerging adults. These are community-based out of someone's house, apartment, or condo throughout the Chicago-land area. They exist to bring redemptive change to their neighborhoods through gatherings, serving initiatives, social events, and discipleship opportunities. This is where life happens in Axis and their dream is to see Missional Community Hubs launched all over our city.

- **Life Transformation Groups** are seasonal, gender-based groups of three to four people that seek to live out the teachings of Jesus in intimate community with focuses on Scripture, prayer, and accountability. These communities are generally born out of relationships with an Missional Community Hub.

- The **Axis Experience** is the place where the entire Axis community gathers for prayer, worship, and to celebrate what has happened in their Missional Community Hubs. This provides the opportunity to connect with each other around our shared language, vision, and values.

- **Generation Axis Videos** on Vimeo: stories, devotions, Bible study, promotion. (http:// vimeo.com/channels/generationsaxistv)

Example: Newsong Third Culture Community, Irvine, CA (www. newsong.net) (http://irvine.newsong.net/ministries/lifestage/youngadults)

Newsong's Young Adult Ministry exists to transform the world by empowering young adults in their twenties and thirties to be radical in their love for God and for people. There are four main elements of young adult ministry:

- **Young Adult Small Groups**. Small Groups meet once a week and live out the third-culture values of loving, learning, and serving (through Bible studies, cultivating relationships, serving the community together). The groups consist of seven to twenty people depending on which group you decide to commit to.

- **Momentum Nights**. Momentum is an event that happens once a month where people connect meaningfully with one another and with God and take steps forward in living out their faith in community. This takes a variety of forms. Some nights this has meant a speaker who delves into a topic relevant to young adults and on other nights this translates into inviting local musicians to come share their art in a café type setting.

- **Travel with a Purpose**. Travel to local and global destinations to experience culture, learn, serve, and live in community for a week. These *Travel with a Purpose* trips take place twice a year for young adults to use their vacation time in a unique way.

- **Service**. Each person is carefully created with unique experiences, pains, gifting, and calling. At Newsong there are many ways to love, learn, and serve. To help people make a difference a FLOW Consult can help people recognize God's unique shaping and calling on their life. FLOW helps people find the passion that God has placed in their heart and bring it to life. Discovery is important but each person's journey is different. There isn't a program or process that fits everyone and that is why it is important for a FLOW consultant to serve as a sounding board to provide a fresh perspective as people tell their stories. They identify obstacles in a person's path and resources to encourage growth.

In addition to these four elements there are also:

- **Message Study Guides** (and audio and video podcasts) provide a way for people to dig deeper into the weekly message from worship gatherings. Each study incorporates questions that will help you examine a Bible text, apply scripture to daily life, and put your faith into action. These studies can be used for small groups or individuals.

- **Connections Dinner** is a non-threatening and fun way to learn about Newsong and to meet several members of the pastoral staff. This introduction to Newsong provides an opportunity to meet new members and share the genesis of the Newsong church community and its vision and how people can participate in the life of Newsong.

- **Foundations—Beginning the Journey** is a six-week class that explores the basics of what it means to be a Christ follower. **Foundations—The Bible** helps people discover what the Bible is all about and learn tools to dig into the Bible for themselves.

- **Justice N.O.W.** is a Night of Worship and music dedicated to bringing light to global issues of injustice that need immediate attention. By catching God's heart for justice through meeting God in passionate worship, people experience the call to a life of justice

Example: St. Vincent de Paul Church, San Francisco, CA
(www.svdpsf.org/youngadults)

The Young Adult Group at St. Vincent's is a community of young adults in their twenties and thirties who value socializing, volunteering, and exploring questions of their faith with others who share a similar Catholic heritage and value system. Their mission is to promote a spiritual, social, and service-oriented community for Catholics in their twenties and thirties. The core events of this group take place on the second and fourth Monday nights of each month. Many young adults also gather for Mass on Sunday at 5:15 pm and social and service activities take place on a weekly basis.

- **Monday events** are the foundation of the young adult community, meeting every second and fourth Monday to explore faith and values in a fun and relaxed atmosphere, get details on upcoming social and community service activities, and make a few new friends. Whether young adults are rejoining the church after a long absence, want to learn more about Catholicism, or just want to meet other Catholics who value their faith and heritage, the Monday events are for them. Every meeting features a new topic and speaker. Generally, most of our topics center around questions and issues facing young adult Catholics in the world today.

- **Service** projects include regular commitments to a retirement community, delivery of food to the homeless, cooking at the soup kitchen, as well as special projects in the community.

- **Annual Retreat** provides an opportunity for reflection, spiritual renewal, fellowship, and more. Desired outcomes for the retreat include: taking an inventory of one's life, exploring one's passions and purpose in life, discerning what God is calling one to do, gaining insight and encouragement from others' experiences, increasing alignment between one's values and actions, and building relationships with other young adults.

- **Small Faith Groups** bring together young adult Catholics to deepen their faith and love of God while fostering fellowship and deepening the ties with the St. Vincent De Paul community. The format involves reflecting on the Sunday's gospel reading with questions to guide people in delving deeper into the scripture and applying it to their lives. Typically, groups decide to meet every three weeks on Sunday evening after our 5:15 pm Mass. The meetings take place at one of the groups members' houses in what often will end up being a pot-luck dinner format. The facilitator or small faith community leader is generally rotated. Groups form after the Annual Retreat, and tend to last a minimum of six months and oftentimes longer.

Additional Congregational Examples

20something (North Coast Church, Vista, CA): www.northcoastchurch.com; http://northcoast20something.com

Kairos and Young Adult Ministry (Brentwood Baptist Church, Nashville, TN): www.brentwoodbaptist.com/karios

Contemporary Roman Catholics (CRC) (Holy Trinity Church, New York City): www.crcnyc.org

The Crossing (St. Paul's Episcopal Cathedral, Boston, MA): www.thecrossingboston.org

Marble Connection (Marble Collegiate Church, New York City): www.marblechurch.org/Programs/20sand30s/tabid/100/Default.aspx

St. Lydia's Dinner Church (New York City): www.stlydias.org

Strategies

Use the following faith formation strategies and customize them for the particular needs and perspectives of Millennials:

- Faith Formation using Digital Media and Web Technologies
- Intergenerational Faith Formation
- Milestones Faith Formation
- Faith Formation in Christian Practices
- Transforming the World: Engagement in and Formation for Service and Mission
- Spiritual Formation
- Multi-Ethnic Faith Formation
- Faith Formation for Spiritual Seekers
- Apprenticeships in Discipleship
- Interfaith Education and Dialogue

Resources

Beckwith, Ivy. *Formational Children's Ministry: Shaping Children using Story, Ritual, and Relationship.* Grand Rapids: Baker Books, 2010.

Changing SEA (Changing Spirituality of Emerging Adults): www.changingsea.org

Children's Ministry in the Twenty-First Century. Loveland: Group, 2007.

Connecting Young Adults to Catholic Parishes. Washington, DC: USCCB, 2010.

Dean, Kenda Creasy. *Almost Christian: What the Faith of Our Teenagers is Telling the American Church.* New York, Oxford University Press, 2010.

Dean, Kenda Creasy, and Ron Foster. *The Godbearing Life—The Art of Soul Tending for Youth Ministry.* Nashville: Upper Room, 1998.

East, Thomas, editor. *Leadership for Catholic Youth Ministry—A Comprehensive Resource.* New London: Twenty-Third, 2009.

Edie, Fred. *Book, Bath, Table, and Time: Christian Worship as Source and Resource for Youth Ministry.* Cleveland: Pilgrim, 2007.

Glenn, Mike. *In Real Time: Authentic Young Adult Ministry as It Happens.* Nashville: B&H, 2009.

Grenz, Linda L. *Transforming Disciples.* New York: Church, 2008.

Hayes, Mike, *Googling God: The Religious Landscape of People in their Twenties and Thirties.* New York: Paulist, 2007.

Haywood, Janice. *Enduring Connections: Creating a Preschool and Children's Ministry.* St. Louis: Chalice, 2007.

Keeley, Robert J. *Shaped by God: Twelve Essential Practices for Nurturing Faith in Children, Youth, and Adults.* Grand Rapids: Faith Alive, 2010.

Keeley, Robert J. *Helping Our Children Grow in Faith*. Grand Rapids: Faith Alive, 2008.

Martinson, Roland, Wes Black, and John Roberto. *The Spirit and Culture of Youth Ministry*. Saint Paul: EYM Publications, 2010. (www.exemplarym.org)

Merritt, Carol Howard. *Tribal Church: Ministering to the Missing Generation*. Herndon: Alban Institute, 2007.

Plant, Marian R. *Faith Formation in Vital Congregations*. Cleveland: Pilgrim, 2009.

Stetzer, Ed, Richie Stanley, and Jason Hayes. Lost and Found: *The Younger Unchurched and the Churches that Reach Them*. Nashville: B&H, 2009.

Stonehouse, Catherine, and Scottie May. *Listening to Children on the Spiritual Journey: Guidance for Those Who Teach and Nurture*. Grand Rapids: Baker, 2010.

White. David F. *Practicing Discernment with Youth*. Cleveland: Pilgrim, 2005

Yust, Karen Marie. *Real Kids, Real Faith: Practices for Nurturing Children's Spiritual Lives*. San Francisco: Jossey-Bass, 2004.

Faith Formation with Generation X

In 2014 the oldest member of Generation X turns fifty years old. Generation X reflects a diversity of adults including single adults, married couples without children, and parents of children, teens, and even college-aged young adults.

Generation X shares many of the characteristics of post-Boomer faith that describe the Millennial Generation, especially the defining feature of *expressive communalism*, which reflects an emphasis on embodiment and community: using one's body in worship; in living out, or embodying, Christian teachings, in service; and in a desire for life in a particular faith community where they can be both personally fulfilled and serve others. Generation X, like Millennials, desire a theologically grounded belief that makes cognitive sense to them and that is also an expressive, embodied spiritual experience.

In *Gen X Religion*, researchers Richard Flory and Donald Miller identify five major characteristics of Generation X religion:

- Generation X religion emphasizes the sensual and experiential, combining the sacred and the profane and incorporating text, image, music, dance, and the body as venues for the expression of religious beliefs.
- Generation X religion is entrepreneurial in finding cultural and institutional space to create new religious expressions based on their existing lifestyle interests.
- Generation X religion is, on the one hand, similar to Baby Boomer religion in that it emphasizes personal identity, religious experience, and spiritual seeking; but it differs in that it roots the quest for religious identity in community, rather than a more purely personal spiritual quest.
- Race, ethnic, and gender diversity and inclusiveness is an explicit goal of Generation X religion.
- There is an insistence on an "authentic" religious experience in Generation X religion, both on the part of the individual and as found in the religious

communities that GenXers choose to join, that acknowledges the ambiguities, trials, and successes of life. (Flory, 234–35)

Generation X is looking for and creating community, belonging, and authenticity. Their desire seems to be first for community and belonging, and second for personal fulfillment. Personal fulfillment comes through commitment to the community, and through the experience of belonging to such a religious/spiritual community.

For Generation X, religious truth, while important, is not a fixed target, and is found through their religious experience, not in texts and doctrines. Truth, for Xers, is best conveyed through stories and myth, and is authenticated through the lived experience of themselves and others, rather than through the pronouncements—and propositional arguments—of external authorities.

Generation X is moving from written text to narrative and image as a basis for religious belief. Image and story have become dominant and text background. Second, there is a move away from proposition truth claims to truth validated by experience in the religious community. There is a move from the essentially individualistic spiritual quest that characterizes baby boomers to a religious/spiritual identity rooted in the larger community.

In his study of Catholic young adults (Generation X), researcher Dean Hoge summarized his key findings, which can easily apply to all Christian churches. He concluded that Generation X will tend to maintain their basic values, beliefs, and faith perspectives as they grow older. Today a religious identity is chosen, not imposed. This brings new personal freedom and autonomy, but it also brings new spiritual needs. Identity must now be chosen through experience and study. Compared with older generations, Generation X will uphold greater individual authority in religious and moral decisions and will desire more lay influence in institutional decision-making. They will tend to distinguish faith in God from obeying the rules of the institutional Church, clinging more to the former than to the latter. The challenge for churches is to encourage young adults to search the richness of the Catholic (Christian) tradition for themselves and to construct a Catholic (Christian) identity which they feel is genuinely inspiring.

In the study *Congregations That Get It* the researchers found that young adults (older Millennials and Generation X) "exercised typical American individualism as they decided about associating with religious communities, sometimes participating in more than one simultaneously" (Belzer, *et al.*, 106). The research team identified the following factors as influencing young adult's participation in a faith community.

- choosing a specific community, rather than committing to a larger denomination
- making choices based on a number of factors, such as interpersonal relationships, worship style, geographic location, opportunities for involvement, and accessibility of leadership

- deciding how often to attend and the extent of their participation
- choosing how much of the official teachings to accept and how much ritual observance to practice
- balancing their individual authority with their identity as members of a community and religious tradition
- seeking a community where there is both flexibility and structure
- being experientially engaged as opposed to a "show up and watch" style of religious participation
- building interpersonal relationships with people who express and explore their religious identities in similar ways; relationship building was a fundamental aspect of young adults' congregational experience (Belzer, *et al.*, 106–7).

Works Cited

Belzer, Tobin, Richard W. Flory, Nadia Roumani, and Brie Loskota. "Congregations That Get It: Understanding Religious Identities in the Next Generation." *Passing on the Faith: Transforming Traditions for the Next Generation of Jews, Christians, and Muslims.* James Heft, editor. New York: Fordham University Press, 2006.

Hoge, Dean, R.; Dinges, William; Johnson. Mary; Gonzales, Juan; *Young Adult Catholics.* Notre Dame: University of Notre Dame, 2001.

Flory, Richard W. and Donald E. Miller, editors. *Gen X Religion*. New York: Routledge, 2000.

Flory, Richard W. "Toward a Theory of Generation X Religion." *Gen X Religion*. Richard W. Flory and Donald E. Miller, editors. New York: Routledge, 2000.

Strategies

Use the following faith formation strategies and customize them for the particular needs and perspectives of Generation X:

- Faith Formation using Digital Media and Web Technologies
- Intergenerational Faith Formation
- Family Faith Formation
- Milestones Faith Formation
- Faith Formation in Christian Practices
- Transforming the World: Engagement in and Formation for Service and Mission
- Spiritual Formation
- Multi-Ethnic Faith Formation
- Faith Formation for Spiritual Seekers
- Apprenticeships in Discipleship
- Pathways to Vibrant Faith and Active Engagement
- Interfaith Education and Dialogue

Resources

Connecting Young Adults to Catholic Parishes. Washington, DC: USCCB, 2010.

Glenn, Mike. *In Real Time: Authentic Young Adult Ministry as It Happens.* Nashville: B&H, 2009.

Grenz, Linda L. *Transforming Disciples.* New York: Church, 2008.

Hayes, Mike, *Googling God: The Religious Landscape of People in their Twenties and Thirties*. New York: Paulist, 2007.

Keeley, Robert J. *Shaped by God: Twelve Essential Practices for Nurturing Faith in Children, Youth, and Adults*. Grand Rapids: Faith Alive, 2010.

Merritt, Carol Howard. *Tribal Church: Ministering to the Missing Generation*. Herndon: Alban Institute, 2007.

Plant, Marian R. *Faith Formation in Vital Congregations*. Cleveland: Pilgrim, 2009.

Faith Formation with the Baby Boomer Generation

In 2011 the first members of the Baby Boomer Generation turn sixty-five years old. In the United States today Americans over sixty-five now outnumber teenagers by nearly two to one. What used to be referred to as the "graying of America" is now understood to be a social revolution. Some thirty-nine million Americans, or 13% of the U.S. population, are ages sixty-five and older—up from 4% in 1900. By 2050, according to Pew Research projections, about *one-in-five* Americans will be over age sixty-five, and about 5% will be ages eighty-five and older, up from 2% now. Nearly every industry in society, from health care to entertainment, is scrambling to respond to this age wave that is crashing onto our shores.

America is in the midst of a demographic revolution, but this revolution is about much more than longevity. It's about the changing perspective of the Baby Boomers as they reach what was traditionally viewed as a time to enjoy the golden years. It's about Americans who have already retired, but are still seeking purpose and productivity. We are witnessing the emergence of a new stage of life between adult midlife–typically focused on career and child-rearing–and old age, traditionally marked by increasing frailty and decline. This new stage of life spans several decades and is characterized by generally good health, relative financial stability, and an active, engaged lifestyle.

Among all adults ages sixty-five and older, nine in ten talk with family or friends every day. About eight in ten read a book, newspaper, or daily magazine; three-quarters watch more than a hour of television; about the same share prays daily. Less than half spend time on a hobby. Roughly one in four use the internet (Pew Research).

Two-thirds of adults ages sixty-five and older say religion is very important to them. Moreover, among adults ages sixty-five and above, a third (34%) say religion has grown more important to them over the course of their lives, while just 4% say it has become less important and the majority (60%) say it has stayed the same.

From research and discussions with adults fifty-five and older, Civic Ventures has identified four major needs and desires among older Americans that cut across all income categories, educational levels, and races or ethnicities. People are seeking:

- Opportunities to explore options for the next stage of life
- Opportunities to retool skills, obtain new training, or pursue educational interests

- Flexible work or service opportunities that use their skills and experience in meaningful ways
- Opportunities to make meaningful connections with others their own age and throughout the community

Civic Ventures believes that this changing notion of aging in America offers the prospect of an "experience dividend" of staggering proportions. In other words, the growing, knowledgeable older population can offer a tremendous return to our society. Never before have so many Americans had so much experience—with so much time and interest in using it.

Gary McIntosh describes the Baby Boomer generation as educated, media-oriented, independent, cause-oriented, fitness conscious, activists, quality conscious, and questioning of authority. He says that as church members Boomers are (1) committed to relationships, rather than organizations; (2) want to belong, rather than join; (3) supportive of people, rather than programs; (4) long to live their faith, rather than talk about it; (5) wish to be seen as unique individuals, rather than a monolithic group; (6) desire to design their own programs, rather than attend ones developed for them; (7) yearn to serve others, rather than only being served; and (8) crave meaningful activity, rather than empty days.

McIntosh makes the following recommendations for ministry with Baby Boomers based on his research:

- Build a ministry for boomers that is adventurous. Consider hiking in the mountains or cross-country skiing. Boomers have always seen themselves as a youthful generation, and they still do.
- Build a ministry for boomers that is fun. Consider catered parties, fishing trips, paint ball competition, and team-building camps. Boomers are not looking for a senior's ministry; they are seeking an older youth ministry.
- Build a ministry for boomers that is significant. Rather than being served, consider serving others by building a home for Habitat for Humanity, assisting missionaries, helping out-of-work people to find a job, or tutoring children. Boomers desire to make a difference in the world by taking on great causes.
- Building a ministry for boomers that is educational. Along with Bible studies, consider CPR, basic first aid, personal health, and managing finances. Boomers are an educated generation, and they wish to continue learning to the end of their days.
- Building a ministry for boomers that is spiritual. Boomers are a mosaic of subgroups, and it will take a multi-dimensional approach to spiritual formation to reach them. (McIntosh, 303)

Boomers tend to be far less driven by programs than the Builder Generation (1945 and earlier). They like activities that seem purposeful to them, that promote health and wellness, and keep them feeling young. They are less interested in attending a meeting "just because they're supposed to" and more interested in involving themselves in something they consider productive and worthwhile. For example, a ministry targeted toward the Boomer Generation might best resemble a day of serving together at a local homeless shelter followed by dinner together and a time of reflection.

Amy Hanson, in *Baby Boomers and Beyond*, proposes three essential components for creative ministries with maximum impact on Baby Boomers: *service, spiritual growth,* and *intergenerational relationships.*

- **Service**: Boomers want to do something interesting and challenging. They are ready to jump into a worthwhile cause where they feel that they can make a significant difference. Boomers want service opportunities that have a mission. They want do to do things that give their lives purpose, meaning, and fulfillment. They want to know their contributions truly matter. There is no greater mission for Boomers to immerse themselves in than the mission of Christ to redeem and heal a broken world. Encourage Boomers to serve in an area where they've always had an interest, and provide them with exposure to a variety of service opportunities. Short term trips can be a great way for people over fifty to discover the one thing they want to invest themselves in. Show Boomers how they might use their past work experiences as tools for service. Help them tap into their passion.

   "Engaging Boomers to make a major impact for Christ in the world should be a primary foundation for ministry with Boomers—if not *the* primary foundation. We have an open window of time right now to help individuals refocus their priorities and recognize how God wants to use them for his purposes in this season of their lives." (Hanson, 143)

- **Spiritual Growth**: There are several fundamental resources why Boomers are responsive to the message of the gospel and to spiritual growth. Later Adulthood is a season of significant life transitions and people are more responsive to religion. A second reason is Boomers quest to find meaning and purpose in life as they enter the second half of life and evaluate the things that really provide lasting fulfillment. A third reason adults are open to faith and spiritual growth is their desire for meaningful relationships. The church can be a primary place of social interaction where people can connect with one another and talk about life issues. "All three factors—help dealing with life's changes, a search for purpose, and a desire for meaningful relationships—can powerfully work together in drawing adults to Christ's saving grace." (Hanson, 151)

   Effective ways to bring older adults into a relationship with Christ include: (1) small group faith formation, (2) hanging out in the places where Boomer adults gather, (3) hosting events that appeal to Boomers' interests and needs, and (4) service opportunities.

- **Intergenerational Relationships**: Ministry with Baby Boomers includes an intergenerational component. Developing intergenerational relationships is one of the best ways to break age-related stereotypes, to share faith across generations, and to help the church become more unified. There are a variety of ways to connect the generations and develop intergenerational relationships: (1) encourage generations to serve together on a worthy cause; (2) form groups according to similar interests rather than age; (3) encouraging adults to intentionally pray for young people and vice versa; (4) host strategic intergenerational events that are fun for all, and have ready-made questions that permit age groups to engage easily in conversation, and encourage relationships to continue after the event is over; (6) ask adults to tell their stories, at workshop or events or programs, and capture them on video and/or in print; (7) develop intergenerational small group and large group programming; (8) integrate all ages in Sunday worship; and (9) educate people as to the uniqueness of each generation.

"As multiple generations work, worship, serve, and play together, the result will be that people lay down their own self-centeredness and take up the attitude of Christ. True, we may have to do church a little differently, but when all ages are regularly interacting and loving one another, God is honored, and we become an example to our hurting world." (Hanson, 185)

Works Cited
Hanson, Amy. *Baby Boomers and Beyond: Tapping the Ministry Talents and Passions of Adults Over Fifty.* San Francisco: Jossey Bass, 2010.
McIntosh, Gary. "Trends and Challenges for Ministry among North America's Largest Generation." *Christian Education Journal* Series 3, 5/2.

Strategies
Use the following faith formation strategies and customize them for the particular needs and perspectives of Baby Boomers:

- Faith Formation through the Life of the Church
- Faith Formation using Digital Media and Web Technologies
- Intergenerational Faith Formation
- Milestones Faith Formation
- Faith Formation in Christian Practices
- Transforming the World: Engagement in and Formation for Service and Mission
- Spiritual Formation
- Multi-Ethnic Faith Formation
- Faith Formation for Spiritual Seekers

- Apprenticeships in Discipleship
- Pathways to Vibrant Faith and Active Engagement
- Empowering the Community to Share their Faith
- Interfaith Education and Dialogue

Resources

Buford, Bob. *Half Time: Moving from Success to Significance*. Revised Edition. Grand Rapids: Zondervan, 2008.

Freedman, Marc. *Encore: Finding Work that Matters in the Second Half of Life*. New York: Public Affairs, 2007. (www.encore.org)

Gentzler, Richard H. *Aging and Ministry in the Twenty-First Century: An Inquiry Approach*. Nashville: Discipleship Resources, 2008.

Grenz, Linda L. *Transforming Disciples*. New York: Church, 2008.

"Growing Old in America: Expectations vs. Reality." June 29, 2009. Pew Research Center. (http://pewresearch.org/pubs/1269/aging-survey-expectations-versus-reality)

Hanson, Amy. "Breaking Down the Age Barriers: How Churches are Becoming Intentionally Intergeneration." Leadership Network. (www.www.leadnet.org/Resources_Downloads.asp)

Hanson, Amy. *Baby Boomers and Beyond: Tapping the Ministry Talents and Passions of Adults Over Fifty*. San Francisco: Jossey Bass, 2010.

Hanson, Amy. "Churches Responding to the Age Way: Top Innovations in Older Adult Ministry." Leadership Network. (www.www.leadnet.org/Resources_Downloads.asp)

Helping Society Achieve the Greatest Return on Experience. Civic Ventures. (www.civicventures.org)

Innovations Documentary Series. Civic Ventures. (www.civicventures.org/publications/booklets/innovations.cfm)

McIntosh, Gary. "Trends and Challenges for Ministry among North America's Largest Generation." *Christian Education Journal*, Series 3, 5/2.

Pettegrew, Hal. "Perspectives on the Spiritual Development of 'Aging' Boomers." *Christian Education Journal*, Series 3, 5/2.

Vogel, Linda. "Creating Learning Environments for Mature Adults that Foster Creating and Faith Formation." *Christian Education Journal*, Series 3, 5/2.

Websites

Amy Hanson (*Baby Boomers and Beyond*): http://amyhanson.org

Christian Association Serving Adult Ministries Network: http://gocasa.org

Civic Ventures: www.civicventures.org

Encore Generation at Leadership Network: www.leadnet.org

Encore Careers: www.encore.org

Half Time: From Success to Significance: www.halftime.org

Older Adult Ministries (United Methodist Church): www.gbod.org/site/c.nhLRJ2PMKsG/b.3784737/k.7977/Older_Adult_Ministries.htm

Faith Formation with the Builder Generation

The present generation of senior adults (the Builder Generation) has probably gone through more changes in their lives and in society than any previous generation. They have gone from horse and buggy days to space travel, to electricity, telephones, computers, VCRs, DVDs, iPods, iPhones, and so many more changes that have effected the way they live, work, eat, play, and worship. They have lived through two world wars, the Korean Conflict, Vietnam, wars in Afghanistan and Iraq, and world terrorism. Through it all, the believers among them have depended upon their spiritual strength to manage the changes, the losses, and the challenges that historical events and the process of growing older have brought upon them.

Today's maturing adults are different from those who came before. They are more motivated by a desire for personal purpose; they tend to be more participatory, more interested in being actively involved with issues that "matter." Continuing their spiritual growth in the later years is crucial—for them and for churches.

Richard Johnson describes several fundamental tasks, overarching units of faithwork, which serve as the scaffolding for comprehensive faith formation programs for maturing adults. These tasks not only guide church leaders in constructing fundamental and functional faith formation ministries, they also act as spiritual development handholds for maturing adults as they work toward a greater realization of God's presence in their lives. (For a description of all sixteen tasks, see Richard Johnson's book and article listed in the resource section.)

1. **Develop basic faith formation competencies with a strong spiritual base**. All maturing adults need to have some basic information, such as about common misconceptions about aging, the fundamental emotional needs of elder adults, common reactions to loss, lifestyle adjustments that come with aging, ways to build relationships that are both nurturing and spiritually, and so on. This information helps form the foundation for the process of "holy aging."

2. **View aging as a spiritual process**. Aging is a spiritual process every bit as much as it is a physical and mental process. In order to understand and personally "own" this expanded view of aging, maturing adults must be given the tools to help them deal positively and constructively with all the issues that aging brings.

3. **Build spiritual companionship skills into the intergenerational patterns of the Christian community**. By forming relationships with diverse groups, across lines of age and other categories, maturing adults can become more aware of the movement of the Spirit in their own lives and in the lives of others. For example, helping maturing adults form mentoring relationships with younger members of the congregation can be a source of positive growth for all involved.

4. **Develop ways to see illness through a lens of faith**. Older adults can grow to see their illness as a normal part of growing older, and as an opportunity to embrace God's love more dearly.

5. **Understand wellness as a spiritually holistic concept**. Wellness is more than the absence of disease; it's a state of being where one is functioning in an optimal manner, physically, mentally, emotionally, and spiritually. Maturing adults need a personal wellness program, a framework that gives them specific guidance on how to achieve wellness regardless of the condition of their objective health.

6. **Learn the essentials of giving care in a way that encourages spiritually growth**. Many maturing adults will be called on to be caregivers. Caregiving is so much more than performing tasks; it's an engagement of the heart as well as the mind, an illumination of the spirit as well as an activity of the soul. Caregivers need to know that their role is a ministry, an opportunity for spiritual growth.

7. **Connect the experiences of the maturing years with God's grace**. The maturing years offer a time of graced and gracious growth. As the body slowly diminishes and shows the signs of physical "dis-integration," the heart and soul have the potential to more fully integrate. The road to spiritual development in the maturing stage is not an easy one; walking it requires continual guidance and enlightenment. This is where an ongoing faith formation program can rise to the occasion.

8. **See all relationships as opportunities for expressing the love of Jesus Christ**. Maturing adults need, and perhaps even crave, the warmth and connection of relationships regardless of whether they are married or single, living at home or in a care setting. Faith formation for maturing adults can raise up all relationships, regardless of how difficult they can sometimes be, as reflections of God's love in action. Maturing adults need to hear the message of love accented again and again so they can reflect the light of Christ in their everyday lives.

9. **Rise to the role of spiritual mentor-coach**. Younger persons in the faith community need the spiritual wisdom of maturing adults. At the same time, maturing adults need the encouragement and skills to carry out the role of mentor-coach.

10. **Enter into a renewed practice of prayer**. In our advancing maturity we discover new urges to find more intimate communion with the divine, and a desire for deeper connection with Jesus. Prayer, our continuous connection with God available 24/7, brings us ever further into the mystery of life, while providing the means for a more peaceful and secure existence.

Consider the following ideas for develop faith formation for the Builder Generation of older adults.

- **Spiritual Enrichment**: "spirituality of aging" programs and retreats, spiritual disciplines and practices, special worship and ritual experiences focused on older adult spiritual and religious needs, prayer groups, retreat experiences, journaling classes, rituals to acknowledge life transitions, and healing services

- **Learning**: book clubs, adult education classes, Bible study classes and groups, small group faith sharing, life review classes, seminars on "end-of-life" issues, trips to museums and other learning venues

- **Nutrition and Wellness:** exercise programs and groups, "walking" together groups, daily exercise resources, good nutrition classes led by a qualified nutritionist, cooking classes for preparing meals with a balanced diet, modeling good nutrition in church meals, nutrition resources

- **Community:** social activities, dinners, travel to religious sites, pilgrimages, intergenerational relationships and programming, trips, intergenerational coaching and mentoring, "movies with a message" programs, field trips

- **Service:** tutoring children, "foster" grandparent program, service projects—local and global, ministry within the church community

---

Works Cited

Johnson, Richard P. "Shaping a New Vision of Faith Formation for Maturing Adults: Sixteen Fundamental Tasks." *Lifelong Faith Journal* 1/1, Spring 2007.

Johnson, Richard. *Parish Ministry for Maturing Adults*. New London: Twenty-Third, 2007.

Strategies

Use the following faith formation strategies and customize them for the particular needs and perspectives of Baby Boomers:

- Faith Formation through the Life of the Church
- Faith Formation using Digital Media and Web Technologies
- Intergenerational Faith Formation
- Milestones Faith Formation
- Faith Formation in Christian Practices
- Transforming the World: Engagement in and Formation for Service and Mission
- Spiritual Formation
- Multi-Ethnic Faith Formation
- Empowering the Community to Share their Faith
- Interfaith Education and Dialogue

Resources

Chittister, Joan. *The Gift of Years: Growing Older Gracefully.* New York: Bluebridge, 2008.

Gentzler, Richard H. *Aging and Ministry in the Twenty-First Century: An Inquiry Approach.* Nashville: Discipleship Resources, 2008.

Gallagher, David P. *Senior Adult Ministry in the Twenty-First Century.* Loveland: Group, 2002.

Grenz, Linda L. *Transforming Disciples.* New York: Church, 2008.

"Growing Old in America: Expectations vs. Reality." June 29, 2009. Pew Research Center. (http://pewresearch.org/pubs/1269/aging-survey-expectations-versus-reality)

Hanson, Amy. "Breaking Down the Age Barriers: How Churches are Becoming Intentionally Intergenerational." Leadership Network. (www.www.leadnet.org/Resources_Downloads.asp)

Hanson, Amy. "Churches Responding to the Age Way: Top Innovations in Older Adult Ministry." Leadership Network. (www.www.leadnet.org/Resources_Downloads.asp)

Johnson, Richard. *Parish Ministry for Maturing Adults.* New London: Twenty-Third, 2007.

Vogel, Linda. "Creating Learning Environments for Mature Adults that Foster Creating and Faith Formation." *Christian Education Journal*, Series 3, 5/2.

Websites

Christian Association Serving Adult Ministries Network: http://gocasa.org

Older Adult Ministries (United Methodist Church): www.gbod.org/site/c.nhLRJ2PMKsG/b.3784737/k.7977/Older_Adult_Ministries.htm

Senior Adult Ministry (Reformed Church in America): www.rca.org/sslpage.aspx?pid=1743

Senior Adult Ministry (Johnson Institute): www.senioradultministry.com

Milestones Faith Formation

Faith formation around milestones, sacramental celebrations, and life transitions provides an excellent way to promote the spiritual and faith growth of all ages and generations, enhance family faith practice at home, and strengthen people's engagement in the church community or invite people to join or rejoin the church community.

First, churches can develop lifelong faith formation around the significant lifecycle milestones, sacramental celebrations, and transitions in the lives of individuals and families across the whole life span from birth to death. Second, churches can develop multi-faceted faith formation (learning, worship/ritual, faith practices) around lifecycle milestones, sacramental celebrations, and life transitions to deepen people's faith, strengthen their engagement in church life, and equip them with practices for living their faith. Third, churches can utilize lifecycle milestones, sacramental celebrations, and life transitions to develop relationships with those who are not actively engaged in the church community. Milestones faith formation provides an important means to address the religious and spiritual needs of all four scenarios.

Lifelong faith formation centered on milestones.

Churches can fashion a plan for lifelong faith formation for home and church around congregational, lifecycle (individual or family), and annual milestones. Congregational milestones include: baptism, welcoming young children to worship, first communion, presentation of Bibles, confirmation, marriage, funeral, commissioning members for ministries and mission trips, and much more. Lifecycle milestones include: entering a new stage of schooling, graduations (middle school, high school, college, or graduate school), getting a driver's license, leaving home for college or the military, first home or apartment, new career or job, moving, retirement, death of a family member, and much more. Annual milestones include birthdays, anniversaries, start of the school year (blessing backpacks), seasons of the church year (Advent, Christmas, Lent, Holy Week), and much more.

A milestones plan for church and home for the first two decades of life could be developed in the following way:

Age	Milestone
Birth	Baptism
Yearly	Anniversary of Baptism
2–5 years old	Prayer
2–5 years old	Welcoming Young Children to Worship
5 years old	Entering School
Yearly	Blessing of the Backpacks
1st–2nd grade	Money & Being a Steward (Allowance)
2nd–3rd grade	First Communion
3rd–4th grade	Bible Presentation
4th–5th grade	Sexuality ("My Body, God's Gift")
5th–6th grade	Entering Middle School
8th grade	Graduation
Teens	Confirmation
Teens	Driver's License
12th grade	Graduation

Multi-faceted faith formation for each milestone.

Churches can incorporate and integrate the following essential elements to provide a multi-faceted faith formation for individuals, couples, families around each milestone:

1. a ritual celebration or a blessing marking the milestone with the whole church community
2. a home ritual celebration or blessing marking the milestone
3. a learning program, often for the whole family or intergenerational, that prepares the individual and the whole family for the milestone and for faith practice at home
4. a tangible, visible reminder or symbol of the occasion being marked
5. resources to support continuing faith growth and practice after the milestone

Example: Plan milestones faith formation that includes: (1) preparation for marking or celebrating a milestone, (2) the experience or celebration of the milestone, and (3) follow-up after the milestone. A milestones plan includes congregational activities and individual/home activities. For example, developing a milestones plan for marriage could include the following elements:

1. Education: marriage course or workshop (theology, life skills, faith practices)
2. Ritual: preparation for the marriage ritual
3. Marriage ceremony
4. Connection to the community: prayers at Sunday worship for the married couple (before and after the ceremony); a "Book of Blessings" from the congregation to the married couple with prayers and words of support and encouragement
5. Continued support: monthly married couples small group meeting; online resources for married couples at the parish web site, a free magazine subscription for the first year of marriage, monthly e-newsletter for married couples
6. Reunion: a reunion breakfast or dinner for newly married couples every six months for the first several years of marriage
7. Anniversary: celebrating marriage anniversaries each month at Sunday worship with a special remembrance and blessing; sending a note of congratulations and a prayer on the anniversary of marriage
8. Resources: Bible readings and reflections for married couples, prayers for a new couple, suggestions for starting a faith-filled home life, ways to be involved in the faith community, ways to be involved in service and justice ministries as a couple

Moments of return.

At each stage of life, significant milestones and life transitions provide churches with "moments of return" when people who have not been involved in church life can return to the church for a ritual experience, family celebration, religious perspective on life's transitions, encouragement, and/or comfort and support. By maximizing these opportunities churches are nurturing people's faith and welcoming them back into the life of the faith community. Marriage, baptism, moments of sickness (personal, family, friends), the death of a loved one, and life decisions are all important milestones or life transitions that provide an excellent opportunity for "moments of return." Marriage and baptism present special opportunities to build a relationship with young adult couples that can lead to an invitation to participate in a church program to guide them in becoming spiritually committed or in renewing their faith as a foundation for deeper growth and more active engagement with the church community. Adulthood is especially filled with transitions: geographic relocations, family formation and re-formation, career changes, empty nests, unanticipated illness, divorce, and the loss of loved ones. In times of transition, people can experience feelings of disorientation and tend to question personal priorities; they may seek to "finish unfinished business" or develop new dimensions of their lives.

Resources

Faith Stepping Stones. Faith Inkubators. (online resource: www.faithink.com).
Family Faith Celebrations. Loveland: Group, 2010. (http://familyfaithcelebrations.group.com)
Haynes, Brian. *Shift—What It Takes to Finally Reach Families Today.* Loveland: Group, 2009.
Keeley, Laura and Robert J. *Celebrating the Milestones of Faith: A Guide for Churches.* Grand Rapids: Faith Alive Christian Resources, 2009.
Keeley, Robert J. *Shaped by God: Twelve Essential Practices for Nurturing Faith in Children, Youth, and Adults.* Grand Rapids: Faith Alive, 2010.
Milestones Ministry Manual for Home and Congregation. Bloomington: Vibrant Faith Ministries, 2007. (www.vibrantfaith.org)

Websites

Faith Inkubators: www.faithink.com
Group Publishing: http://familyfaithcelebrations.group.com
Legacy Milestones (Brian Haynes): www.legacymilestones.com
Vibrant Faith Ministries: www.vibrantfaith.org

Faith Formation in Christian Practices

Churches can offer people of all ages a compelling vision of a Christian way of life that is worth living and then guide them in developing that way of life. The recovery of historic Christian practices—honoring the body, discernment, dying well, forgiving, healing, hospitality, keeping Sabbath, managing household life, praying, reading the Bible, testimony and witness, transforming the world (caring for creation, doing justice, peacemaking, serving), singing our lives—provides a way to shape and focus faith formation for all ages. These are practices in which Christian communities have engaged over the years and across many cultures. Christian practices have helped people to understand their continuity with the Christian tradition—an important matter during this time of change and in the midst of a culture infatuated with what is new. These Christian practices have endured over time and can help contemporary people to treasure their continuity with the past. Faith formation in Christian practices equips people to apply these practices to everyday life in our own time and place. Those who embrace Christian practices engage in them in the light of God's presence and in response to God's grace as it is known in Jesus Christ.

Churches can make Christian practices central to faith formation for all ages and generations, at church and home, by focusing on these historic Christian practices. Craig Dykstra writes,

In my view, an essential task of education in faith is to teach all the basic practices of the Christian faith. The fundamental aim of Christian education in all its forms, varieties, and settings should be that individuals—and indeed whole communities—learn these practices, be drawn into participation in them, learn to do them with increasingly deepened understanding and skill, learn to extend them more broadly and fully in their own lives and into their world, and learn to correct them, strengthen them, and improve them. (Dykstra, 71)

Christian practices can be incorporated into all of church life and faith formation through a holistic formation process of teaching the practice, listening to God's Word and celebrating the practice at worship, experiencing the practice in the life of the church community, living/acting on the practice at home and in the world, and reflecting upon the lived experience. Churches can form people in Christian practices through educational programs, apprenticeships, and immersion experiences that give people a firsthand experience of a Christian practice, equip people to live the Christian practice in their daily lives, and guide reflection on living the practices. Faith formation can offer a wide variety of programs for all ages and generations to teach Christian practices, such as family and intergenerational programs, summer camps, workshops, courses, retreats, children's Liturgy of the Word and discussions after Sunday worship, field trips, action projects, and small groups.

As churches become intentional about Christian faith practices, a renewed sense of identity and mission is fostered in the whole community. Engaging in Christian practices elevates the sense of intentionality throughout the congregation that leads to greater vitality and spiritual depth. The church becomes intentional about teaching practices by how it lives—teaching the practice of hospitality by how it welcomes the stranger, teaching about the place and significance of Scripture by how it is read in worship, treated in sermons, and held in the communal and personal lives of church members.

IDEAS

Formation in Christian practices.

Churches can design educational programs for all ages and generations that are designed intentionally to teach people how to live the Christian practices in their daily lives. Utilize a learning process that incorporates the following elements in an educational program:

- *Yearning*: tap into people's hunger for living meaningfully using real-life stories.
- *Reflecting*: give people an opportunity to become aware of how they experience

the hunger for the Christian practice in their own lives, and how they may already be living this practice.

- *Exploring*: present the biblical teaching on the practice, how the practice addresses basic human need and hungers, and why the practice is important for living a Christian life.
- *Living*: provide people with a variety of ways to live the Christian practice and integrate the practice into their daily lives.

A variety of different program formats, tailored to needs of different ages and generations, can be used to teach Christian practices: family and intergenerational programs, courses and workshops, retreats, summer programs (Vacation Bible School and summer camps), youth meetings, small group learning, and Bible study groups. For example, by organizing Christian practices small groups with each one focused on a different Christian practice, a church can offer people a variety of learning topics on different days of the week, at different times of the day, and in a variety of places (home, restaurant, coffee shops) that can fit their busy lives. A church can publish, in print and online, a menu of Christian practice groups, times, and places.

A church can develop a one-year plan Christian practices faith formation plan which integrates a monthly intergenerational learning model for all ages with a connection to the Sunday worship (Scripture readings, music, and sermon), household Christian practice activities, and a churchwide "practices project." In addition the monthly Christian practice can also be taught in other settings such as a youth meeting and small groups. Here's an example of a one-year plan on the theme of "Living Faith: Real Faith for Real Life."

September: Caring for the Body

October: Celebrating Life

November: Discernment

December: Eating Well

January: Forgiving

February: Keeping the Sabbath

March: Managing Household Life

April: Praying Well

May: Reading the Bible

June: Transforming the World

(This example uses the *Living Well: Christian Practices for Everyday Life* resource.)

Apprenticeships.

Churches can develop Christian practice apprenticeships where people of all ages can learn how live a practice from "Practice Mentors"—living embodiments of a Christian practice, such as of service or hospitality or prayer. Structure learning opportunities around "Practice Mentors" in individualized and small group settings where mentors guide people in learning about the practice from Scripture and the tradition, doing the practice with them, and reflecting upon the lived experience of the practice. For example, if people wanted to learn how to serve people in need at the local homeless shelter, they can accompany the "practice mentor" when he or she works at the shelter, and learn about homelessness and the practice of hospitality and serving others. Each apprenticeship can include a study component with independent reading from the Bible and descriptions of service. This model of mentoring can be applied across the entire church and become integral to all learning programs in the curriculum.

Christian practice immersion experiences.

Churches can develop immersion experiences for people of all ages using the faith community's lived experience of the Christian practices. Each immersion experience begins with a direct experience of the practice—within the church or in the wider community—followed by reflection on the experience, education about the practice, and resources for living the practice in daily life. Churches can offer a variety of immersion experiences throughout the year in various program formats and timeframes, or integrate immersion experiences into an existing program. Immersion experiences can include field trips to see and experience Christian practices in action, such as dying well at a hospice center or praying at a monastery or hospitality at a soup kitchen or homeless shelter.

Christian practices in current faith formation programming

- **A Focus for the Whole Year**: Make a Christian practice a focus for the whole year through all education programs, worship, preaching, and service/action, for example: reading the Bible, praying, hospitality, and transforming the world.

- **A Focus for a Season**: Make a Christian practice the focus for a season of the year through all education programs, worship, preaching, and service/action, for example: during the Lenten Season focus on the practice that is in keeping with the theology, liturgies, and Scripture readings of the season, such as forgiving or discernment or praying or transforming the World.

- **A Focus for a Month**: Focus on a Christian practice each month for a whole year or more in family-intergenerational programming, aligned with Sunday worship and preaching, action projects, and so on. For example: If the family-intergenerational program is focused on Ritual-Celebration-Worship the following practices could become the focus of learning programs: celebrating life, eating well, keeping Sabbath, praying, and reading the Bible.

- **A Connection to Worship**: Connect the Sunday lectionary readings and preaching to Christian practices and offer educational programs on Christian practices to prepare for or follow-up on the particular Sunday.

- **A Connection to Milestones**: Connect Christian practices to milestones and life transitions. Every milestone presents an opportunity to teach a Christian practice that directly connects to what is happening in the life of the individual or family. For example, confirmation (or high school graduation) is for teaching the practice of discernment and transforming the world; marriage is an opportunity for teaching managing household life.

Resources

Allender, Dan. *Sabbath*. Nashville: Thomas Nelson, 2009.

Barton, Ruth Haley. *Sacred Rhythm: Arranging Our Lives for Spiritual Transformation*. Downers Grove: Intervarsity, 2006.

Bass, Dorothy C., editor. *Practicing Our Faith: A Way of Life for a Searching People*. Revised Edition. San Francisco: Jossey-Bass, 2010.

Bass, Dorothy C. *Receiving the Day: Christian Practices for Opening the Gift of Time*. San Francisco: Jossey-Bass, 2001.

Benson, Robert. *In Constant Prayer*. Nashville: Thomas Nelson, 2008.

Chittister, Joan. *The Liturgical Year*. Nashville: Thomas Nelson, 2009.

Dykstra, Craig. *Growing in the Life of Faith: Education and Christian Practices*. Second Edition. Louisville: Westminster John Knox, 2005.

Foster, Charles. *The Sacred Journey*. Nashville: Thomas Nelson, 2010.

Gallagher, Nora. *The Sacred Meal*. Nashville: Thomas Nelson, 2009.

Hicks, Douglas A. *Money Enough: Everyday Practices for Living Faithfully in the Global Economy*. San Francisco: Jossey-Bass, 2010.

Jung, L Shannon. *Sharing Food: Christian Practices for Enjoyment*. Minneapolis: Fortress Press, 2006.

Keeley, Robert J. *Shaped by God: Twelve Essential Practices for Nurturing Faith in Children, Youth, and Adults*. Grand Rapids: Faith Alive, 2010.

LeBlanc, Douglas. *Tithing*. Nashville: Thomas Nelson, 2010.

Long, Thomas. *Testimony: Talking Ourselves into Being Christian*. San Francisco: Jossey-Bass, 2004.

McLaren, Brian. *Finding Our Way Again: The Return of the Ancient Practices*. Nashville: Thomas Nelson, 2008.

McKnight, Scott. *Fasting*. Nashville: Thomas Nelson, 2009.

Newman, Elizabeth. *Untamed Hospitality: Welcoming God and Other Strangers*. Grand Rapids: Brazos, 2007.

Peterson, Margaret Kim. *Keeping House: The Litany of Everyday Life*. San Francisco: Jossey-Bass, 2007.

Paulsell, Stephanie. *Honoring the Body: Meditations on a Christian Practice*. San Francisco: Jossey-Bass, 2003.

Pohl, Christine D. *Making Room: Recovering Hospitality as a Christian Tradition*. Grand Rapids: Eerdmans, 1999.

Saliers, Don, and Emily Saliers. *A Song to Sing, A Life to Live: Reflections on Music as Spiritual Practice*. San Francisco: Jossey-Bass, 2005.

Wirzba, Norman. *Living the Sabbath*. Grand Rapids: Brazos, 2006.

Wolfteich, Claire. *Lord Have Mercy: Praying for Justice with Conviction and Humility*. San Francisco: Jossey-Bass, 2006.

All Ages

Faith Practices. United Church of Christ. Cleveland: Pilgrim, 2010. (www.faithpractices.org) (Online resources for every age group and setting in your congregation with at least twenty-four different faith practices—each practice has more than six hundred activities, fifty activities per age group)

Family and Adult

Martineau, Mariette. *Living Well Children's Workbook*. Naugatuck: LifelongFaith Associates, 2009. (www.LifelongFaith.com)

Roberto, John, editor. *Living Well: Christian Practices for Everyday Life*. Naugatuck: LifelongFaith Associates, 2009. (www.LifelongFaith.com)

Youth

Bass, Dorothy C. and Don Richter, editors. *Way to Live*. Nashville: Upper Room, 2002.

Young Adult

Bass, Dorothy C. and Susan R. Briehl, editors. *On Our Way: Christian Practices for Living a Whole Life*. Nashville: Upper Room, 2010.

Adult

Living the Good Life Together: A Study of Christian Character in Community. Nashville: Abingdon. (www.livingthegoodlifetogether.com)

Websites

Faith Practices (United Church of Christ): www.faithpractices.org

Living Well: Christian Practices for Everyday Life (LifelongFaith Associates): www.LifelongFaith.com

Practicing our Faith: www.practicingourfaith.org

Way to Live: www.waytolive.org

Transforming the World: Engagement in and Formation for Service and Mission

Church can place engagement in mission and service at the center of all of its efforts. Tapping into the tremendous interest and passion in all generations, but especially the youngest, for service to the world, faith formation can educate and empower families and individuals of all ages for the Christian mission to the community and world: serving the poor and vulnerable, working for justice to ensure the rights of all people, being a peacemaker, and caring for creation. As Jim Wallis observes, "Two of the most powerful forces in the world right now are service and spirituality. The growing influence of both is evident almost everywhere, and together they provide the most potent combination for changing our communities. Service and spirituality are growing streams of energy, which, as they begin to flow together, could create a mighty river of action."

First, churches can make formation for service and engagement in local and global action projects an essential component of faith formation for all age groups and families every year: serving the poor and vulnerable, working for justice to ensure the rights of all people, being a peacemaker, and caring for creation. An annual "mission involvement catalog" can be created, in print and online, to provide descriptions of the diversity of projects.

Second, churches can incorporate an educational component into all service/ mission projects that includes knowledge of the justice issues being addressed, the teachings of Scripture and the Christian tradition on the issues, skills for the specific service/mission project, and reflection on the service/mission involvement.

Third, churches can sponsor local and global service/mission projects that are designed for the participation of people from the wider community, providing a public presence of the church in the community—from local efforts to feed the hungry, house the homeless, and improve education by adopting a public school to global projects that build schools, care for AIDS victims, and provide wells for water. The church partners with other churches and agencies to establish a serving presence in the community where people who are passionate about transforming the world, but not involved in church life, can work side-by-side with church members and see the gospel in action.

IDEAS

Service and mission projects for all ages.

Churches can organize service/mission projects for individuals of all ages, the whole family, and multiple generations that are developmental in scope with projects geared to different levels of involvement and challenge:

- local mission projects lasting anywhere from a few hours to one day in length
- short-term mission trips lasting anywhere from two to five days and requiring an overnight stay on location
- weeklong mission trips within the United States as well as to foreign countries, designed for those who are ready to take the next big step in service
- global expedition trips of ten to fourteen days that provide the opportunity to be immersed for a longer period in the targeted community and culture
- personalized small group mission trips, organized around the interests and time of the group

Research and utilize existing projects and organizations—locally, nationally, and globally—to offer a variety of involvements for people of all ages and for families at different times during the year and in varying lengths. Develop an annual "catalog" of all service/mission opportunities for children and parents, teenagers, adults, families, and all generations. Integrate service/mission projects into the existing faith formation programming for families, children, teens, and adults or build faith formation programming around service/mission projects.

Example: Ginghamsburg Church (Adult Mission Trips)
http://ginghamsburg.org/missions

Education and reflection with service and mission projects.
Churches can incorporate social analysis and theological reflection with action projects to guide people in developing a deeper understanding of the causes of injustice and the teachings of Scripture and the Christian tradition. The process includes: (1) connecting to a social issue (Experience)—how people are personally affected by an issue or how the issue affects others; (2) exploring the social issue (Social Analysis) to understand the causes and underlying factors that promote or sustain the issue; (3) reflecting upon the teachings of Scripture and the Christian tradition (Theological Reflection) to develop a faith perspective on the social issue and how people of faith can address the issue; and (4) developing ways to address the issue (Action) by working for social change and serving those in need as individuals, groups, communities, and/or organizations.

The process can begin with a service involvement, leading to social analysis and theological reflection *or* it can begin with people's experience of a social issue, leading to analysis of the issue, connecting the issue to the faith tradition, and developing action projects of direct service to those in need, and social change and advocacy.

Resources

Holland, Joseph and Peter Henriot. *Social Analysis—Linking Faith and Justice.* Maryknoll: Orbis, 1983.

Semmens, Dave, O. Carm. *The Pastoral Circle—Explained.* Video. Washington, DC: Center of Concern. (www.educationforjustice.org/interact/PastoralCircle/player.html)

Wisen, Frans Jozef Servaas, Peter Henriot, and Rodrigo Mejia. *The Pastoral Circle Revisited: A Critical Quest for Truth And Transformation.* Maryknoll, Orbis, 2005.

Annual churchwide service project.

Churches can mobilize the whole faith community through an annual churchwide justice and service project with local-global connections. Focus on a project, such as adopting a local or global action project organized by an organization, or focus on an annual theme, such as poverty, care for creation, or peacemaking. For each annual theme develop a comprehensive set of programs and resources (often available from organizations you partner with) for all age groups, families, and the whole community, including:

- worship and prayer experiences focused on the particular theme or project
- educational sessions including social analysis of the issues and reflection on the teachings of Scripture and the Christian tradition
- household activities on the theme or project: prayers, learning resources, action suggestions
- local action projects, if you focus on a theme
- international action projects, if you focus on a theme
- a website with the resources, activities, action projects, and features to allow people to share what they are doing
- special presentations by experts on the issues and by people engaged in action on the issue

An example of this type of churchwide involvement is *Faith in Action Day* sponsored by World Vision and Outreach, Inc. *Faith in Action* is a four-week, churchwide campaign that creates an outward focus and a heart to serve in your congregation. *Faith in Action* culminates on a Sunday on which the entire congregation engages in service projects in and with the community. (www.putyourfaithinaction.org)

Service with the wider community.

Churches can sponsor local and global service/mission projects that are designed for the participation of people from the wider community, providing a public presence of the church in the community—from local efforts to feed the hungry, house the homeless, and improve education by adopting a public school to global projects that build schools, care for AIDS victims, and provide wells for water. The church partners with other churches and agencies to establish a serving presence in the community where people who are passionate about transforming the world, but not involved in church life, can work side-by-side with church members and see the gospel in action.

Study-action small groups.

Churches can develop small groups that combine study of justice and social issues with experiential hands-on action projects. Groups can be organized around issues or themes. One example of a small group program that weaves study, small group learning, retreat experiences, and action projects is JustFaith (www.justfaith.org).

JustFaith is a thirty-week justice formation and transformation process that focuses on discipleship—engagement in the life of Jesus—and the call to be about God's dream of justice and compassion in a world scarred by the domestic and global crisis called poverty. Meeting weekly, small groups of 10–15 people employ books, videos, discussion, prayer, retreats and hands-on experiences. Opening and closing retreats are part of the commitment each participant makes to the group. Four immersion experiences provide face-to-face contact with people living on the margins of society, and include social analysis and spiritual/theological reflection. The intent of Just-Faith is to provide a tapestry of learning opportunities that emphasize and enliven the healing work of God's compassion found in scripture, church history, teaching, and faithful witnesses.

Resources

Barker, Ash. *Make Poverty Personal: Taking the Poor as Seriously as the Bible Does.* Grand Rapids: Baker, 2009.

Cannon, Mae Else. *Social Justice Handbook—Small Steps for a Better World.* Downers Grove: Intervarsity, 2009.

Clark, Chap and Kara E. Powell. *Deep Justice in a Broken World: Helping Your Kids Serve Others and Right the Wrongs around Them.* Grand Rapids: Zondervan, 2007.

Clawson, Julie. *Everyday Justice—The Global Impact of Our Daily Choices.* Downers Grove: Intervarsity Press, 2009.

Daley-Harris, Shannon, Jeffrey Keenan, and Karen Speerstra. *Our Day to End Poverty: Twenty-Four Ways You Can Make a Difference.* San Francisco: Berrett-Koehler, 2007.

Delio, Ilia, Keith Douglass Warner, O.F.M., and Pamela Wood. *Care for Creation*: A *Franciscan Spirituality of the Earth.* Cincinnati: St. Anthony Messenger Press, 2009.

Greer, Peter and Phil Smith. *The Poor Will Be Glad—Joining the Revolution to Lift the World Out of Poverty.* Grand Rapids: Zondervan, 2009.

Haugen, Gary A. *Just Courage: God's Great Expedition for the Restless Christian.* Downers Grove, IL: IVP Books, 2008.

Jegen, Mary Evelyn. *Just Peacemakers: An Introduction to Peace and Justice.* New York: Paulist Press, 2006.

McLaren, Brian. *Everything Must Change: Jesus, Global Crises, and a Revolution of Hope.* Nashville: Thomas Nelson, 2007.

McLaren, Brian, Elisa Padilla, and Ashley Bunting Seeber. *The Justice Project.* Grand Rapids: Baker Books, 2009.

Massaro S.J., Thomas. *Living Justice: Catholic Social Teaching in Action.* (Revised Edition) Lanham: Rowman and Littlefield, 2008.

Peters, Rebecca Todd, and Elizabeth Hinson-Hasty, editors. *To Do Justice.* Louisville: Westminster John Knox, 2008.

Powell, Kara E. and Brad M. Griffin. *Deep Justice Journeys: Moving from Mission Trips to Missional Living.* Grand Rapids: Zondervan, 2009.

Powell, Kara E. and Brad M. Griffin. *Deep Justice Journeys: Fifty Activities to Move from Mission Trips to Missional Living.* Grand Rapids: Zondervan, 2009.

Richter, Don. *Mission Trips That Matter: Embodied Faith for the Sake of the World.* Nashville: Upper Room Books, 2008.

Rizzo, Dino. *Servolution: Starting a Church Revolution through Serving*. Grand Rapids: Zondervan, 2009.

Russaw, Rick and Eric Sawnson. *The Externally Focused Church*. Loveland: Group, 2004.

Russaw, Rick and Eric Sawnson. *The Externally Focused Quest: Becoming the Best Church for the Community*. San Francisco: Jossey-Bass. 2010.

Sagawa, Shirley. *The American Way to Change: How National Service and Volunteers Are Transforming America*. San Francisco: Jossey Bass, 2010.

Service-Learning in Community-Based Organizations: A Practical Guide to Starting and Sustaining High-Quality Programs. Minneapolis: Search Institute. (Download from www. search-institute.org)

Sleeth, J. Matthew *Serve God, Save the Planet: A Christian Call to Action*. Grand Rapids: Zondervan, 2007.

Stearns, Richard. *The Hole in Our Gospel: The Answer that Changed My Life and Might Just Change the World*. Nashville: Thomas Nelson, 2009.

Thompson, J. Milburn. *Introducing Catholic Social Thought*. Maryknoll: Orbis Books, 2010.

Van Schooneveld, Amber. *Hope Lives: A Journey of Restoration*. Loveland: Group, 2008.

Websites
Catholic Relief Services: www.crs.org
Catholics Confront Global Poverty: www.usccb.org/sdwp/globalpoverty
Center of Concern: www.educationforjustice.org
Church World Service: churchworldservice.org
Compassion International: www.compassion.com
Externally Focused Network: http://www.externallyfocusednetwork.com/
Habitat for Humanity: www.habitat.org
Heifer Project: www.heifer.org
Inspired to Serve—An Online Toolkit for Interfaith Action: www.inspiredtoserve.org
International Justice Mission: www.ijm.org
Lifetree Adventures: www.lifetreeadventures.com
NETWORK: www.networklobby.org
ONE Campaign: www.one.org
Saddleback Church: The PEACE Plan (www.saddleback.com/lakeforest/adults/peace) (www.thepeaceplan.com)
World Vision: worldvision.org

Spiritual Formation

Churches can respond to the hunger of people of all ages for growing in relationship and intimacy with God and exploring more deeply the life of the Spirit by providing formation in spiritual disciplines and practices. Churches can engage individuals and families in learning about and practicing historic Christian spiritual disciplines, and in developing a "rule of life" that allows for regular space for the practice of the spiritual disciplines. Churches can offer spiritual formation for individuals, families, and multiple generations that includes education in the spiritual disciplines and practices, retreat experiences, spiritual guides who serve as mentors on the spiritual journey, and resources on the spiritual disciplines and practices.

IDEAS

Formation in spiritual practices and disciplines.

Churches can develop the spiritual life of all age groups and families through the intentional teaching of spiritual practices and disciplines in age-appropriate ways. Focus on essential spiritual practices such as Lectio Divina, Scripture reflection, spiritual reading, contemplation, fixed-hour prayer, the examen, solitude and silence, Sabbath, praying with art and music, discernment, fasting, and prayer styles and traditions. Select one practice or develop a program with multiple spiritual practices. Utilize a variety of models to teach spiritual practices and disciplines, such as individualized growth plans, online spiritual formation centers and resources, one-on-one spiritual direction or mentoring, small group spiritual formation, retreats, Lenten programs, and large group programs (courses, workshops).

Spiritual formation small groups for teens, young adults, and adults provide a flexible way to explore and experience the spiritual practices and disciplines, and apply them to daily life. Offer small groups in a variety settings (church, home, coffee shop) and times, and lengths suited to people's lifestyles. Offer a variety of content topics such as "Spiritual Disciplines Bible Study Groups" focused on the core spiritual practices in the Bible (see *Spiritual Disciplines Companion: Bible Studies and Practices to Transform Your Soul* by Jan Johnson); and small groups focused on a single spiritual practice, such as Sabbath, prayer, contemplation, fasting, Scripture reflection, pilgrimage, discernment, and liturgical year.

Set aside a prayer room stocked with resources about prayer and spiritual practices and connect people to online spiritual formation and prayer resources, as well as to online communities that nurture spiritual formation.

Churchwide program for spiritual formation.

Churches can engage all ages in the congregation in a small group spiritual formation process that explores spiritual practices, and develops new daily patterns that will open people's lives to a deepening relationship with God. This can be done in a small group format or in more structured teaching format. One example of the small group format is Companions in Christ (Upper Room Books), a twenty-eight-week study of five topics: spiritual formation, scripture, prayer, vocation, and spiritual companionship. Each week of study includes a reading by a recognized author in spiritual formation, reflection questions, and daily scripture readings to guide private reflection, culminating with a two-hour group session where people share their thoughts, reflect together, and take part in diverse group learning experiences. Exploring the Way (Upper Room) is structured more as a class, meets for just one hour each week, and includes 6 weeks of sessions. The participants are asked to engage in personal reading and reflection after (not before) the group meeting. Topics include: grace, blessedness, forgiveness, transforming discipleship, prayer, and discernment. The Way of the Child (Upper Room) is designed for ages six to eleven, calls children to recognize their own relationship with God and to create quiet space in which to listen, and includes 39 modules that can be used as a whole or in sections. The Way of Pilgrimage is a five-volume, thirty-week experiential, peer study with video, designed for youth in high school and college freshmen, that engages them in ancient spiritual practices of prayer and contemplation, helping them discover new ways to go deeper spiritually. Topics include: way of pilgrimage, the Bible, prayer, companions on the pilgrimage, and stepping into the world.

Resources

Chambers, Sally, Jonathon Norman, Gavin Richardson, Kyle Dugan, Craig Mitchell, Ciona Rouse, Jenny Youngman, Steve Matthews and Kara Lassen. *The Way of Pilgrimage.* Nashville: Upper Room, 2007.

Dawson, Gerrit Scott, Adele J. González, E. Glenn Hinson, Rueben P. Job, Marjorie J. Thompson, and Wendy M. Wright. *Companions in Christ: A Small-Group Experience in Spiritual Formation.* Revised Edition. Nashville: Upper Room, 2006.

McGregor, Wynn. *Companions in Christ: The Way of the Child.* Nashville: Upper Room, 2006.

Website

Companions in Christ: www.companionsinchrist.org

Spiritual formation in all faith formation programming.

Churches can utilize existing faith formation programming with children, teens, adults, and families to teach spiritual practices and disciplines. Select a spiritual practice as a focus for each month and incorporate the teaching, demonstration, and experience of the practice in all faith formation programming and church meetings, provide a resources for individuals and families to live the practice in daily life (print or online), reinforce the practice through Sunday worship. Introduce prayer, silence, and a slower pace to faith formation programs and to all congregational meetings and programs. Incorporate prayer practices, contemplation, reflection, and discernment into service projects and mission trips.

A contemplative approach to faith formation.

Churches can nurture the spiritual life of all ages and generations by infusing a contemplative approach to faith formation—spiritual disciplines and contemplative practices—into all faith formation programming. Utilize the seven principles and their corresponding practices developed by Mark Yaconelli and the Youth Ministry and Spirituality Project in developing a contemplative approach to faith formation.

- **Sabbath**. A contemplative approach is grounded in a Christian community committed to the sacred balance between work and rest. A life that honors Sabbath rest helps us to be more in touch with our heart and soul, more aware of the Spirit of God, and more available for relationships of love.

- **Prayer**. A contemplative approach is rooted in desire for intimacy with God in Christ through a life of prayer. Practice and teach many forms of prayer, especially regular periods of *contemplative* prayer in order to be healed, inspired, and guided by the power of the Holy Spirit.

- **Covenant Community.** A contemplative approach is practiced within a covenant community of Christian disciples. Encourage, support, and practice small covenant groups who sense a common call to spiritual growth and meet regularly in covenant communities for sharing, prayer, Scripture study, and discernment.

- **Accompaniment.** A contemplative approach is focused on discipleship through accompaniment, for example, initiating young persons into mature Christian faith through relationships with elders who join them in living the way of authentic discipleship and offer them friendship, guidance, and listening hearts as they make the passage through adolescence into spiritual maturity.

- **Discernment.** A contemplative approach is guided by discernment. Teach and practice the disciplines of individual and group discernment so that people can learn to be fully available and responsive to the movement of God's grace in their covenant communities.

- **Hospitality.** A contemplative approach seeks to welcome, bless, and joyfully integrate all people into the whole church community—the full inclusion of people and their many gifts into every dimension of church life: worship, teaching, proclamation, fellowship, and service.

- **Authentic Action.** A contemplative approach seeks to engage people in authentic actions that reflect God's mercy, justice, and peace. Communal practices of Sabbath, prayer, discernment, and accompaniment find their fulfillment in actions with youth that make visible the gifts of the Holy Spirit.

(For a complete description of the seven principles see chapter 4 in *Growing Souls* by Mark Yaconelli.)

Resources

Yaconelli, Mark. *Contemplative Youth Ministry: Practicing the Presence of Jesus.* Grand Rapids: Zondervan, 2006.

_____. *Growing Souls: Experiments in Contemplative Youth Ministry.* Grand Rapids: Zondervan, 2007.

_____. *Downtown: Helping Teenagers Pray.* Grand Rapids: Zondervan, 2008.

_____. *Wonder, Fear, and Longing: A Book of Prayers.* Grand Rapids: Zondervan, 2009.

Spiritual guides or mentors.

Churches can identify people who model discipleship and live the spiritual practices to serve as spiritual mentors or guides for people of all ages on their spiritual journeys. Prepare people through a retreat experience focused on their spiritual life, spiritual practices, and guiding others on their spiritual journeys. Create a community of spiritual mentors/guides who meet regularly for sharing, prayer, Scripture study, and discernment in the service of their ministry of spiritual formation. Engage the spiritual guides or mentors in one-on-one or small group spiritual formation by adding a spiritual mentoring component to existing spiritual formation programs and small groups.

Spiritual formation opportunities for the wider community.

Churches can develop opportunities for spiritual formation by taking existing programs and activities, or creating new ones, that are targeted to spiritual seekers in the wider community. Stillpoint—A Centre for the Practice of Christian Spirituality in Oxford, England was created to serve both spiritually searching people who would not previously have considered the Christian way as a path to deepen their spiritual search, as well as people who already identify themselves as Christians but are looking for opportunities to learn practices that will deepen their interior journey. Stillpoint offers conferences, courses, classes and group work, resources, artistic and cultural events, and spiritual direction and mentoring that are open to the whole Oxford community (www.thestillpoint.org.uk).

Resources

Allender, Dan. *Sabbath*. Nashville: Thomas Nelson, 2009.

Barton, Ruth Haley. *Sacred Rhythm: Arranging Our Lives for Spiritual Transformation*. Downers Grove: Intervarsity, 2006.

Benson, Robert. *In Constant Prayer*. Nashville: Thomas Nelson, 2008.

Calhoun, Adele Ahlberg. *Spiritual Disciplines Handbook: Practices that Transform Us*. Downers Grove: Intervarsity, 2005.

Caliguire, Mindy. *Discovering Soul Care*. Downers Grove: Intervarsity, 2007.

_____. *Spiritual Friendship*. Downers Grove: Intervarsity, 2007.

_____. *Simplicity*. Downers Grove: Intervarsity, 2008.

_____. *Soul Searching*. Downers Grove: Intervarsity, 2007.

Chittister, Joan. *The Liturgical Year*. Nashville: Thomas Nelson, 2009.

Foster, Richard. *Life with God: Reading the Bible for Spiritual Transformation*. San Francisco: HarperOne, 2008.

_____. *Prayer: Find the Heart's True Home*. San Francisco: Harper/San Francisco, 1992.

_____. *Celebration of Discipline: The Path to Spiritual Growth*. 20th Anniversary Issue. San Francisco: HarperCollins, 1998.

Gallagher, Nora. *The Sacred Meal*. Nashville: Thomas Nelson, 2009.

Johnson, Jan. *Spiritual Disciplines Companion: Bible Studies and Practices to Transform Your Soul*. Downers Grove: Intervarsity, 2009.

Jones, Tony. *The Sacred Way: Spiritual Practices for Everyday Life.* Grand Rapids: Zondervan, 2005.

MacBeth. Sybil. *Praying in Color: Drawing a New Path to God.* Brewster: Paraclete, 2009.

_____. *Praying in Color: Kids' Edition.* Brewster: Paraclete, 2009.

McLaren, Brian. *Finding Our Way Again: The Return of the Ancient Practices.* Nashville: Thomas Nelson, 2008.

McKnight, Scott. *Fasting.* Nashville: Thomas Nelson, 2009.

Redmont, Jane. *When in Doubt, Sing: Prayer in Daily Life.* Notre Dame: Sorin, 2008.

Rhodes, Tricia McCary. *Sacred Chaos: Spiritual Disciplines for the Life You Have.* Downers Grove: Intervarsity, 2008.

Rolheiser, Ronald. *Longing for the Holy: Spirituality for Everyday Life.* Plainfield: RENEW International, 2009. (www.renewintl.org)

Rupp, Joyce. *Prayer.* Joyce Rupp. Maryknoll: Orbis, 2007.

Stonehouse, Catherine, and Scottie May. *Listening to Children on the Spiritual Journey.* Grand Rapids: Baker Academic, 2010.

Thompson, Marjorie. *Soul Feast: An Invitation to the Christian Spiritual Life.* Westminster/John Knox, 2005.

Vennard, Jane E. *A Praying Congregation: The Art of Teaching Spiritual Practices.* Herndon: Alban Institute, 2005.

Wicks, Robert. *Prayerfulness: Awakening to the Fullness of Life.* Notre Dame: Sorin, 2009.

Wilhoit, James C. *Spiritual Formation as if the Church Mattered: Growing in Christ through Community.* Grand Rapids, Baker Academic, 2008.

Willard, Dallas. *The Divine Conspiracy.* San Francisco: HarperCollins, 1998.

Wolpert. Daniel. *Creating a Life with God: The Call of Ancient Prayer Practices.* Nashville: Upper Room, 2003.

_____. *Leading a Life with God: The Practice of Spiritual Leadership.* Nashville: Upper Room, 2003.

Yust, Karen Marie, and E. Byron Anderson. *Taught by God—Teaching and Spiritual Formation.* St. Louis: Chalice, 2006.

Websites

Metamorpha: www.metamorpha.com

Online Retreat: A 34 week retreat for Everyday Life. Creighton University. http://onlineministries.creighton.edu/CollaborativeMinistry/cmo-retreat.html

Renovare: www.renovare.us

Shalem Institute for Spiritual Formation: www.shalem.org

Soul Care (Mindy Caliguire): http://soulcare.com (Mindy Caliguire Spiritual Formation videos on YouTube: www.youtube.com/view_play_list?p=C0CEC630CFA4D9E8)

Spiritual Directors International: http://sdiworld.org/home.html (videos about spiritual direction and how to find a spiritual director)

Spirituality and Practice: www.SpiritualityandPractice.com

Transforming Center: www.thetransformingcenter.org

Triptykos: www.triptykos.com/home

Upper Room: www.UpperRoom.org

Multi-Ethnic Faith Formation

Americans are diverse in terms of race and ethnic origins. Almost every white congregation by 2020 will have at least some Latino, Asian, or African American presence. Bicultural, multicultural, and ethnic churches are fairly common today in all Christian traditions. Cultural diversity is a normal part of congregational life in the United States. The culturally diverse church can provide a healthy environment, hospitality and welcoming, and a sense of community so that people of all cultures feel inclusion and acceptance. The church can encourage ethnic festivals, religious traditions, and feasts. Ethnic religious traditions can be woven into a tapestry of church life and faith formation. All ages and generations can experience the various aspects of another culture and begin to experience its richness.

Peter Phan describes the current relationship of ethnic cultures to American society in the following way:

> What is distinctive about the newest arrivals to the United States is that they come mostly from non-European countries, especially from Africa, Asia, and Latin America, and bring with them languages, customs, and cultures vastly different from those of their host country. Most importantly, unlike their predecessors, these immigrants intend to preserve their native traditions. While working hard to move into the economic and political mainstream, culturally and religiously, these new immigrants refuse to be assimilated into the white, Anglo-Saxon culture. Rather, they want to maintain, for themselves and their descendants, their own languages, customs, and cultures. In addition to various cultures, the immigrants also bring with them a different brand of Catholicism (Christianity) and a different experience of being church. (Phan, 155–56)

Given this new approach to assimilating and inculturating, Phan presents two challenges for churches in the United States. First, churches need to help immigrants maintain and transmit, especially to their children, their languages, customs, and culture, which are the glue that binds the immigrants together. Second, churches need to embrace "inculturation," which "is the double process of incarnating the already culture-laden gospel into the various cultures and of bringing the cultures into the gospel whereby *both* the gospel and cultures are transformed and enriched" (156). Phan continues,

> Inculturation involves the interplay of five components: the message of gospel itself (divine revelation); the cultures (for example, Semitic, Hellenistic, Roman, Germanic, and so on) in which the gospel has been transmitted (the Christian Tradition); the American culture (mainly white, Anglo-Saxon, Enlightenment-inspired); the culture—predominantly pre-modern—of a

specific ethnic group (for example, the Vietnamese); and the cultures of other ethic groups (for example, African-American, Mexican, Cuban, and so on.). The areas in which inculturation takes place include all aspects of church life: liturgy, catechesis, spirituality. (Phan, 156)

Churches can develop faith formation that is inclusive of a diversity of ethnic cultures and their religious traditions and expressions: offering *culturally-specific faith formation* that inculturates the gospel message and Christian tradition so that it is proclaimed and taught in the language and culture of the people; *intercultural faith formation* that brings ethnic communities together for learning, relationship building, faith sharing, praying, serving, and celebrating; and providing a hospitable, welcoming, and *inclusive community* for people of all ethnic cultures.

Culturally-specific faith formation.
Faith formation recognizes the uniquely lived experiences, needs, and aspirations of people from each cultural ethnic community in the church, and offers culturally-specific faith formation for the ethnic communities in the church. Culturally-specific faith formation inculturates the gospel message and tradition so that it is proclaimed and taught in the language and culture of the people. It presents the teaching of the faith in a complete and authentic way in dialogue with the language, customs, and practices of those to whom the gospel is presented. The inculturation of the gospel involves listening to the culture to discover the seeds of the gospel that may already be present in the culture; knowing and respecting the essential elements and basic expressions of the culture in the lives of people; and using the language and culture of the people as a foundation to express the common faith of the gospel and Christian tradition.

Intercultural faith formation.
Faith formation offers intercultural faith formation that brings the whole church together intergenerationally for learning, relationship building, faith sharing, praying, serving, and celebrating. An essential element of intercultural faith formation is listening to the stories, perspectives, and preferences of people from the different cultures and ethnicities present in the church. Teaching skills for intercultural communication is important so that intercultural experiences will be positive and enriching for all cultures. Also important is cultivating respect for and appreciation of the cultural heritage and religious traditions of people from the different cultures in the church. These intercultural opportunities between Christians of diverse cultures, including mainstream culture, are transforming opportunities that bear the fruits of Christian unity in the spirit of a new Pentecost. Churches bring people face to face with the contrasting realities of middle class/working class, post immigrant/new immigrant, citizen/foreigner, mainstream white/Black, Hispanic/Latino, Native American, Asian, and Pacific Islander cultures. Bringing these very different realities together provides an opportunity for building the reign of God right at home.

Intercultural faith formation provides an opportunity for ethnic cultural awareness to correct ethnic and racial myths and stereotypes by providing people with accurate information on the histories, lives, and cultures of ethnic groups; facilitating the development of attitudes and values conducive to living in an ethnically diverse church and world. Intercultural faith formation can help people develop openness, flexibility, and receptivity to cultural diversity; enrich human experiences through the study of different ethnic groups; accept and prize diversity, and reduce anxieties about encountering different ethnic groups, their life styles, value preferences, and behavior patterns.

Each ethnic group teaches the whole church about what it means to be a people of faith, and the church affirms these special gifts and welcomes them into the whole community. As an example, Hispanic/Latinos bring to the church religious practices that can enrich everyone: blessings, promesas (prayer promises), the celebration of quinceanera, the altarcito (home altar), the celebration of Los Posadas in Advent, and Our Lady of Guadalupe, to name a few. They also bring to the U.S. church small Christian communities (or CEBs), a model of church from Latin America, where people meet in homes to discuss the weekly Scriptures and how best to apply them to daily life. The small Christian communities also come together to pray, learn, respond to issues of social justice, and mutually support one another.

Culturally-inclusive faith formation.

Faith formation incorporates a diversity of ethnic faith traditions and expressions into existing programming and experiences. Infuse an ethnic cultural perspective into your congregation by adjusting programs to incorporate specific content from one or more ethnic cultures, such as a prayer tradition, ritual, devotional practice, song, artwork, or story. In this sense, faith formation for all ages and generations can become culturally inclusive and expand everyone's experience of the richness of ethnic cultures.

Works Cited

Phan, Peter. "A New Way of Being Church in Asia: Lessons for the American Church." *Inculturation and the Church in North America*. T. Frank Kennedy, editor. New York: Crossroad, 2006.

Resources

Aguilera-Titus, Alejandro. "Ministry with Youth in a Culturally Diverse Church." *Leadership for Catholic Youth Ministry*. Thomas East, editor. New London: Twenty-Third, 2009.

Bowers, Laurene Beth. *Becoming a Multicultural Church*. Eugene: Wipf and Stock, 2007.

DeYmaz, Mark, and Harry Li. *Ethnic Blends: Mixing Diversity into Your Local Church*. Grand Rapids: Zondervan, 2010.

DeYmaz, Mark. *Building a Healthy Multi-Ethnic Church*. San Francisco: Jossey-Bass, 2007.

Livermore, David A. *Cultural Intelligence: Improving Your CQ to Engage Our Multicultural World*. Grand Rapids: Baker Academic, 2009. (See also: http://davidlivermore.com)

Talvacchia, Kathleen T. *Critical Minds and Discerning Hearts: A Spirituality of Multicultural Teaching*. St. Louis: Chalice, 2003.

Faith Formation for Spiritual Seekers

Churches can address the spiritual needs and hungers of people by developing a guided process for spiritually hungry people to become spiritually committed and join in small communities with other seekers for spiritual growth and support, thus creating new expressions of Christian community designed especially for spiritual seekers.

IDEAS

Formation Process for Spiritual Seekers.

Churches can offer a guided process for spiritually hungry people to become spiritually committed and join in small communities with other seekers for spiritual growth and support. One example of this process is an "Introduction to the Christian faith" program—an opportunity for people to investigate the claims of the Christian faith in an informal, no pressure, non-judgmental, and friendly environment. The emphasis is upon exploration and discovery in a relaxed and informal setting, and does not assume any background knowledge of or belief in Christianity. It can be offered in a variety of settings, formats, and times.

Alpha (http://alphausa.org) is an opportunity to explore the meaning of life in a relaxed, friendly setting. The Alpha course usually meets once per week for ten weeks, and includes a one-day or weekend getaway. Each session, people enjoy great food, laughter and learning in a fun and friendly atmosphere where no question about life or God is seen as too simple or too hostile, questions like—Is there a God? Why am I here? Where did I come from? Where am I going? Alpha is for anyone who thinks there may be more to life than meets the eye. People attend from all backgrounds, religions, and viewpoints. They come to investigate questions about the existence of God, the purpose of life, the afterlife, the claims of Jesus, and more. Some people want to get beyond religion and find a relationship with God that really changes life. Others come for the close, long-lasting friendships that are built during the Alpha course. Many guests have never been to church, others may have attended church occasionally but feel they have never really understood the basics of the Christian faith.

Each gathering begins with a meal or refreshments—a chance to get to know others. Then there is a short talk which looks at a different aspect of the Christian faith each week. This is followed by a time of discussion in small groups, where everyone is welcome to contribute their opinion and ask questions. People usually stay in the same small groups for the duration of the course so they can get to know each other, continue discussions, and deepen friendships. The emphasis is upon exploration and discovery in a relaxed and informal environment. The talks each week cover the following topics, acting as a springboard for the small group discussions:

Introduction Dinner: Is there more to life than this?

Week 1: Who is Jesus?

Week 2: Why did Jesus die?

Week 3: How can we have faith?

Week 4: Why and how do I pray?

Week 5: Why and how should I read the Bible?

Week 6: How does God guide us?

Week 7: How can I resist evil?

Week 8: Why and how should we tell others?

Week 9: Does God heal today?

Week 10: What about the Church?

Weekend: Who is the Holy Spirit? What does the Holy Spirit do? How can I be filled with the Holy Spirit? How can I make the most of the rest of my life?

The Alpha course is available in eighty-one languages such as Spanish, French, Chinese, Korean, Arabic, Portuguese, and Vietnamese.

Websites
Alpha (UK): http://uk.alpha.org
Alpha (USA): http://alphausa.org

New Expressions of Christian Community.

Churches can create new expressions of Christian community designed especially for spiritual seekers. Here are two examples of Christian communities, developed by established Christian churches, and their faith formation offerings targeted specifically for spiritual seekers in their twenties and thirties.

The Crossing, St. Paul's Episcopal Cathedral, Boston (www.thecrossingboston.org)

The Crossing is a community that seeks to walk in the life-changing, world-changing Way of Jesus, sharing the love, hope, beauty and justice of God in the city of Boston. People gather for transformative worship, spiritual practice, and authentic community. The community fuses the wisdom and mystery of ancient traditions with that of urban mystics, artists, and activists; and moves out to join God in healing, freeing, and blessing all people, communities, and the earth.

Worship. Every Thursday from 6-7:30 pm at St. Paul's Episcopal Cathedral, people gather for a transformative encounter with God that leads people to act a bit different in the world. Here's what the community experiences: (1) R&B grooves laid out under monastic chant, gospel, spirituals and Episcopal hymns, (2) silence and intentional spiritual practice as part of worship, (3) reflections on the gospel, usually led by a lay person, plus some brief talk-back time, (4) open space to catch your breath and let God's word sink in, (5) Eucharist (or communion) with a groove, where everybody is welcome to celebrate the mystery of Jesus alive among us, (6) post-worship: crank the stereo and share snacks and community, (7) post-post worship: usually a field trip to a local restaurant for very cheap food or a potluck with community formation.

Small Groups and Formation. Sundays @ the Crossing
- Every Sunday @ 3-4:30 pm: An Intro to the Episcopal Church
- 1st Sundays, 5-7:30: Artist Expressions
- 2nd Sundays, 5-7:30: Bible Study
- 3rd Sundays, 5-7:30: Crossing Community Dinners
- 4th Sundays, 5-7:30: Bible Study

During the Week
Monday-Wednesday Evenings: Neighborhood Action/Reflection Groups (justice and service action/reflection), and Covenant Groups (small discipleship circles centered around prayer and stories, four to six people per group)
Thursdays after Worship: Dancing with Jesus (monthly) and Everybody Does Theology (monthly)

Rule of Life. The Crossing is a community of sisters and brothers offering a compassionate, progressive, creative, generous, radically welcoming expression of God's life and love in the city of Boston. From that community has grown this Rule of Life, which like the Rule of a monastic community spells out our commitment to discipleship. We believe we are called to follow in the footsteps of the ancients and live the way of Jesus: nurturing God's Spirit in and among us; gathering everybody for prayer and celebration at God's table; bearing the good news of hope and resurrection into the world; and spreading God's mission of healing and transformation. But we know we cannot live this dream alone. We need each other. We need authentic, concrete spiritual practices that form our lives in the shape of Jesus' life. We need to make real commitments to God and to each other as we journey together closer to the heart of God and to the deepest callings on our own lives. This Rule for Real Life describes a way of walking together, and following Jesus together and making something extraordinary, holy, and whole of our daily and (seemingly) ordinary individual lives.

Justice and Service.

- The Hope in Action Campaign: a young adult justice effort led by Relational Evangelists at eight ministries throughout the Boston area to develop programs of public service and social justice based on the needs and interests of the community
- Monday Lunch Program at the Cathedral
- Boston Faith and Justice Network: build awareness, relationships and action around fair trade and justice issues, locally and globally
- Saint Francis House: prepare and serve meals every day
- Haley House: soup kitchen, food pantry and clothing room, bakery café and corner shop, youth culinary classes, noonday farm
- Ecclesia Ministries: social services to homeless people in concert with spiritual companionship and community

Kairos and Young Adult Ministry, Brentwood Baptist Church, Nashville (www.brentwoodbaptist.com/kairos)

- **Kairos** is a come-as-you-are Tuesday night worship experience geared toward energetic young adults who share a passion for growing together in the Word of God. Kairos is designed to challenge young adults on both a personal and spiritual level and teach them how to uniquely apply the scriptures to their life. Kairos provides a relaxed atmosphere to make new friends and enjoy the live music as young adults connect with a loving God who has a plan and purpose for your life.

- **Kairos Podcasts** contain the audio programs of the Kairos message each week.

- **Kairos Roots** is a deeper experience, using the same Kairos setup—complete with tables, chairs, and candles. There will be a time of worship and a message with a small group table discussion regarding the topic of the night as a part of the worship experience.

- **Intersect** groups provide opportunity for young adults to socialize, learn, and grow together with like-minded people in an authentic community that seeks to find and follow Christ. New groups start several times during the year on a wide variety of young adult relevant topics, for example: Breathing New Life into Your Career; In a Pit with a Lion on a Snowy Day (book study); Life in the Journey Living Beyond Yourself; Me, Myself, and Lies; New to Fitness; Steps in Soul; TrueFaced; Unfamiliar Christianity; Unleashing Courageous Faith; and Your Bible Isn't Scary.

- **Impact** is service to the local and global community with a variety of projects including providing beds for orphans and abandoned children in

Haiti, Uganda, and Moldova; working at the Nashville Rescue Mission; and providing meals and supplies for the homeless.

Read more about Kairos in the book by pastor Mike Glenn: *In Real Time: Authentic Young Adult Ministry as It Happens* (Nashville: B&H, 2009).

Apprenticeships in Discipleship

Churches can offer an apprenticeship in discipleship for spiritually hungry people who want to grow in relationship with Jesus Christ and the Christian way of life. An "apprenticeship process" is designed to help people who are hungry for God develop a robust discipleship by helping them understand who God is, what it means to be a Christian, and what it means to live in community as part of God's kingdom. The apprenticeship process fosters transformation by contrasting the God Jesus revealed with commonly held beliefs about God; explores how beliefs about God, self, and the world shape people's lives; encourages soul training, spiritual practices to help people experience God's love; and nurtures accountability in a small group setting. Through the apprenticeship process people's understanding of God is strengthened and healed through spiritual practices, helping people more naturally live the life Jesus described in the Sermon on the Mount. An apprenticeship often incorporates one-on-one mentoring, small group sharing, personal study, prayer, and retreat experiences.

IDEAS

The Apprentice Series. James Bryan Smith.
(www.apprenticeofjesus.org)

- *The Good and Beautiful God: Falling in Love with the God Jesus Knows.* Downers Grove: Intervarsity, 2009.
- *The Good and Beautiful Life: Putting on the Character of Christ.* Downers Grove: Intervarsity, 2010.
- *The Good and Beautiful Community: Following the Spirit, Extending Grace, Demonstrating Love.* Downers Grove: Intervarsity, 2010.

The Apprentice Series is designed to help people in their efforts to grow in Christlikeness. The series is built on a basic formula for transformation that includes a mental side (changing narratives), a physical side (practicing spiritual exercises), a communal side (doing the first two in the context of community), and a spiritual side (the work of the Holy Spirit). Real transformation must be holistic, taking into account the many dimensions of human life. When people engage in all three of these activities—under the leading of the Spirit—transformation is not only possible but also practically inevitable. The three core books (above) follow a logical progression.

The books are intended to be used in the context of community—a small group, a class, or a few friends gathered in a home or coffee shop. The weekly formation process suggested in the Apprentice Series includes: (1) reading a chapter, (2) journaling on the reflection questions in the chapter, (3) completing the weekly exercises in the chapter, (4) interacting in a small group setting around the journal reflections, (5) encouraging each other between sessions using email or social networking.

Soul Revolution and the 60-60 Experiment
(www.soulrevolution.net)

The idea behind *Soul Revolution* is to challenge people to do a very simple sixty-day experiment in faith, going all-out in a radically-responsive relationship with God. This experiment has proved itself in the lives of thousands of people. People experience how moment-by-moment connection to God with wide-open willingness fulfills their deepest longings and transforms them into life-giving people. The sections of *Soul Revolution* four major themes:

- Our longings: What shallow strategies do we use to get our deepest longings met? What are God's deepest longings for us?
- Loving God minute by minute: How do we follow God's lead to experience a growing love for God?
- Growing in character: How does God grow our character as we make ourselves willing?
- Moving toward others: How will God lead us into new, life-giving ways of relating to one another as we follow Him moment by moment?
- Impacting the world: What unique contributions did God create you to make? How might you and your friends impact the world as you follow God's lead?

Soul Revolution is designed for a sixty-day experiment, inviting people to try to stay in a continuous, honest conversation with God, willing to do his will moment by moment. The experiment involves setting a watch or alarm to beep every sixty minutes, and putting up sticky notes and reminders around the home, car, and office, as a reminder to stay connected. One of the big ideas behind using something that beeps is to remind people about the 60-60 experiment or people are likely to stay in their daily routines. People often need an external reminder, like a watch, timer or computer alarm. Though something active that beeps is the best, passive items (like sticky notes, signs, a dot on your watch, and so on) can also be used. People are encouraged to turn their thoughts back to God all throughout the day, as often as they can. This simple conscious contact with God isn't easy, but it's all people have to do—everything else will begin to fall into place over time. Every sixty minutes people stop and recall "God is with me right now" and they allow that to propel them to ask God, "Show me your will this next moment. I want to be willing to do your will as an act of love toward you."

Another feature of *Soul Revolution* is Spiritual Running Partners who provide encouragement, pacing, and motivation for people's spiritual goals. Spiritual Partners agree to walk together for a season in complete honesty to help each other grow spiritually to be more like Christ. Spiritual Partners agree to listen, to care, to pray for one another, to point out patterns they see, and to urge each other to keep moving forward in growth to become all God intended them to be. The goal is to think, live, and act more and more like Jesus would if he were living my life, working at my job, and in my relationships. Spiritual Partners agree to "run together" for a defined period of time, set a time and place to meet or have a phone appointment weekly, and agree to meet face-to-face at least monthly. They take turns asking each other the "How Are You Running" questions.

There is also a curriculum guide for using *Soul Revolution* in a small group setting. The website (www.soulrevolution.net) has a variety of resources for the 60-60 experiment, for Spiritual Running Partners, and for developing groups. There is also an online community at the website.

Resource

Burke, John. *Soul Revolution: How Imperfect People Become All God Intended.* Grand Rapids: Zondervan, 2008.

Additional Resources

Chalke, Steve. *Apprentice: Walking the Way of Christ.* Grand Rapids: Zondervan, 2009.

Epperly, Bruce G. *Holy Adventure: Forty-One Days of Audacious Living.* Nashville: Upper Room, 2009.

Johnson, Jan. *Invitation to the Jesus Life: Experiments in Christlikeness.* Colorado Springs: NavPress, 2008.

Moon, Gary W. *Apprenticeship with Jesus: A Thirty Day Experience.* Grand Rapids: Baker, 2009.

Smith, Stephen W. *The Lazarus Life: Spiritual Transformation for Ordinary People.* Colorado Springs: David C. Cook, 2008. (http://lazaruslife.com)

Smith, Stephen W. *Living the Lazarus Life: A Guidebook for Spiritual Transformation.* Colorado Springs: David C. Cook, 2009. (http://lazaruslife.com)

Pathways to Vibrant Faith and Active Engagement

Churches can offer formational processes for the Spiritual but Not Religious (Scenario 2) and the Participating but Uncommitted (Scenario 4) who desire to deepen their relationship with Jesus Christ, engagement in church life, and practice of the Christian faith. Churches can offer a multi-step formation process consisting of a series of courses, small group programs, or retreat experiences that gradually deepen people's faith and engagement in the church community. A second option is to offer a yearlong process, modeled on the baptismal catechumenate.

IDEAS

Multi-Step Formation Process.

Churches can offer a multi-step "Basic Training" program (large group or small group or one-on-one) as a introduction or refresher for people who want to learn how to develop and deepen a relationship with Christ, learn the foundational teachings of the Christian faith, and live the fundamental Christian practices, such as reading the Bible, praying, and serving. This process can serve as a foundation for deeper learning and spiritual growth and engagement in church life. (See the examples below of "step" processes.)

Example: CLASS at Saddleback Church (www.saddleback.com/lakeforest/adults/class)

CLASS (Christian Life and Service Seminar guides people in taking their next step spiritually. This could mean getting baptized, committing to digging into the Bible each day, discovering how God wants to use you to help others, or just learning more about God's plan for your life. Saddleback's classes guide people through the following steps:

- *Class 101* is the basic introduction to the Saddleback church family and is designed to clearly explain who and what our church is. People learn about the church's beliefs on salvation, statements of purpose, and the church's strategy and structure. They will hear about the history of the church, and how the five biblical purposes are necessary to fulfilling God's calling for a person's life. At the end of class, people are given the opportunity to decide whether to complete the membership process by filling out and signing the membership covenant.

- *Class 201* helps people develop the habits they need to jump-start their spiritual growth. It provides an overview of the three basic spiritual habits every Christian needs in order to grow: daily time with God (prayer and Bible study), giving, and fellowship.

- *Class 301* helps people discuss that God created them with special gifts intended for God's purposes. God didn't design ministry for just a few; God made each person a minister. At Class 301, people learn how God can use their Spiritual Gifts: Heart, Abilities, Personality, and Experiences (SHAPE) to minister to the needs of others.

- *Class 401* helps people discover their life mission and how to be a part of God's plan to reach out to the world. This class will helps people develop a personal perspective of the gospel message, develop their personal story of how God has worked in their life, build confidence in sharing their story, and understand the PEACE Plan—Promote reconciliation, Equip servant leaders, Assist the poor, Care for the sick, and Educate the next generation—and how they can begin to be a part of it.

Example: Our Lady of Soledad Parish
(www.soledad-coachella.org)

Our Lady of Soledad Parish provides a step-by-step process to help parishioners deepen their faith, so they don't just enter the front door only to drift quietly out the back door later. The discipleship program mirrors the process developed by Rick Warren (Saddleback Church). It consists of five mini-retreats. Each mini-retreat includes prayer, ice breakers, talks, faith sharing, and food. Held on a Sunday when most parishioners are off work, the first session begins at 3 p.m., late enough to allow for both Sunday Mass and family time. Retreats end at 8 p.m., early enough for participants to be rested for the next day. The parish provides child care. Each mini-retreat is self-contained; no one must return to complete it. This practice eliminates absenteeism and distinguishes the retreat experience from a class. Lay teams lead the mini-retreats, which are offered in English and Spanish and repeated frequently throughout the year. Each mini-retreat focuses on a different aspect of spiritual growth:

- *Mini-Retreat 101: "Catholics Alive!"* begins with the question, "What does it mean to be a follower of Christ?" Retreatants discuss the difference between a relationship-centered faith and a rules-centered faith; consider the importance of church as a family, instead of a privatized, Lone-Ranger Christianity; and note similarities and differences between Catholic and non-Catholic Christians. The group discusses the importance of serious commitment to the Catholic faith, as well as the commitments asked of parish members. Participants are asked to sign a simple membership covenant if they wish to join the parish as registered members.

- *Mini-Retreat 201: "Alive and Growing Spiritually!"* focuses on maturation in the Catholic faith. Retreatants discuss prayer, Bible study and the importance of belonging to a small faith community. There is also a presentation of Catholic moral teachings.

- *Mini-Retreat 301: "Alive and Gifted!"* helps retreatants discern how to serve God in ministry. The activities follow the acronym Shape, as developed by Warren, where "S" is for spiritual gifts; "H" represents the "heart" or passion and desire to serve; "A" stands for natural abilities; "P" is personality; and "E" represents life experiences. This mini-retreat helps participants discover how God has uniquely shaped them for ministry. Parishioners take up a ministry based on their gifts, not just on parish needs.

- *Mini-Retreat 401: "Alive in the World!"* helps participants live as witnesses for Christ, as contagious Catholic Christians. The group discusses evangelization, as distinguished from proselytizing. Retreatants learn how to defend the Catholic faith. They also discuss Catholic social justice teachings and specifically how this parish is active in community organizing.

- *Mini-Retreat 501: "Alive to Praise God!"* focuses on Catholic worship and the sacraments. It begins with a Taizé-style prayer, followed by a guided tour of the church during which sacred spaces, vessels, and vestments are explained. Next, retreatants rotate through four workshops on the sacraments, the liturgical year, and church traditions. The retreat concludes with a shortened Seder-like meal that leads into an explanatory Mass.

Example: S.T.E.P.S. at Impact Catholic Ministry (http://impactcatholic.com/steps.html)

S.T.E.P.S. is the "Formation for Life Process" of Impact Catholic Ministry. These steps are designed to lead people towards greater maturity in their Christian life and equip them for rewarding involvement in the life of this Church community. The S.T.E.P.S course is designed to help people grow in understanding and experience of faith and the Christian life. As people discover their own faith through these steps, they can also find their place in this community where they can grow and enjoy life.

- *STEP 100: All about Christ.* This is a first look at who Jesus is and how He can impact our lives. The course covers the basics of the message of Christ. If people are interested in investigating the Christian faith for the first time or looking to rediscover the foundation of faith, this course is for them.

- *STEP 200: All about Church.* The Christian life is never lived alone; people are designed to support one another. Church is that gathering of people who walk together in faith. This course focuses on the Impact church family. Here people find out about the statements, strategies and structure of Impact Catholic Ministry.

- *STEP 300: All about my Character.* Personal growth occurs when people make a deliberate and informed decision to put certain practices into action. This is a discipleship course that examines some of the key practices of the Christian life. People learn practical, everyday ways to grow in maturity in your faith.

- *STEP 400: All about my Capacity.* People are gifted in unique ways. This course takes people through a process of self discovery as they identify their unique gifts and abilities, dreams and desires, temperament and personality. Finding their gifts allows people to better understand their place in the community of faith.

- *STEP 500: All about the Cause.* The message of Jesus has a transforming power. Individual lives, communities, and nations have been radically changed by that message. As followers of Jesus each person can be part of that cause. This course looks at how Jesus is working in our world and how his followers can be part of what he is doing.

- *STEP 600: All about our Commission.* Jesus' last instruction to His followers before he returned to his Father was that they should share what they have received from Him with others. His followers today share the same task as those first followers. This course covers how people can share what they have experienced in a loving and respectful way.

- *STEP 700: All about the Cross.* This final step is really the beginning of a whole new life. At the cross, Christians find an invitation to commit themselves to God in a deeper way. Here people will learn how to live intimately with God. They embark on a daring adventure into the life God has always dreamed they would live.

Example: Awakening Faith (www.awakeningfaith.org)
Seeking Christ (www.pncea.org/programs/seekingchrist.aspx)
Paulist National Catholic Evangelization Association

Awakening Faith: Reconnecting with Your Catholic Faith, is a conversation-based, small group process that helps inactive Catholics return to the Church. The group meets once a week for six weeks of conversation and socializing. The conversations are based on short, easy to read essays about spirituality, Jesus, the Holy Spirit, God's mercy, the Mass, and the Church. The meetings foster reflection, prayer, and honest sharing in a setting of hospitality and acceptance. A small community is formed and over the weeks that community becomes a bridge to the larger church community. Additional, optional essays allow the group to continue to meet if desirable for another four weeks to discuss faith, love, marriage and divorce, and money. The process is simple and inviting. A parish can offer *Awakening Faith* any time of the year and repeat it year after year.

Seeking Christ aims to solve the problem parishes face when people inquire about the Catholic Church, but the parish has no way to begin receiving them. *Seeking Christ* includes eight sessions that can be used in a variety of ways to welcome and engage people who are inquiring about becoming Catholics. After an initial interview, the program offers eight possible sessions dealing with human seeking, our words and the Word of God, faith, Jesus, the Holy Spirit, the church as the community of Jesus, freedom, and conversion. Depending on inquirers' needs, a parish chooses which sessions would be most helpful. Each session involves a short DVD reflection, a scripture passage for discussion, and a take-home session which allows the inquirer to begin seeing Catholic approaches to various life issues. The inquirer receives a booklet for reflection and journaling.

Catechumenal Formation Process.

This can be a yearlong process, modeled on the catechumenate and Christian initiation process, to guide people in exploring, nurturing, and renewing their commitment to Jesus Christ and living as a disciple of Christ. The process can begin by exploring Scripture, worship, prayer, and sacraments; then exploring the presence of God in the world and in daily life; and then going deeper into the Biblical stories as a preparation for an affirmation of faith or affirmation of baptism at the Sunday worship (for example, Easter Vigil or Easter Sunday). Continue the process by moving to the practice of living the Christian life by exploring faithful responses to care for the earth, for humankind, relationships and daily work.

Example: The WAY at Phinney Ridge Lutheran Church (www.prlc.org/belonging/the-way)

The WAY encourages, challenges and invites a deeper life of faith. The WAY refers to a style of life in which both believing and living are centered in Jesus Christ. At Phinney Ridge Lutheran Church, the WAY is an opportunity for faith to be explored, nurtured, and renewed, a commitment to Jesus Christ affirmed, and a walk as a disciple of Christ to be established or re-established in the life-giving waters of Holy Baptism or the Affirmation of Baptism. The WAY is a process over the seasons of the year:

- Autumn: Sunday evening meetings begin in October and end with an Advent Celebration in early December. The autumn meetings explore topics of interest such as scripture, worship, prayer, and sacraments.

- Winter: Sunday evening meetings resume in early January. In both small and large group conversations, participants continue to explore the presence of God in the world and in daily life.

- Early Spring: Throughout the weeks of Lent, participants "dig deeper" into the Biblical stories that prepare for Baptism and Affirmation of Baptism at the Vigil of Easter.

- Late Spring: After Easter, the WAY looks toward the practice of living the Christian life as we explore faithful responses to care for the earth, for humankind, relationships and daily work.

(See: "Forming Faith," by Paul Hoffman in *From Nomads to Pilgrims*, edited by Diana Butler Bass and Joseph Stewart-Sicking, Herndon: Alban Institute, 2006.)

Faith Formation in Third-Place Settings

Churches can establish a Third-Place gathering space for faith formation in the community that offers hospitality, builds relationships, hosts spiritual conversations, provides programs and activities, and nourishes the spiritual life of people, especially those who are Spiritual but Not Religious (Scenario 2) or Unaffiliated and Uninterested (Scenario 3). "The Third Place is the informal public space between home and work that connects people to each other, allows them to recharge, pause, and then reengage the world. They are places in which participants feel strong, positive emotional ties because they are creating rewarding, meaningful social experiences and a warm community environment" (Herring, 123). Bookstores with a café, spaces for reading, guest speakers and programs, and reading groups are examples of contemporary Third Places.

Churches can utilize the potential of a Third Place for faith formation. In the words of Lee Sparks, "What if we could create a comfortable place and time for people to gather weekly to explore life and faith? What if it looked and felt like the kind of place we'd typically meet a friend for food and drink and fun? What if the atmosphere encouraged conversations, questions, and personal stories? What if the conversations about life somehow led to an "ah-ha" of God's real presence and genuine love?" (Sparks, 37).

Third Places offer those who are not involved in a church community—spiritual seekers and the uninterested and unaffiliated—an informal gathering place to feel at home, nourish relationships, promote companionship, and help create a sense of place and community. In this neutral setting, faith formation can offer a variety of programs and activities, varying in purpose, scope, and depth, providing a way for people to discover their hunger for God and the need for community.

A Third Place is the ideal setting for groups to gather, each with their own focus. Some groups emphasize studying the Bible and deepening knowledge of the faith, others emphasize expressive and artistic activities (making music, creating art, or writing poetry), others are organized around a lifestyle or common interest. Some are on a contemplative path (gathering for evening prayers or spiritual exercises), while others are on an active path (working at soup kitchens, tutoring kids, building houses).

Churches use the Third-Place concept to offer a variety of programs and activities for the wider community. Programs and activities can be sponsored by the church and conducted by people and groups in the community, such as an after-school program for children, an art gallery for local artists and art classes, a "faith and film" series, music concerts by local musicians, children's storytelling hour, book reading groups, guest speakers, and so on. A church's Third Place serves as a venue for faith formation programming and an entry point for those who are not engaged in church life. Program offerings can include spiritual formation programs, life-centered clinics and workshops (for example, marriage enrichment, parenting, divorce and separation, bereavement, life and career planning, financial planning, recovery programs, dealing with depression), and the "introduction to the Christian faith course" (see "Faith Formation for Spiritual Seekers" for ideas).

Some churches locate their Third-Place facility in the "marketplace"—at a coffee shop, a café, or a store in a mall, while other churches re-design space within their existing church facilities, transforming an old fellowship hall into a café where people can meet during the day and night and an indoor play area where children can play while parents gather. Churches are "building" their Third Places with a café (coffee and food), bookstore, play space, and rooms for small group gatherings; and equipping their Third Places with Wi-Fi, flat screen televisions, computers, and couches.

Example: Lifetree Café
(www.lifetreecafe.com)

A Lifetree Café offers people the opportunity to gather in warm and hospitable venues to explore life and faith. The hour-long Lifetree Café experiences feature stories of real people, guided conversation, biblical insights, time to build relationships with new and old friends, laughter, fun, and opportunities to serve. Lifetree Café offers a casual physical environment, warm hospitality, a safe place for questions and doubts, and an encouraging atmosphere for participants to share their own stories. Lifetree stories dig into the big and little stuff that shapes people's lives: family, friends, fears, busyness, balance, money, materialism, health, heaven, peace, and purpose. Through the exploration of these stories people discover that God is active today and looking for a close relationship with them—through all that life has to throw at them. (For more information about developing a Lifetree Café contact Group Publishing at www.lifetreecafe.com.)

Example: The Lighthouse
(www.freshexpressions.org.uk)

The Lighthouse is a beacon for the unchurched on the outskirts of Bristol, England. It arose out of the prayers of two women, each a member of a different church. Their vision was the provision of a relaxed environment where people could come together to share food and share their lives. The Lighthouse meets for a meal at 6.30pm on Fridays. The focus is on sharing one another's lives and their problems. Numbers vary from twelve to forty, most of whom would not describe themselves as Christians. Men and women, old and young, children with parents, come because they find something special. The Lighthouse has been described by them as a "lifesaver," somewhere with "warmth," and a place where "we find God." Members have begun to ask for more Christian content to the evenings. This is a result of the clear Christian welcome and strength of relationship offered at the Lighthouse. It is provided through videos and interactive learning rather than acts of worship. Some members choose to attend a monthly Sunday evening service in a local community centre. Through the offering of a safe space, a new community has formed which gives local people a place to experience Christian love.

Example: Sidewalk Van
(www.sidewalk.org.uk)

Inspired by a year working with Metro Ministries in New York, Barry and Camilla Johnston are connecting with non-churched children and youth in their area by going to where they are. Every Saturday for eight months of the year (spring/summer/autumn), they take their yellow Sidewalk van to the same local park where local children gather to play. The team run an hour of activities that include songs, games, a memory verse, a drama based on a Bible story, three object lessons and a life lesson (cartoon story tying it all together). Though aimed at the children, parents and older siblings tend to watch from the back. Some are increasingly helping in minor roles and making suggestions of what would make it better. For all the children they befriend, appropriate longer-term discipleship of those who want to know more about the Christian faith is one that the Sidewalk community takes responsibility for. They make regular visits to the families of the children that come and are starting to look to establishing a community house as a base for some who are involved. The Sidewalk community who facilitate this ministry meet weekly for food and fun. They meet in the park to continue to build relationships with families there and then gather in a team member's home.

Example: Zac's Place
(www.freshexpressions.org.uk/stories/zacsplace)

Zac's Place began in the late 1990s when Sean Stillman moved to Wales and conducted a couple of funerals for members of motorcycle clubs, who in turn began to ask very deep questions and wanted to know more about God, but couldn't see how mainstream church was relevant to them. So Sean booked a function room in a local bar every Sunday night to answer some of these questions and many came including bikers, musicians, and those on the fringes of society—the vast majority of whom had very little church connection what so ever. The gatherings aimed to provide opportunity for expression of and enquiry into the Christian faith in a relaxed pub environment. The format consisted of quality live music and other performance art and straight talking in languages and images that relate at street level. Over the next seven years, somewhere in the region of three hundred events took place, using dozens of musicians, storytellers, and artists, and a significant number of people benefited from the community that surrounded them. Some folk were encouraged in their recovery from addictions, working alongside local and national agencies. Others, whose faith had been battered by negative church experience, had their wounds tended. Still more found a level of communication they could relate and respond to, to see their Christian faith develop. Zac's Place now continues to meet in their own venue in the Gospel Hall. As people have grown and matured in their walk following Jesus, this community of faith has emerged into being a church—a church for ragamuffins. The venue is used by different groups for different events throughout the week including offering a daily breakfast for the street homeless, a weekly Bible study, and an evening soup kitchen.

Example: The Playhouse
(www.freshexpressions.org.uk/stories/playhouse)

As a member of Howden Clough Methodist Church, Birstall (England), Caroline was faced with the challenge of a dwindling congregation and a community that appeared to have no need for the traditional church building on their doorstep. "Seeing all those children in these awful places to play made me really stop and think," says Caroline. "I thought, 'why don't we do something like this at Howden Clough?'" Her dream has become an amazingly successful reality—thanks to the efforts of a dedicated volunteer team, key sponsors, and a church willing to take what was seen as an enormous risk. "We now have three thousand square feet of play area, a café that operates alongside it, and a supportive local community who have taken it to their hearts and now use the Wesley Playhouse as the venues for birthday parties and celebrations. We've even had several Christenings there as a result of people feeling so much part of what has very much become their own fresh expression of church." Since its launch in 2007, the project has seen over twenty-four people come through its doors. Services take place in a room re-designed as a chapel downstairs every Sunday morning, and a Playhouse Praise is now a regular event on the first Sunday of the month. "It's fantastic to see how many people have struck up friendships and are happy to be part of this community," says Caroline. "People have asked to have their babies christened here and been amazed to discover that we can do this in the Wesley Playhouse. I explain that we may have climbing frames and all sorts of things all over the place but we are a church, and we're here because we love God and we love them." The Playhouse seeks "to lead people to faith and disciple them; to help them find out why we've done what we've done with this project and encourage them in their own walk with God."

Example: Night Church
(www.freshexpressions.org.uk/stories/nightchurch)

Make your way to Exeter Cathedral on a Friday night and you may be surprised at what you'll find in this ancient place of worship. Near its medieval entrance, the weekly barbecue provides food for visitors—whether they're cathedral regulars, the homeless, or the downright curious. Inside, and "the congregation" for Nightchurch is meeting in small chapels and spaces throughout the building. Night Church meets on Fridays from 8 to 10:30 pm. The initial aim was to help those born after 1960, Generations X and Y, to find a way back to God. But of course it is open to all and if it grows, Nightchurch will become another part of the cathedral community. Their values, or DNA, are to be an inclusive community with Christ at its heart; and to learn how to be generous with hospitality, creative in spirituality, and passionate about justice. At Friday night gatherings people explore social justice, enjoy the creative arts in poetry or music, and become involved in discussion, prayer and meditation, and lots of other things. Every two to three months everyone involved in Nightchurch invites their friends and have a bigger than normal Friday night in the cathedral.

Resources
Croft, Steven, Ian Mobsby, and Stephanie Spellers, editors. *Ancient Faith, Future Mission: Fresh Expressions in the Sacramental Tradition.* New York: Seabury, 2010.
Fresh Expressions: www.freshexpressions.org.uk
Lifetree Café: www.lifetreecafe.com

Empowering the Community to Share their Faith

Churches can empower people of Vibrant Faith and Active Engagement (Scenario 1) in the church community—individuals, small groups, and the whole faith community—to share their faith with those "who not involved" in the church community or spiritually committed. By developing programs, processes, and resources to equip the faith community to share its faith, the church develops another means for reaching people in the other three scenarios—an approach called "everyday evangelism." Everyday evangelism can be described in this way: "evangelism is anything you say or do to help another person move into closer relationship with God, or into Christian community" (George Hunter III); "the heart of evangelism is having an alive relationship with God, being part of a church you love, and caring that people outside the church find what you've discovered" (Martha Grace Reese); and "evangelism is to cooperate with the Holy Spirit and others to bring one person one step closer to Christ" (Lisa Orris).

IDEAS

Mobilize the Whole Faith Community: "The Unbinding the Gospel Project" (GraceNet: www.gracenet.info)

The process and integrated set of resources from Unbinding the Gospel Project empower the faith community—people of Vibrant Faith and Active Engagement—to share their faith with those who are not engaged in the church community and/or are not growing in faith. This process and the accompanying resources help the whole church change its habits to reflect practices of members and leaders of highly effective churches. They begin to pray daily, to talk about their faith with each other, and to take steps toward significant faith conversations with friends without a faith/church relationship.

The process was developed based on a four-year, Lilly Endowment study of superb evangelism that included over 1200 interviews, fifty site visits, and a major survey of congregations doing the best job reaching unchurched people. The study found fascinating things about churches that are doing a wonderful job with all different types of evangelism: (1) evangelistic churches exist all along the theological spectrum; (2) all sizes of churches are doing great evangelism—throughout the country; (3) leaders and members love Jesus—their spiritual lives keep growing; (4) these churches help their people articulate their faith—they encourage faith sharing; and (5) pastors maintain a laser-like focus on evangelism, on reaching out to people beyond church walls.

The process moves through the following steps:

- Step One. Church Leader's Study: *Unbinding the Gospel*. Designed for pastors, key congregational leaders and evangelism teams *Unbinding the Gospel* helps committed leaders deepen and start sharing their own faith, understand their cultural context, and begin to plan for authentic congregational faith-sharing. It works best as a seven- to ten-week small group study. Each chapter concludes with questions, scripture suggestions, and group exercises.

- Step Two: All-Church Saturation Study: *Unbinding Your Heart: Forty Days of Prayer & Faith Sharing*. This is a six-week, churchwide, small group E-vent that can be conducted during Lent, summer, or fall study for all established classes and small groups, and new ones formed just for the E-vent. The purpose of an all-congregation study is to help people strengthen their own faith and to learn to talk about it with each other first, and then others outside the community. Each week, for forty days, people will (1) pray each day's scripture and prayer exercise and work with a prayer partner; (2) study a chapter of the book with their small group, and (3) worship with sermons, music, and prayers centered on the week's chapter. *Unbinding Your Heart* enriches the church's community life. It helps individuals risk face-to-face encounters with God. The entire congregation begins to talk about their faith. The E-vent creates momentum in the church.

  (Support for Steps One and Two: *Unbinding Your Church* is a collection of fully integrated resources to help churches work and pray through the process seamlessly, including worship resources and sermons, music plans, step-by-step planning tools, and integrated web sections for easy downloads.)

- Step Three: An Experiment in Prayer and Community: *Unbinding Your Soul*. Many people who aren't connected with a church would love to try a no-obligation experience of substantial spiritual discussion, prayer, and community. *Unbinding Your Soul* prepares church members to invite their friends into a four-week small group experience with short study chapters, an individual prayer journal, prayer partner activities, and group exercises. Groups can choose an additional four-week segment: "Faith and Courage."

Resources
Reese, Martha Grace. *Unbinding the Gospel: Real Life Evangelism*. St. Louis: Chalice, 2006.
_____. *Unbinding Your Heart: Forty Days of Prayer and Faith Sharing*. St. Louis: Chalice, 2008.

_____. *Unbinding Your Church*. St. Louis: Chalice, 2008.

_____. *Unbinding Your Soul: Your Experiment in Prayer and Community*. St. Louis: Chalice, 2009.

Website
GraceNet: www.gracenet.info

Share Faith in Daily Life—Prayer, Care, Share: "What's Your One Step"
(Evangelical Covenant Church: http://whatsyouronestep.com)

People today are looking for stories, experiences, and connections to God. These realities compel church leaders to reinvent how they practice sharing the good news about Jesus. There is need to articulate a biblical view of evangelism because people in our culture are not responding and because people in our churches are not excited or engaged. Evangelism is to cooperate with the Holy Spirit and other Christians to bring one person one step closer to Christ. The call for evangelism today must be about investing in relationships, incarnating the gospel, and inviting people to the mission of Jesus. Evangelism is about participating in the work that God is already doing in the lives of people. Therefore, any spiritual conversation, any act of kindness can bring someone one step closer to Christ than where they were before. This is evangelism!

What's Your One Step is a process, a small group series, and a website to share ideas, stories, and practical tools as church members seek to help bring friends, neighbors, and families one step closer to Christ through *prayer, care,* and *share*. Evangelism is a process that usually involves a lot of little steps. This one step could be praying for someone, caring for the needs of others, or verbally sharing one's faith. The small group series is designed to take people on a journey to be encouraged, challenged, and open to the leading of the Holy Spirit and to discover how God is calling them to be a partner in helping someone become a follower of Jesus. The study does not require a formal leader but simply calls for people to gather in a small group, open their Bibles, and begin to learn together about evangelism and how they can take one step to help friends, family, neighbors, and coworkers take one step closer to Christ.

Website
What's Your One Step. http://whatsyouronestep.com

Additional Resources

Kujawa-Holbrook, Sheryl, and Fredrica Harris Thompsett. *Born of Water, Born of Spirit: Supporting the Ministry of the Baptized in Small Congregations*. Herndon: Alban Institute, 2010.

Osborn, Larry. *Sticky Church*. Grand Rapids: Zondervan, 2008. (http://stickychurch.com/what-is-sticky-church)

Interfaith Education and Dialogue

We live in a religiously diverse world and people of diverse religious traditions are interacting with one another on a daily basis. The United States may be the most religious diversity country on the planet. Consequently, there is a tremendous need for interfaith understanding and dialogue—for the good of the society and religious congregations. Rabbi Justus N. Baird, director of the Center for Multifaith Education at Auburn Theological Seminary in New York City, explains that the case for multifaith education stands on three things: the *news*, the *pews*, and *religious views*.

First, the *news*. News headlines are dominated by events that are, at least in part, the result of religious ignorance or misunderstanding. Because news stories like these are the primary source of information about other religious traditions for most Americans, it is not surprising that so many of us are misinformed or have biased opinions about people of different faiths. Religion's high profile in the media puts the responsibility on religious leaders to offer quality instruction about other religious traditions to their flocks. If we don't answer this call for multifaith learning, we will raise another generation of people of faith schooled in misunderstanding, stereotypes, and bias.

News stories are a constant reminder that religion and misunderstanding about religion play a role in conflict around the world. Humanity's ability to resolve conflict is in part predicated on our ability to create better understanding between peoples of faith; our own security—our physical safety—is directly related to building relations across religious divides.

The news is a daily reminder that the world remains a broken place. People of faith have a responsibility to take part in repairing the world by reaching across religious divides and working together on issues of shared concern. For all these reasons—the misunderstanding and bias created by learning about other faiths from the news, the role of religion in conflict that affects our security, and the reminder of injustices that demand cooperative action—the news is a major part of the case for multifaith education.

The second reason to engage in multifaith education is the *pews*. "Pews" refers to the religious diversity in our neighborhoods and in our congregations. The religious diversity in our neighborhoods spills over into the pews of our congregations. Each time I lead prayers or give a sermon in my own synagogue, I have to think about how the prayers or the sermon will be understood not only by my Jewish congregants but also by the many non-Jewish people in the room. These are not curious visitors—these are the partners and spouses of congregants, many of whom regularly come to the services. And almost half of the people in the pews of American congregations grew up in a different denomination: the 2008 United States Religious Landscape Survey by the Pew Forum on Religion and Public Life reported that 44% of Americans have left the denomination of their childhood for another denomination, another faith, or no faith at all. Most clergy find a wide variety of backgrounds represented in the pews: lifelong adherents, less affiliated newcomers shopping for a religious community, and people of a different faith altogether. Family members of different faiths turn up during a visit to the hospital, at weddings, and at funerals. Do clergy know enough about other religious traditions to serve non-adherents well? Do lay leaders know how to embrace people from other religious traditions without saying embarrassing things? Can congregations serve families made up of a variety of religious affiliations? To effectively serve our communities—to lead our congregations faithfully—we must have a better working knowledge of other faith traditions.

The news and the pews are the two high-profile reasons for engaging in multifaith continuing education. The third reason, *religious views*, is more subtle and personal: engaging in multifaith education enriches one's own faith. Those who spend time learning about different religious traditions report that they come to understand their own tradition better and that they are stretched to grow spiritually. A familiar maxim teaches that "to know one religion is to know none." Religious traditions did not evolve in a vacuum—they are interrelated, and many aspects of our faith traditions cannot be understood without knowledge of other religions. Learning about other religions helps us make sense of our own. Encountering other faiths also directs our attention to muted theological strands in our own tradition. Religious practices or ideas that are strongly emphasized in one tradition may be more hidden in another. We can experience what theologian Krister Stendahl called "holy envy;" that is, we can appreciate new languages to praise God while being faithful to our own tradition.

No longer can we ignore the religious diversity that influences our world and reaches deep into our communities. Because of a great lack of education about other faiths, stereotypes and misunderstanding continue to proliferate, which fuels conflicts around the world and at home. Religious leaders and laypeople must better understand other faith traditions in order to serve their own communities and engage in righteous acts with others. And as we travel the path toward greater understanding of other religions, we will grow in our own relationship to God.

Faith formation can strengthen the distinctive Christian identity of church members so that they know who they are and what they believe, and are able to honestly encounter religious differences, understand people of other faiths, and explore areas of mutuality. Faith formation can enable people to discern authentic religious life and practices in a broad spiritual marketplace; teach the practices of discernment and theological reflection; and encourage Christians to work together with others in a multi-faith world on projects and activities that advance the common good. Christian churches can engage in ecumenical and interfaith dialogue, worship, and learning experiences that develop understanding of other faiths and traditions, and develop a new understanding and appreciation of one's own tradition and its gifts.

IDEAS

Courses and Field Trips.

Faith formation from adolescence through adulthood can include the study of other religious traditions and encourage direct encounter with these traditions and people. This can include field trips to the synagogue, mosque, or ashram, and study of their traditions. The intent of such interfaith faith formation is not simply to "learn about" other traditions, but more to "learn from" them. This means studying them with appreciation, alert for the resonances and differences, seeking for what can enhance our understanding of other religious traditions and of our faith (Groome).

A local church an teach a course, face-to-face or online or both, using the print and video resources at Patheos.com, an online resource center to engage in the global dialogue about religion and spirituality and to explore and experience the world's beliefs. Patheos is the website of choice for the millions of people looking for credible and balanced information or resources about religion. Patheos brings together the public, academia, and the faith leaders in a single environment, and is the place where people turn on a regular basis for insight into questions, issues, and discussions. Patheos is designed to serve as a resource for those looking to learn more about different belief systems, as well as participate in productive, moderated discussions on some of today's most talked about and debated topics.

Art of Spiritual Conversation.

Faith formation can train people in the art of spiritual conversation, including listening with openness to learn from others, and then sharing in ways faithful to Christian teachings and practices. It is important to be honest in recognizing differences. Nothing is achieved by the pretense of being "the same, really" when that simply is not so. People need to listen and talk "between the lines," looking out for the deeper meanings and values that lie beneath formulas of belief (Groome).

Shared-Values/Service Learning.

The Interfaith Youth Core seeks to nurture the interaction among religiously diverse young people in the direction of strengthening religious identity, encouraging understanding between religious communities, and facilitating cooperative service for the common good. The Interfaith Youth Core uses an interfaith shared-values/service-learning model. They bring together diverse fourteen- to twenty-five-year-olds, mostly through their congregation- or campus-based youth groups, to discuss how their different traditions "speak to" shared values such as hospitality, service, pluralism, and peace; and participate in service projects which put those values in action. Sometimes the discussion comes first, sometimes the projects come first.

The simple genius of the shared values approach is that it highlights things people share universally while creating the space for each community to articulate its unique understanding of the value. In a discussion on the shared value of hospitality, Muslims might cite what they do for *iftar* and the hadith of the Prophet, Jews might talk about their Shabbat practice and scripture from Exodus, and Christians might discuss their church's tradition on Christmas and the example of Jesus in Matthew 25. By speaking from their own traditions, participants find their faith deepened. This directly addresses the most pressing fear that parents and religious leaders have regarding interfaith youth work—the "you better not turn my Muslim into a Buddhist" problem. It also avoids the pitfall of immediately getting into competing claims—the "it was Isaac, no it was Ishmael" problem. They also find that shared values is a language of faith that is relevant to the world of "inter." Jews, Muslims, and Christians can all cite how their scriptures and holidays command them to provide hospitality. They discover that their stories can live side by side, even mutually enriching one another, and motivate them towards cooperative service together.

Special Events.

Churches can partner with other religious congregations and communities to sponsor a multifaith speaker series with discussion and interaction; multifaith worship and ritual experiences; artistic programming including music, sacred art, and video; multifaith festivals and holidays, and multifaith service programming.

Works Cited

Baird, Justus N. "The Case for Multifaith Education." The Alban Institute. (http://www.alban.org/conversation.aspx?id=8866)

Groome, Thomas. "Catechesis Amidst Religious Pluralism." *Catechetical Update* 19 (Jan-Feb), 2008.

Resources

Campbell, Cynthia. *A Multitude of Blessings: A Christian Approach to Diversity.* Louisville: Westminster John Knox, 2007.

Websites

Belief Net: www.beliefnet.com

Graduate Theological Union—Centers of Distinction: www.gtu.edu/centersandaffiliates

Interfaith Youth Core: www.ifyc.org

Interfaithing: www.interfaithing.com

Patheos: www.patheos.com (world religions)

Read the Spirit: www.readthespirit.com

Spirituality and Practice: www.SpiritualityandPractice.com

Faith Formation 2020
Website & Training

Website: www.FaithFormation2020.net

Visit FaithFormation2020.net for free resources to accompany each chapter in the book and for updates to the ideas and resources in the book. Find the following resources online:

- Additional information on the important trends and forces affecting faith formation and websites to help you stay informed on the latest trends
- Planning tools and reproducible handouts for creating a Lifelong Faith Formation Network as described in chapter 2
- Leadership tools and online training for leading Faith Formation 2020 in your church
- Models, examples, program resources, and websites for implementing the sixteen strategies in chapter 4

Subscribe to the free Faith Formation 2020 e-newsletter by going to www.faithformation2020.net.

Workshop: "Designing the Future of Faith Formation 2020"

- Bring a one-day workshop to your church, regional church body (diocese/synod/district), or regional/national conference.
- Introduce leaders to the vision of Faith Formation 2020 and guide them in designing creative innovations to address the spiritual and religious needs of people in all four scenarios over the next decade.

Contact: John Roberto at jrlifelong@gmail.com

About the Author & Project Coordinator

John Roberto is president of LifelongFaith Associates (www.lifelongfaith.com), editor of the journal *Lifelong Faith*, and coordinator for the *Faith Formation 2020 Initiative* (www.faithformation2020.net). John also works on the Vibrant Faith Ministries team as project coordinator of the *Faith Formation Learning Exchange* (www.faithformationlearningexchange.net). John works as a consultant to churches and national organizations, teaches courses and conducts workshops in faith formation, and has authored books and program manuals in youth ministry, family ministry, and intergenerational faith formation. John created the theory and practice of *Generations of Faith*—an intergenerational, lifelong approach to faith formation; and administered the five-year Lilly Endowment funded project to develop lifelong faith formation in Catholic parishes across the U.S. His latest publications include *Living Well: Christian Practices for Everyday Life, Becoming a Church of Lifelong Learners*, and four volumes of intergenerational learning programs in the *People of Faith* series. John was the founder and director of the Center for Ministry Development, where he worked for 28 years.

LifelongFaith Associates: www.lifelongfaith.com